Bobby B[...]

8/27/14

2014 U.S. OPEN

HIDING INSIDE THE BASELINE

by Bobby Blair
and Barry Buss

Thank you For your
Support.
Together We Strive For
Equanity + Acceptance
For All.

United We Ensure We
Are on the Right Side
of History.

HIDING INSIDE THE BASELINE

by Bobby Blair
and Barry Buss

Editor

Jim Martz, author of eight books on tennis and University of Miami football and baseball, has been publisher-editor of *Florida Tennis Magazine* and editor of *CaneSport Magazine* since 1992. A sports writer/editor for 22 years with the *Miami Herald* and three years with the *Des Moines Register*, he has written for several tennis magazines and the *Sporting News and Sport.*

Editor, Second Edition

Linda Pentz-Gunter was an editor and journalist for 20 years. She was an editor and reporter for *Tennis Week*, as well as a freelance writer for Reuters, *The Times* (UK) and other news outlets. She also served as a television commentator and interviewer for USA Network. In 1998 she shifted her focus to environmental advocacy and in 2007, founded Beyond Nuclear, an anti-nuclear environmental nonprofit just outside Washington, DC.

Cover photo of Bobby Blair

Dennis Dean continues to make his mark as an internationally known photographer. He is credited for his creative abilities, strong composition, and dramatic lighting. Dennis's work has earned numerous awards and has been featured in several magazines worldwide. His photography has been seen in a plethora of art publications, including G. A. Hauser erotic novels, as well as countless exhibitions, including two in London at the Adonis Art Gallery. Dennis is contributing photographer for *Passport* & *Guy* magazines, and Creative Director for the apparel brands, Five Star Monkey & Ruff Riders. Dennis is proud to be partnering with Royal Palms Resort & Spa in Fort Lauderdale, Florida showcasing his photo works in all the rooms, bar and grill, the spa and fitness center.
See more of his work at www.dennisdean.com.

ISBN-13: 978-0615974064 (Custom Universal)

ISBN-10: 0615974066

BISAC: Biography & Autobiography / Gay & Lesbian

Book Website:
HidingInsideTheBaseline.com

Email:
Bobby@BobbyBlair.com

Facebook Fan Page:
"Hiding Inside the Baseline"

CONTENTS

Dedicated to
my incredible mother Margaret,
my brother Joe
and my life partner Brian.

Nicholas J. "Nick" Bollettieri

Nick Bollettieri is one of the most influential people in the world of tennis and a legend who has transcended the sport. In 1978, he founded the Nick Bollettieri Tennis Academy (NBTA) in Florida. The NBTA was the first full-time tennis boarding school to combine intense training on the court with a custom-designed academic curriculum. What was once a program of primarily on-court training has evolved into a multi-faceted approach which includes blending the technical and strategic on-court training with specialized performance physical training and mental conditioning. The Bollettieri approach not only builds athletes on the court, but more importantly, prepares them for a successful life off the court as well.

It was this proven method that Nick used to coach ten #1 players in the world – Agassi, Becker, Courier, Hingis, Jankovic, Rios, Seles, Sharapova and Venus and Serena Williams, as well as a multitude of other world-class players, including: Haas, Kournikova, Arias and Vaidisova, to name a few. The NBTA quickly became synonymous with tennis excellence and its coaches and students continue to reflect Nick's passion for excellence and the game. In 1987, Nick expanded his vision when he joined forces with IMG to turn the Tennis Academy into a multi-sport training facility, now known as IMG Academies. Located on over 400 acres, the IMG Academies complex trains over 13,000 junior, collegiate, adult and professional athletes annually, including families and corporate groups, from over 75 countries annually. At 80 years old, Nick is still going strong, rising at 4:20 am every morning to get to the gym by 5:00 am. He starts coaching at 5:30 am, stopping only for a quick lunch before finishing his last lesson at 7:00 p.m. Nick teaches private lessons, as well as oversees the progress of numerous professional players, the Elite Juniors, and the general Academy groups. He also travels around the country and internationally on an annual basis conducting clinics, making appearances, and giving motivation speeches for all audiences.

Nick brings his own passionate style to everything he does and a message that cannot be ignored. He has always relied on his resilient and positive attitude and unique strengths to enable him to attain his current level of success. He is a strong advocate and role model for living a healthy lifestyle. Nick demands a lot out of himself, all those who work for him, and those who train with him. Nick is extremely zealous about giving back to the community and is especially inspired by programs that help children. He is currently involved in a number of great opportunities for children who may not be as fortunate as others. Nick has written numerous books on tennis, contributed to many television and video programs and is recognized for his promotion of the sport, especially among youth. The Bollettieri name is recognized worldwide as a leader and innovator in the world of sports.

In 2014, Nick was inducted to the International Tennis Hall of Fame.

FOREWORD
by Nick Bollettieri

I was surprised - and excited - when I was asked to write the foreword for Bobby's book. There are dozens of reasons why he should have asked someone else to perform this honor. Just to name a few, I've been married eight times; I built the first dedicated tennis academy in the world and was responsible for looking after girls and boys from around the world; I knew nothing and still know very little - about the LGBT lifestyle. But it is for these very reasons that I agreed to write this foreword and to try to put my experiences with Bobby into words.

I can still remember Bobby showing up at the Nick Bollettieri Tennis Academy in Bradenton, Florida. It was Labor Day in 1980. He was driven to succeed, in spite of very difficult circumstances at home. His mom was suffering with cancer and his dad was an alcoholic. His financial resources were less than zero. It didn't take long for me to recognize his raw talent and his incredible work ethic, so I offered him a full scholarship.

My initial instincts about Bobby were accurate and he didn't disappoint me. He went from an average player to one of the finest junior players in the U.S. In fact, he reached the final of the Boy's 18 National Clay Court Championships and lost to Aaron Krickstein, a player who would later become one of the top 10 players in the world. He was, without a doubt, one of the most improved players in my academy.

I can't imagine how difficult it must have been for Bobby to conceal his homosexuality. I can state unequivocally that neither I, nor any of my staff, nor any of his roommates ever had a hint about it. I can still remember when I was in college and a group of us would go out on the weekends to meet women. I wonder how that would have worked if I were hiding an innate attraction to men. Anyway, that was decades ago, long before the LGBT community became established as a major civil rights agenda item. Since those days, athletes from major sports like boxing, basketball, football, hockey and wrestling VII have come forward to publicly express their sexual independence.

In a very real way, the timing is perfect for Bobby's book. It might serve as a catalyst to energize another generation of youngsters to trust that they can reach their potential if they only remain true to themselves. Bobby's experiences may give them the courage to feel free to be themselves and to live that truth with their parents, family, friends, teachers and coaches. His story may soften these hearts, and those of sponsors and fans, helping people to understand the challenges encountered by gay and lesbian athletes, ultimately breaking down barriers and building stronger support teams.

To that end, Bobby has created a not-for-profit foundation with a cadre of mentors that will help LGBT boys and girls to negotiate the challenges that are sure to arise and help them remain focused on achieving whatever goals their talent and determination will permit. I know Bobby's determination and enthusiasm first hand; I hope that you will agree that his story, and his commitment to this new foundation, will help those who are striving to pursue their dreams and to live their lives, openly and honestly, to the fullest.

> *"People fail to get along because they fear each other; they fear each other because they don't know each other; they don't know each other because they have not communicated with each other."*
> — *Martin Luther King Jr.*

INTRODUCTION

April 29th, 2013. Sports Illustrated breaks the big scoop. The first male athlete in a major American team sport is to announce he is gay. Rumors of such an announcement had swirled for weeks. Who would it be? Which sport? Would it be well received? Would this be the beginning of more and more gay athletes coming out across the athletic spectrum?

The story breaks. It's professional basketball player Jason Collins. Within 24 hours the media circus is in full effect. All the usual suspects chime in with their words of support. Even the President gets in on the act with a high-profile public phone call. Oh, the evolution of it all.

I was so excited that the first major professional sports star to come out was an athlete like Jason Collins. A super-talented player but not a superstar in the NBA. Thousands of young athletes from every city and small town in America dream of playing in the NBA. I feel because Jason is not a superstar that parents, family, friends teachers, sponsors and the fans can better relate to Jason Collins because he is just slightly removed from being an everyday guy. Jason is trying to live his dream with his God-given talent and passion, which is basketball. He relates to the thousands of athletes who are hiding in the closet not living their truth as they pursue their dream in a way that holds them back in so many ways. Jason showed the world that living your truth allows people like us to live a full life in a way God created us to live. When the media took a different direction with this monumental moment within 24 hours of his announcement, my heart broke.

He came out after his season was over. He was a free agent and did not have a contract for next season, meaning he really was not the first active athlete to come out in one of America's four major team sports. All the talk of this being some kind of game-changing moment just didn't seem justified to me, and now I was starting to see why.

It didn't take long before some high-profile media figure failed his tolerance test. Chris Broussard, an anchor at ESPN, pretty much declared that Collins was going straight to hell, according to Broussard's Christian orthodox views. Super. Now this was the story less than 48 hours after Collins' coming out. I sensed the gravity of the moment slipping away as the attention shifted to Broussard's backward views. Thousands of young gay male athletes hide in plain sight daily from the intolerance and homophobic cultures that are male team sports. How was this ever going to change when the media can't stay with the true story for more than a news cycle? I put my head down that night encouraged by Collins' courageous step but disheartened by what appeared to be another individual act of heroism with no real follow-through to affect a wider impact.

I've followed the process of male athletes coming out for some time. Every act of coming out rings powerfully to me. In many ways, though, each time I hear of somebody coming out, it seems like the righting of a profound wrong. It's addition by subtraction, the truth emerging from the removal of a big lie. These acts of individual courage are sporadic, random, unorganized, with no cohesive plan of action associated with them to make the environment that is professional sports a safer, more inclusive place for young gay male athletes. I would wonder: Could the LGBT community get better organized behind these random acts, to employ a mentoring program of support for all the closeted gay athletes suffering in silence in sports worldwide?

The LGBT community keeps waiting for a marquee name to come out at the pinnacle of his sporting career. But what if that name athlete doesn't appear? What if he doesn't exist? Society runs the numbers and assumes statistically he is there. Matter of fact, they're near certain about it. But I know a few things about trying to become an elite athlete. I played some serious tennis back in my day; was one of the top American junior and college tennis players of my era; had a victory over a Grand Slam tournament champion at a former Grand Slam venue.

To be the best at something, an athlete needs to have a resolute belief in him- or herself. I know intimately the complexities of trying to build a strong and unflappable sense of self while living a lie. I am absolutely certain my development as a young professional athlete was hampered by my not feeling safe to live my truth in my sport's culture. I'm also certain about how comforting it would have been if more athletes during my era had come out like Jason Collins did. To know I was not alone in loving how I loved. What source of strength that would have been for my young in-the-closet self. The end-all goal for all of us in the LGBT community is complete social acceptance. The path to acceptance goes through tolerance first. Tolerance; a concept that gets thrown around by all sorts of successful people when the cameras are rolling. But tolerance is more than an ideal. Tolerance plays out for those of us in the LGBT community in every encounter, every conversation, every handshake, every look and glance far away from the tape recorders and bright lights of our mass media. Day after day, week after week, year after year.

Most in our day and age are increasingly hip that gay people are no different than anyone, deserving all the same rights and protections our straight brethren possess. Our fears lie in the potential repercussions from those who are not hip with the fact that we are exactly like you in every way, except in who we were born to love. It's those repercussions, the smears, the bullying, the ostracizing, the hate, or even worse, that we fear in coming out. We fear the safety nets are not in place for us to come out and be our true selves. It can be such a lonely place, living in the closet and knowing that if I can't get over my fears of who I truly am, how can I ever expect you to get over yours of who I am either?

I knew the LGBT community needed to do more. Then I realized I am the LGBT community. I am 49 years old, in a serious partnership for 10 years, owner of a gay media business for seven years, principle director of a foundation in my community that helps those less fortunate than myself get the proper healthcare for HIV-related illnesses. But I needed to do more.

I've been out to my family, friends and in my professional life, but not in the tennis community in which I spent so many productive years of my life chasing excellence. I needed to tell my story to the tennis community, but not as some isolated act of coming out courage, but as the first important act in a XI program of concerted action to help make professional sports, and in particular my sport of tennis, a safe, inclusive and tolerant environment for the next generation of young up-and-coming gay athletes.

For the numbers are staggering. Thousands of young players at the junior, college and professional ranks, and barely a single gay male tennis player out in the open about his sexuality. And not just tennis. It's thousands in all sports. All sports culture has so many in plain sight. Tennis culture can say whatever it wants about being tolerant of those with different sexual orientations. The gaping disparity between the openness of gay women associated with our sport compared to men speaks loudly that all is not safe for gay males trying to live lives of dignified authenticity. A lot needs to change; I have set my sights on being an integral part of that change. First by telling my story. Second by being part of future courses of action to change tennis culture so young tennis players no longer have to hide inside the baseline, living in shame and fear while pursuing their athletic dreams.

Coming out is not about you getting to know everything about my private life. Nor is it about not having to keep private one of the most important aspects of my life. It's about no longer having to hide an essential part of who I am while standing in plain view. It's about being able to tell my story to you here, now, about being able to share my experience with you today in the hope that it helps generate empathy and understanding for the next generation of aspiring gay athletes who live in fear among you. It's about being able to declare with pride and confidence that my name is Bobby Blair, a former professional tennis player, and a gay male...

And this is my story.

1

THE EARLY YEARS

July 24, 1983...Louisville, Kentucky...Sunday 11:00 a.m. The crowd settles in. The umpire calls out: "Players ready? Play." The match is about to begin. I'm in the finals of my first ever major national tournament. The national Boys' 18-and-under Clay Courts. Win this match and I go on to the National Championships at Kalamazoo the number one-ranked junior tennis player in the United States. Across the net from me is Aaron Krickstein, future top 10 in the world professional. Playing Aaron on a normal day in itself is an enormous task. Today is no normal day.

The stands are full of people. People from all areas of my life. At courtside sits my Junior Davis Cup Coach, Brad Louderback. Next to him sit half a dozen of my teammates. Quietly some of them are rooting for me, some against me. You're never exactly sure who. I'm part of a traveling team of the United States' best junior tennis players. We pound on each other by day, hang out and house together by night. Rivalries and resentments come with the environment. It's a big deal to be a part of this team; and I'm honored.

Next to them is my tournament housing host Jim, a gregarious 43-year-old heavy equipment dealer by day, manipulative sexual predator type by night. He had been showing an intense interest in me for over a year now. I had succumbed finally to his advances just two nights prior. Now he sits front row, cheering for me as if what happened was perfectly normal. I look at him. I look away, back to myself. Not one single thing feels normal about what transpired between us.

1

Right next to Jim is my girlfriend, Mary Claire. I invited her to Louisville to protect me from Jim. That didn't go so well, he kicking her out of my housing the first evening in town, to have me all to himself. He got her a hotel room. She is still here, oblivious to the nature of the man beside her. Equally oblivious to the reality of her boyfriend, who himself is just starting to understand he's not like all the other straight men he's been playing tennis against his whole young life.

On the other side of the stands sits my coach from the Academy, Nick Bollettieri. He has chosen to sit with my opponent's father, Dr. Krickstein. This stings a little. Nick always said stick with the winners; I see who he thinks will prevail today. It will take my best effort today to pull him back over to my side.

Sitting to the right of my coach is mom. She is terminal. Cancer. My heart is so heavy I can barely stand to look at her. But this may be the last day I ever get to see her alive. Jim knew this. Unbeknownst to me, he flew my mom in for the semifinals, where she helped will me to victory. Could we work our magic just one more time on this most complicated of days?

My thoughts race as the match begins. How did I get here? From a two bedroom house on an Orlando dirt road to a borrowed racket at the public parks, to the world-class Nick Bollettieri Tennis Academy, to here playing for my first national championship? So many forces pulling at me. Some of circumstance, some of my own doing.

My thoughts race more as the match begins. I have a major secret I know little of what to do with. I'm 18 years old and I'm not like my fellow tennis players. I'm a gay man in a straight sport. My awareness of this is near certain. What is also certain is nobody is to know anything about my secret. Away from tennis, I will be hiding in the closet. On the tennis court, I will be hiding inside the baseline, in plain view for all to see. How will this play out in my life, being too afraid to live my truth in 1980s America?

Join me now as I share my story...and you will see...

I was born October 24 1964, the first son of Margaret Shields and Thomas Blair. All indications are I was not part of anyone's master plan.

My mother had great athletic potential. In her 20s she was playing in a developing professional women's basketball league. Her parents made her quit the league right at her athletic peak. My grandfather argued that the league was full of lesbians and that my mom needed to snap out of it if she was going

2

to make anything of her life.

Well snap she did, but not out of it. She fell into a deep depression thereafter. Was the depression from the taking away of her sporting dreams? Or was it from the severing of the close connections she felt to her fellow players? I'll never know. What I do know is she spent her 20s in a great deal of pain, fueled by the pressure to marry and live the devout Catholic life. The treatment for depression then was shock treatment; the same treatment the psychiatric community applied to people struggling with their sexuality. I wish I could turn back time to learn what she was really treated for.

My father rolled in to town at age 25. Apparently he had had a full life before meeting my mother. The story is that at age 25 he stole his mother's Cadillac in Fort Wayne, Indiana, leaving his wife and two boys high and dry as he set off to Florida for a fresh start. Did he leave them? Or was he chased out of town? We'll never know. My dad liked to drink and gamble. He was good at the former, not so good at the latter. Meaning he had to leave town a lot.

Later, when I was 14, my two half brothers were to appear at our front door, the first time my brother Joey and I even knew they existed. One of them, Billy, eventually settled with his family nearby and we developed a close bond over the years that continues today.

Both my parents were going through tough times when they met. My mother, my father. She 31, he 25. They met at the *Elbo Room* in Fort Lauderdale Beach, Florida. There is no fairy tale romance to relay to you. They met. Not much later, I was born. All indications are they were not married when at the time. They shored that up by the time they had my younger brother Joe a couple of years later. If there was such a thing as a loveless marriage, my parents embodied that. No hand holding, no affection, not a single loving emotion expressed toward each other in all my youngest memories.

So there we were. A poor family of four getting by on my father's odd jobs of painting and wall papering. When dad worked he could make a little money. The problem is he spent it just as quickly. Booze and gambling and fighting led to erratic work and lots of moving. My mom would try to pick up the income slack when dad proved unemployable, but to little avail. It seemed all chaos all the time; the perfect breeding ground for high anxiety. Which at first sounds terrible, but being a kid in early 1970s America, having a bunch of nervous energy to burn each day, was not the worst thing.

Every day outside in my neighborhood was like the Olympic Games. 3

Kids everywhere, running around, playing sports. There always seemed to be a park nearby where I could go to play pickup games all day. Once settled in Orlando, I grabbed a little structure, joining little league, quickly becoming one of the best baseball players in the city.

Before long I was being entered in track meets to run the sprints. I don't recall losing very often. What I do recall is how much I loved winning. More than the winning was the attention I got for being the best. At least for a moment I could forget I was the poor kid from the house of nothing. I could forget I had a drunk, abusive dad at home who didn't seem to give two cares about supporting his family. I could forget all the yelling and fighting and drama and the fear that not all was well in our fracturing home life.

Interestingly, it was those early athletic years when my dad was not around that I began to see there existed a different life. My friends in sports would invite me over to hang out and play. This is where I began to see that other families had more than we did; larger homes, nicer cars, swimming pools, all kinds of luxuries we just couldn't afford. More than the material differences, these families welcomed me in to their homes, showing me what a supportive household looked like. I was immediately fascinated by how other families operated, beginning early in life to see that through success there was another way to live. For make no mistake about it, I was only welcomed in these homes because I was a winner.

My childhood seemed broken up into two experiences. Inside the house, outside the house. Outside the house was a world of seemingly endless adventure, with bountiful opportunities for success and validation. Inside the house was chaos. My father was alcoholic. He would come home. We never knew what we were going to get. Was he going to yell, was he going to be playful, was he going to just walk right in and out of the house like we never existed?

I came to expect the yelling, the drama, likely because it was most prevalent. In an odd way it was easier to deal with. It was more predictable. He had certain things he would say, often profane and denigrating. Knowing they were coming didn't make them hurt any less. What made them tolerable was knowing that when he was done, my mom would come in to make everything better. For every shaming put-down from dad, Mom would be right there with supportive talk, calling me special, smart, talented, and telling me that I would accomplish amazing things. I had little idea what she meant specifically; she never gave exact details. What I did know was that I liked the way my mom could make me feel. I saw how soothing her words could be.

And so the turmoil. The drama playing out before me daily, often a battered and bloodied father stumbling drunk into our house. His only words being, "You should see the other guy." Not exactly the words scared kids with their moms want to hear from the man entrusted to provide for them. I grew up with two strong voices in my life, both trying to define me in such different ways.

Through it all my mom, brother and I developed a tight bond; a survivors' connection. We were all stuck in a traumatic episode we had little to no control over. Nor could we leave the scene. My mom's Catholicism forbade her from divorcing him. It wasn't easy for my mom protecting us from him. After a particularly tough experience, I was crying to my mom about how bad dad was when she would calmly say to me, "Now Bobby, you and your brother are the two best things in my life, and your father was a part of both of you happening."

I was too young then to understand the sadness in those words, that the only positive thing my mom could say about my dad was that he gave us life. Period. But that is what she said, and that is how I felt for long stretches of my childhood.

In the home, a dynamic began of my having to be the caretaker. I was young, really young, yet always seeming to be putting my mom and my brother back together by cleaning up, or through soothing words. It all felt so out of control.

But perhaps it was the example my mother had shown me —when she would come in to my room after one of my dad's latest blowups to assure me all would be alright. Somehow, when a new crisis hit, I found the words to comfort her; to lessen the pain.

I would tell my Mom if she wanted to leave any time, that would be OK. Whatever decision she needed to make, I would support. I didn't care if we moved if that's what it would take to get away from him. But leaving just wasn't an option for her. The emotional turmoil was terrible. But it brought us closer together. And maybe, in the end, it fueled my determination to succeed; to be a winner.

How I hated the effect he had on our household. Everything stopped when he entered. Our peace and serenity being smashed so unnecessarily. I needed that one activity that could be all about me, that could heal and soothe me. That I didn't have to depend on two full teams showing up. That I didn't have to depend on anyone else for my well-being. I had that at home already. Intuitively, I wanted to play alone, by myself, outside the house where I would be provided with all the things I wasn't getting at home.

I wouldn't have to wait too much longer to find it...

CHAPTER

2

FIRST EXPOSURE TO TENNIS

Summer 1973...Enter tennis. Sitting around one nondescript weekend afternoon, mom and I were watching television. Anytime it was just mom and me was a special time for me for how we clicked, but also for how pleasant it was to not be subject to my father's abusiveness. Tennis was on, women's tennis to be exact. Billie Jean King and Chris Evert were playing. Mom had developed a strong interest in tennis and loved to watch local kid done great, little Chrissie Evert, do battle.

"Bobby, next time we go visit Nana in Fort Lauderdale, would you
like to go by and see where Chris Evert plays?'"

"Seriously??!!" I could barely contain myself.

"Absolutely. It's a huge park in Fort Lauderdale where her father runs the shop and people play tennis all day and night. I think you'll love it"

"Right on mom!!! Can we go now?"

"Yes Bobby, this weekend, I promise"

"Way cool. Thanks mom!!!"

Boy, was I excited. At this point in my life, I was all of nine years old with little exposure to the world of tennis. Mom and I descended upon the Holiday Park and at my first glance I could not believe my eyes. On television, you see only one tennis court. Here at the park were dozens of courts, all full with players, some playing singles, some playing doubles, with courts and players extending as far as my eyes could see. What a sight I remember.

But what really stuck with me were the sounds.

7

My first tennis racket: with Princeton Park Director Tony Mazza in center and Joe (far right), as we hit our first tennis ball.

If you're a tennis fan you know exactly what I'm talking about. There's a distinct sound a well hit tennis ball makes. It's somewhere between a pop and a crack, clearly distinguishable from most every other sound you will hear in your day-to-day life. This wasn't the isolated, intermittent, well-hit ball though. This was dozens of players hitting simultaneously, all within ear shot of each other. That day and even now, no other feature about tennis makes me want to run out and play more than the noise of a well-hit ball.

Even though I was young, I had been watching sports with my family for some time now. I wanted to be an athlete so badly in my younger years; all the attention of people cheering for me all the time. Though I grew up watching Notre Dame football and other team sports, I was not drawn to them. I didn't want to share the attention with any other kids. There was something about the individuality of tennis that attracted me to it. I was also drawn to being totally in control of the outcome. Maybe it was also growing up in a household where depending on others for positive attention and support was so lacking that drew me to the autonomy of tennis. I did know after spending the whole day at the park, watching Mr. Evert running the tennis shop with all the people playing on the courts, having fun playing board games between matches with everyone being well dressed and polite and playful with each other. It just seemed like such a healthy place to be.

When I put my head down to rest that evening and closed my eyes, the sound of those tennis balls being cracked ran through my head all night long. I knew from that day forward, I wanted to grow up to be a tennis player.

My first tennis problem was that I had never hit a ball before. Enter mom. Mom was quite athletic in her time. She could have played professional basketball if in her day the WNBA had existed, so I had an athletic gene pool to draw from. That Christmas of 1973, my mother got my brother Joe and I our first rackets, beginning my young tennis career. Joe and I would go to Princeton Park in Orlando to meet up Tony Mazza for our first classes. Mom had a hunch tennis was going to play a role in my young life, christening the moment with a photo.

Those first six months after Christmas, mom and I made that trek often to the public courts. She patiently taught me the beginning skills of our sport. It became apparent to me early on, from all the countless hours of time and sacrifice my mother spent with me and my tennis, that she wanted only one thing from her life; that her children would have a better life than she did. She knew my father was out of control and not about to get better. Her Catholic upbringing made it impossible for her to divorce him and possibly have a better life for herself too. I don't remember much tennis from those early sessions; I'm sure I sucked pretty good. But my early awareness of what parental love and sacrifice for one's children looked like never left me. My Mom was determined to ensure that I had a way out of our home life; a way out she did not have the luxury of. And that way out was to be tennis.

That half year from Christmas to the end of school went quickly and before long it was the summer of 1974. I had six months of tennis under my belt with my mom. Enough of a skill set was in place where she felt it safe to enroll me in summer tennis camp at the historic Orlando Tennis Center. I don't recall direct conversations with my mother about how to comport myself at the camp. What I do recall was having this driving impulse inside of me already that tennis was somehow going to be the activity for me that would change my life. I had no concept of what being a successful player was all about and all that came with it. What I did sense immediately from my experience in Fort Lauderdale and here at the OTC was that these people appeared to be living a happier existence than the one that was consuming me. Here was an opportunity to live a different life than the one I seemed destined to. Combining my love of attention, my fierce desire to escape my home life, and my growing love for this new activity of tennis, you can just imagine how hard I worked at my first ever tennis camp that summer.

Running that camp was a 26-year old teaching pro named Jim Kelaher, the first live tennis pro I had ever met. Many images flashed through my mind that day. The first was he was the coolest guy I had ever met.; he was a professional at the sport that was to be my ticket out, so I had to do everything in my power to get his attention early and often. Second thing was that there were a lot of other kids there vying for his same attention, kids who pulled up in Mercedes and Cadillacs that were all members of the club. One of those kids was a boy named Robert Sojo. He became my instant rival at the workouts in every way. I was struck by how supportive his father was for his tennis, for in those early formative days, my father was nowhere to be found. Robert came from a successful family; big house, fancy car. But more than their affluence, they treated me so generously and kindly, like I was a member of their family. It was my first lesson learned in the tennis community; that kids I would compete fiercely with by day would also be my closest friends on my journey.

Another boy I met there was Joey Perry. A quality guy, he was a better player than me, becoming my early nemesis. Yet I was able to keep him close as a good friend too. Joey became my rite of passage; all my dreaming of playing on the big stage someday went through Joey Perry. If I couldn't beat him, nobody else mattered. He was how I judged my development; it would be years before I would reel him in.

Coach Kelaher soon had his hands full with my young inspired self. When asked to get in line, I would always win the sprint to be first. When asked to run three sprints, I would do four. When asked to pick up the balls, I would always pick up the most and the quickest. When it came time to sweep the court at camp's end, I would literally get in fights to wrestle the broom away from the other kids. Back then, I did little in silence. My enthusiasm for the opportunity before me was heralded by my outgoing and boisterous personality. Call me a kiss ass or the teacher's pet, either way, it worked like a charm. After summer camp concluded, Jim agreed that I might have the right stuff to become a pretty good little player. Knowing my family's financial predicament, Jim agreed to teach me for free and my life as an aspiring young tennis player had begun.

The next two years saw me spending every day riding my bike the two and a half miles from home to the club, barely able to contain how excited I was knowing tennis awaited me. Every day after school and all weekend long at the Orlando Tennis Center, my new coach Jim and I worked hard at developing my game. I was making new friends and the OTC took me under its wing as the club mascot, for my hard work and great attitude were infectious. I kept improving under the watchful eye of my first coach until that big day came. Jim pulled me aside after my lesson and handed me a book.

"What's this Coach?"

"This is the other bible. The tennis players' bible. This is the FTA Yearbook with all the tournaments and rankings for all the tennis players in the state of Florida."

"Cool. But why are you giving it to me?"

"Because I want you to have it. Because I want you to read it. Because I want to see your name in this very soon."

"How's that gonna happen?"

"Because I spoke to your mom Bobby and we've entered you into your first tournament in Lakeland in a couple weeks."

"Me in a tournament??!! Like on TV with trophies and big checks and all those people watching and stuff?"

"Well, not exactly. You're a couple years from all that, kid. But I think you're ready to compete."

I opened the book to pages and pages of tournaments and even more pages of rankings. I saw the Evert name with practically every flip.

"Look, Chris Evert's name is in here."

"I know. And I want your name in there, too."

"Right next to Chris Evert's in Florida."

I had no idea what that really meant at the time, but it sounded pretty cool. What I did know even at my young age was this guy Jim Kelaher, who I idolized more than anyone I had ever met, saw something special in me. I was the only kid at the OTC that he was having this conversation with and the fact that he had already spoken to my parents about it meant this was serious.

"You think I can hang, coach?"

"No. I know you can hang Bobby. Keep that book, read it every night. Learn the names and the places and all the rules and how all this tournament stuff gets done 'cause you're going to be spending a lot of time doing this in the years to come. Just keep working hard like you've been doing with me in your tournaments and the sky is the limit for you. Your tournament tennis education begins now."

My mom picked me up from the club and I hopped in to the car clutching the yearbook Jim had given me. Mom noticed it immediately and pulled the car over.

"Jim spoke to you?"

"Yeah mom"

"What do you think?"

"Of course I like it, but what about you and dad and Joey? Can we afford this? These tournaments are all over the place and all the time"

"We're gonna work it out honey." My mom paused as she looked over and held my stare. "We're gonna work it out. There are people that want to help you."

She reached across and grabbed my hand that day, not unlike she had done before, but she held it a little longer than normal that time. This was my ticket. To a better place. To a better life. And my mom knew that and she was going to do whatever it took for me. And tennis was to be that vehicle. Tournament tennis. Florida junior tennis tournaments. Did I have the right stuff to be successful? I would find out soon enough.

CHAPTER

3

GROWING PAINS

October 1975. To say I was excited to play my first sanctioned tournament would be criminally understated. I was three weeks shy of my 11th birthday and really enjoying the new tennis life I was growing into at my club. Tournament tennis was to be a whole new set of personal challenges for me. I was at a vulnerable age where I found it hard not to compare myself with all the other kids and families I had been meeting in Orlando. I could live with being the poor kid, for my mother and grandmother were instilling in me a work ethic at my young age that ensured I would make my own way in the world when my time came. What was hard to bear was my father's dysfunctional alcoholic behavior. Not a week would go by in which he wouldn't humiliate me by saying something offensive in public. He was getting a reputation for causing problems, either for myself or my mother, often in front of my new tennis friends from the club. Issues of my family's class and standing were becoming apparent to even my pre-teen self.

An interesting dichotomy was developing among the wealthier families from my club. They loved having me around as a positive influence for their kids because of how hard I worked. They hoped my enthusiasm would rub off on their less inspired children. The message I also heard in their conversations was that while people who came from my background were welcome in their homes, they would never be welcomed into their families. Being poor represented some sign of bad breeding or weak morals that could never be outgrown. I was getting a sense that my family life was not going to turn around; 13

that being poor subjected me to assistance, but not a rescue. If I wanted to have a better lot in life, I was going to have to earn it and tennis was the place to make that happen.

So yeah, I was pretty excited when the Blair family station wagon pulled in to the parking lot of the Lakeland Tennis Center for my first ever junior event. As usual, our mode of transportation distinguished us from my fellow competitors, but there were other class markers separating us. Everyone had multiple rackets, as well as the latest in matching outfits and sneakers. I remember how intimidated I would get by kids who appeared to have more than me. I, on the other hand, looked exactly like what I was; a poor little park player playing their junior tournament; my presence was dependent on the graciousness of more fortunate others. Early on I learned one of the unique aspects of tennis -- that once the balls were rolled out, and all the jewelry and bling got put away, it didn't matter what kind of car you drove up in or how many extra rackets you had. Tennis was simply two players squaring off in a veritable steel cage match, bound by the same conditions and same rules, and though a player might have perfectly groomed country club strokes, there were no style points awarded in tennis. I learned early that different types of assets were required to win tennis matches. Tenacity, conditioning, intensity, effort, attitude, desire, and I had all of those in spades. I was assured by my coach that though I was a late starter, I would catch up to my more experienced and physically mature peers, and that my attributes of tenacity and desire would eventually pay off. In tennis, one walks away the victor, the other the vanquished, in one of sport's truly zero sum games. You're all winner or all loser in tennis competition. I would learn early at these tournaments which of those results best suited me.

In my first match, I would come up against a player named Jeff Stokes, who had more experience and more game than my young playing self. I didn't get embarrassed though, fighting hard and being demonstrative at every turn of good fortune I had. My mom also got in on the cheering game. Right from my first match, my Mom set the standard for how the engaged tennis parent behaved. She did not care one iota what you thought of her as she yelled and cheered and encouraged her son. She sat front and center for every match of mine she could make over my whole career, making friends and leaving impressions on everyone she met. If you wanted to defeat me on a tennis court, you were going to have to do it over my mom's rabid cheering. We went in to battle together. She became somewhat of a not-so-secret weapon. In the most individual of all sports, having someone in your camp, or player's box, was an extra asset in one's quest for success.

My winning shots were met with fist pumps by me, and cheers from Mom. Unfortunately, in my first match, there weren't quite enough of those, as my over-eager tennis self attempted a winner on every shot. Though I lost, I saw early that to be on the wrong side of our cheering section could not have been fun. This was just another plus in my tool kit, in the ultra-competitive world that was junior tennis. My opponents knew going in they were to be playing us both. I would be remiss if I didn't give my mom's cheering the credit it deserved for unsettling a few of my less mentally tough opponents. She did her cheering in a respectful manner though, winning the affections and allegiances of all the tennis families and tournament directors we would meet along the way. I would lose that first match but mom and I walked away from that event having left a mark that we would be coming back another day to fight again.

My spirits were also lifted during this time because my mom and dad were suddenly spending more time together, leaving for appointments during the day and sometimes even overnight. My brother Joey and I felt sure that, at last, our dad must be getting help for his alcoholism. Even if he wasn't there for me at the tennis courts, I knew things would be easier at home if he just stopped drinking. How bitterly different the truth would turn out to be.

In spite of my energy and efforts, I didn't exactly set the world on fire with my early results. I was able to get enough wins in 1975 to get my first ever Florida ranking of 35 in the 12-and-unders. One of the hardest things about playing junior tennis was there was no guidebook on how to do go forward. Everyone was doing the journey by the seat of their pants. To be successful you had to be all in from such a young age, and I'm not just talking about the player himself. I'm also referring to his family and even his siblings, for what limited parenting skills my parents may have had, all resources and time were being channeled toward my tennis.

The reality of Florida junior tennis was there were thousands of kids making the exact same investment that I was, and that was just in Florida. Across the country the numbers were in the tens of thousands, all working just as hard and equally hungry. What would the determining factors be that separated the top from the rest? Was it hard work? Was it athletic prowess? Or did resources play a determining role in one's success? The professional era and all the rich- 15 es that could be won was beginning to take form. With the stakes being quite high for those achieving success, the professional and elite training techniques and academies were beginning to sprout up. Did any one of these hold the secrets to future success? We all watched what the others were doing with rapt attention, for one of these new systems was going to prove to be superior to the others. Which would it be?

One of the players who was going about this tennis thing differently than me was future top 10 in the world player, Jay Berger. One of the great things about playing my early tennis in such a tradition-rich section as Florida was being able to see and play against many of the most famous names in our sport during their earliest years. Jay was two years younger than me, but his reputation as an up-and- coming phenom preceded him to our match site. I was nervous but also excited to see how I matched up against all the hype that was Jay Berger at the time. When Jay gave me a good beating in our first encounter, I started getting upset over how I was to compete against these kids who had all these high-tech training techniques. I literally was growing up on the other side of the train tracks. Again, my upbringing began to wear on me. If this was my ticket out, how was I going to get ahead against these kids and families who had superior means compared to mine?

As my frustrations on the court began to mount, so did my expression of that frustration. I soon became that kid you would never want your kid to be. Loud, cocky, temperamental. When matters started to go south on the tennis court, I made it very clear to all within earshot how I felt about it. The pressure to succeed on the court was starting to mount. Ignorance was bliss when I was just hacking it around at my club; now I was playing among the elite in my state, which also meant the elite in the country. And though I was in the mix and getting my fair share of decent results, it was becoming apparent that most of these kids were better, and were coming from healthier more supportive homes. And if this was going to be my ticket out of my home life, something was going to have to change and change quickly for what was happening wasn't going to cut it. All of sudden, my little enthusiastic hard-working club mascot status was in jeopardy as I smashed racket after racket and started letting my newly learned profanity fly at every opportunity. My coach soon started to get a bit distant with me, and understandably so, I thought. I was being a punk and I knew it, but the internal discord I was feeling about just not measuring up to the other boys my age was starting to catch up to me. I soon found my coach's distancing from me had other origins. Jim had applied to law school and was accepted. This meant more than just losing my coach and mentor; this meant losing the OTC as a club where I could play and train. But Jim being a good friend and mentor to my family and me had arranged a junior tennis membership at the very wealthy Orlando Racquet Club. It wasn't going to be cheap but my family worked out the finances as Jim set me up with the new coach who I was to train with.

Adding to my discomfort of feeling different was the subject of girls. I was 13 at the time and all my school friends and tennis friends were talking quite openly about all the cute chicks and the feelings that ensued. Not only was I not feeling the feelings they were so openly expressing, I found myself increasingly drawn to my guy friends. I just wanted to be around them, hang out with them, be like them and find out all the things they liked and try to be just like them. It was becoming apparent to me even at the early age of 13 that I was far more interested in my guy friends liking me than in attracting the attention of the young girls in our surroundings.

I didn't know the first thing about what same sex attraction was really all about except what I had been hearing on television all those years from the likes of Florida's own Anita Bryant and from the Catholic teachings I had received from my mother and grandmother, who were quite devout. At the time, my understanding of being gay was that it was some kind of mental illness or some kind of choice that immoral and depraved people made. As I chronicle my history of being in the closet and the effects it had on my ability to be the best tennis player I could possibly be, I can look back and attribute my exhibition of on-court anger to many sources. Home life, feeling inferior to others, and general teenager growing pains were the obvious suspects. But not everyone else around me was having on court meltdowns. The internal confusion and angst about the possibilities that I might be gay began to fill me with a dread I could barely contain and often didn't.

One late afternoon after practice, when my mom picked me up, we took a detour over to the Orlando Airport instead of going straight home. This usually meant dad was raging at home and she was riding out the storm. I wanted to talk to her about these feelings I was having; to ask her what they meant for me, for my future, for my salvation before the eyes of God. I kept hearing the word sin associated with having a same sex attraction. Was I doomed to eternal hell for feeling so? Geez, I was 13 years old and really didn't sign on for this. 17

Mom parked in our normal spot at the end of the airport where the planes took off. The last couple of years we had come to this spot, partly to stay away from the house, partly to have some time together. We would watch the planes take off, mom staring at the first few for a while with a distant longing in her eyes. Mom used to always point out the planes taking off and tell me that if I kept working hard at tennis I would be on one of those planes one day. I would be going somewhere, anywhere, but, more importantly, leaving Orlando and getting away from my home life.

But mom wasn't pointing out the planes that day. We sat quietly in the car like we had done so many times before. I felt something heavy in the air between us. Normally I could talk to her about anything anytime, but for some reason I withheld my questions about the feelings I was having. I switched in to caretaker mode with my family. Mom hadn't been herself lately, as far as I noticed, but she was never one to complain about her lot in life. I looked over at her staring blankly ahead as another plane took off unacknowledged.

"Mother? You ok?"

She didn't respond, continuing to stare straight ahead.

"Mom? What's up? You're not yourself."

Again she didn't answer. But now her hands had started shaking quickly as her face tightened to hold back tears.

"Mom??!!" I reached over to her and grabbed her hand. She grabbed mine back, uncertainly.

"Bobby...I've got some bad news to tell you. I've been trying to keep it to myself and take care of it myself and not let it interfere with my raising you and your brother Joey and supporting your tennis and being able to take you to your tournaments each weekend." She paused briefly to catch her breath and compose herself. She took a deep breath, grabbed my hands tighter and said, "I haven't been honest with you about where I've been going these past few months. Your father and I have been going to the doctors in town. I haven't felt myself lately. They ran a bunch of tests and I have cancer, honey."

I saw my world pass before my eyes. We both started crying. I had been here before, having to be the caretaker to my mother, but this just didn't seem fair. I needed her to tell me everything was going to be OK like she had so many times before when we would escape to our spot, but that assurance was not coming from her.

I was able to compose myself first and blubbered out as best I could.

"Mom, are you going to die?"

Which just made my mom cry even harder. This wasn't going well.

"Mom??!!"

"I don't know Bobby. I don't know. It's treatable but it's not good. I'm going to be pretty sick for awhile. They have to start pretty aggressive chemo this week and when all that's done, we just have to pray they get it all and that it doesn't come back. But nothing is going to happen to me now other than I'm going to be really sick for awhile and just not able to do my normal load. Your dad is going to do his best to be better and I need your help with your brother. I know you and dad haven't been getting along but you two need to pull together and we can pull through this as a family, OK?"

The rest of that day remains a hazy memory for me, the shock of what was happening to my young life all at once was overwhelming. My concern for myself and all the awkward feelings I was having would have to wait. Now I was faced with a much greater challenge; the prospect of life without mom. It was almost too awful to bear.

My mother might die. She would need my help. So would Joey. Should I abandon my dreams of a professional tennis career and just stick close to home? How would we cope if my mother died, with my dad as good as not there at all? I was being called upon for a higher purpose. It was time to step up once again and fulfill a role way beyond my years. It felt like a lot with which to be burdening my young shoulders. Everything I had been working so hard to achieve now hung precariously in the balance as my beloved mother began the fight to save her life.

CHAPTER

4

A TOUGH LOVE LETTER BEFORE ITS TIME

The Orlando Racquet Club was another step up from the Orlando Tennis Center in wealth. The club was host to the Virginia Slims women's professional tennis event that came through Orlando. I was familiar with the club, for I had been sneaking in to watch the tournament for a couple years now. My father got some work painting and wallpapering the clubhouse; we both knew the ORC was the place to be. We also knew it was a place we would never be able to afford to join. So when I was able to secure a junior membership to train there, I could see how my tennis success could open doors for me if I continued to get better.

During my mom's illness, my mom's brother, Uncle Jim, would visit quite a bit. He made it clear to me that my family was of good stock, that my father's alcoholism was an exception to our families. My mom was a Shields, she came from a family of winners. My uncle always tried to assure me that everything was going to work out well for me, but that I had to make my own success. My Mom and my Dad had their own battles to fight. Uncle Jim always left me with a $50 bill, telling me if I ever needed any advice, he was there for me. My tennis results continued to improve under the watchful eye of my new coach, Murray Hough. I had just turned 14. We had just moved to 4628 Andrus Avenue, a two bedroom one bath house, just north of downtown. This was not moving on up. The great news was our new home was five blocks from the ORC. Even better news was my two-and-a-half mile bike ride to play tennis was now shortened to a really fun ride through woods on my new motorbike. My dad saw that I was engaged with a pretty high class crowd at my new club. He wanted my brother and me to not feel so inferior around the other kids who seemed to have everything. So he got us motorbikes. I remember how great it felt in those awkward years to have something that my other friends did not. My dad was trying. With my mom sick, dad was trying to be the father he had struggled for years to be.

The ORC was a beautiful setup, with a lovely veranda overlooking a series of indoor courts and 14 clay courts outside. I developed a thing for playing on the first court back in those days. I loved the attention; all the encouragement from those successful members was quite inspiring. And they loved my enthusiasm. Before long, I became the club mascot in much the way I had been at the OTC.

Tennis can be the most psychological of sports. You become an egomaniac with an inferiority complex. The one-on-one of tennis competition creates a clear stratified system; you always know just where you stand in the tennis food chain. Results are all or nothing. There is very little gray space or nuance. Right next to you there could be two players you handle easily. You feel that power over them. You know you are better than them. Part of the psyche of tennis is to maintain that competitive advantage every way you can, by keeping a little distance, a little space, still polite. We always acknowledge but we don't always engage. There is nothing to be gained by becoming extra friendly with those who'll be trying to beat your brains in mere moments later.

Conversely, just steps to your left can be a guy who, every time you play him, beats you badly. You pine for that player's attention, to be noticed, to forge a connection of sorts, anything to shorten the competitive gulf that exists between us. You want him to respect your game and your attitude and your desire. Although he may be better than you now, he can easily see you as a peer someday, equals even, hell, maybe even friends. For few others can understand and appreciate this unique way of growing up better than another fellow player.

So the psychology of the young up-and-coming player is one of posturing and poses. Nobody is ready to admit defeat, or fear, or overtly concede their inferiority to anybody, even though in private we quake in our boots at being publicly humiliated by those who have our number. Though we will never ever show that. Generally, the more grounded a player is in his sense of self, the quieter he is. A quiet confidence, you might say. I was not amongst this quiet, confident group. In the compare and contrast world of Florida junior tennis, there were few areas where I felt I measured up to my fellow players. They were wealthier, had healthier and more supportive home environments, and always had the latest of everything. The better kids were much better or had top line coaches who taught perfect technique. And as far as results went, quite a few of them were better and ranked higher than me. To say nothing of this gnawing feeling inside of me that had me overly fascinated by members of my own sex as compared to members of the opposite. But I was not about to let all those pesky little details get in the way of how I carried myself in public, no sir.

Thinking back on how I cavorted around back in those awkward formative years makes me cringe. I couldn't get half way through a conversation with any tennis person before expounding on how good I was, or how much better I was than everyone else, or how I could just kill the player being discussed if we ever played. And while playing? Oh boy. I pity those who had the misfortune to walk by my court if I was having an off day. Oh, the theatrics. Every missed shot would be met by loud exclamations for everyone to hear that "I never miss that shot!!" or "No way!! That was so easy!!" And the worst of them all, when losing to what I considered an inferior opponent, "I can't believe I'm losing to a guy this bad!!!" And other lovely commentaries (is it too late to make a blanket apology to everyone I ever smeared so?) I wince now in that I really thought I had everyone fooled, like people weren't savvy enough to understand what I was really saying. That below all the arrogance and braggadocio was just a fractured, scared young boy, mortified that people might find out that I didn't quite have it all figured out while my inner world became increasingly confusing.

For the record, none of these outbursts were planned or premeditated. Quite the contrary. Spontaneous, involuntary, almost a Tourette's type of thing, they would just come out. Loud, annoying, there was nothing charming or engaging about them. To the outside observer I just came across as another punk kid with a huge sense of entitlement who felt the world owed him something. Nothing could have been farther from the truth. I was really just a young boy trying to find his way in a sport and in a world where nothing felt natural or comfortable. I was playing this sport thanks to the sheer benevolence of others. I feared it all could get pulled away in a flash if I was deemed not good enough. Or if there was another new kid to come around in a similar bind like mine who had a little more charm, a little more game, a little more 23 potential; or with what was becoming apparent to me, a little less baggage.

Having my ability to compete in tennis all the while dependent on the generosity of others cut both ways, though. It called for an accountability and responsibility to my dedication to tennis at a very early age. In many ways this invoked a maturity that was well beyond my years. There was also the pressure that the people from my club wanted to see a return on their investments. There were a lot of kids and causes they could give their time and resources to. The fact that they chose me and my tennis to invest in was something I could not take for granted, nor would they let me. So I tried to placate and please as many of them as I could, as often as I could.

Early days competing on the Florida Junior Tennis Circuit.
On the right, *Orlando Sentinel* tennis writer Jim Carfield walks with me before
we sit down for an interview.

But something happens to young players when they start to move up the ranks in such a demanding sport. It can be uncomfortable inside at times. All those nagging questions of self worth and self doubt get magnified. 'Am I really this good?' I would ask myself after a good stretch of results. Or was my tennis clock to strike 12 and I would come crashing back to my middle of the pack mediocre self? I was improving and I knew it and with each leap forward

24   came increased expectations from myself and others. My playing stature had

gone from being a bad loss to a good win, with my ego starting to show it. For in tennis, the rankings didn't lie. I was now one of the best kids in all of Florida and for a kid who didn't grow up with much, who was obsessed with comparing himself to everyone else, that ranking meant a lot to me.

So it came as little surprise when my behavior started to spiral out of control and I began to develop a reputation in the tennis community, that someone was going to sit me down and have a talk with me. I sensed it was coming, I knew I was losing it out there and starting to disappoint some of my new supporters. But when I received a letter from my old coach and mentor, Jim Kelaher, who I had been apart from now for a few of months, well, that I was not expecting.

I had promised to write Jim often when he went away to law school. I had not. Should I have? Jim had done an awful lot for me and I was eternally grateful for all he did. But I knew the kind of principled guy he was, and just the mere thought of Jim and what he represented had me feeling guilty for how I was conducting myself now that I was not under his daily supervision. So as I opened up the hand-written letter, I was not surprised to read in the first paragraph that I probably wasn't going to like what he had to say.

In my defense, Jim obviously did not know all the internal discord I was experiencing regarding my sexual confusion at the time. But in Jim's defense, even if he did know, he would not have cared. Understanding why I was acting like I was acting wasn't going to change anything about how I was acting. Jim wasn't a big fan of reasons and excuses; he was an action guy from the start. He used to always implore me to be on time and be reliable because people really didn't care why you were late or didn't show up, all they cared about was whether you were on time and honored your word. So acting like the punk I was would have little impact on Jim. But to Jim's credit, he cared enough to write the most important letter I would ever receive in my life.

Jim Kelaher's letter:

Dear Bobby:

Sorry I didn't get a chance to see you but I talked to your folks a while on Sunday and when I called the ORC they said you were on the court. You probably would not have liked what I would have said, anyway. The rest of this letter is going to be unpleasant, so you can either finish reading it or 25 *throw it out now.*

At 14 you're getting to the stage where it becomes harder and harder to change habits and personality problems. In other words, you'd better grow up quickly. No one owes you anything in this world, and the sooner you realize that, the better off you'll be. Hanging around the people at the ORC is great for your game, but unless you keep the right attitude, you'll be much worse off in the long run. Most of the people at the ORC have a lot of money; you don't. Your folks are trying very hard to make sure you get what you need in tennis equipment, but they're not wealthy and you're going to have to realize that. Your mother told me when she's able she is going to have to get a job to keep you in tennis shoes, string, going to tournaments, etc. Do you really think she owes this to you? Of course not! She's doing this because she wants you to have things the ORC kids have. The only difference is, the parents of the ORC kids don't undergo any special hardships to give their kids the things they want. You must be very, very happy and appreciate every little thing your folks get you. Don't take anything for granted. Learn now to be grateful for what things they get for you.

Now do you think other people owe you just because you're Bobby Blair? Do you think Dr. Wood owes you anything? You act like you're mad just because Dr. Wood hasn't worked with you yet. Why does he have to? Why did I have to do what I did with you? Dr. Wood doesn't, and I didn't either. To make a long story short, nobody owes you anything and you had better be thankful for everything you get, even from your folks.

Next: the problem about your head? It's too big. Don't think you're the only kid who can hit a tennis ball. Just because you've improved a little bit in a short period of time doesn't mean you're hot stuff. It just means you're on about the third rung of a two-story ladder. You've got a long way to go. This means that you don't have any reason to be stuck up. When a little wimp like Joey Perry beats you, it's back to the minor leagues. This also means that any display of any emotion (remember our long talks when you first started playing) is childish and grandstanding. When you get mad and whack your racket, you think you're telling the people around you "look at me folks. I'm really better than this. I'm playing badly." Instead, you're telling them "I don't pay for this racket. My hard-working folks do. I just beat it around because I'm a spoiled brat." This is the truth. No one respects a kid with a bad temper. I

mean nobody. Everyone (even your mother) told me that your attitude is get-

ting bad and you need to clean up your act. Don't start your tennis career out on the wrong foot. Work on this hard and clean up your act. I want you to do the following: 1) Start doing everything around your folks house that you can do (sweeping, taking out the garbage, mowing the yard, raking leaves.) You don't show your folks you love them by saying "thanks for the warm up" and "I love you." Anybody can do that in two seconds. You've got to show them by respecting them and by working around the house. That's the only way to show love and appreciation. And quit asking them to bring you things you don't absolutely have to have! Maybe your folks would like to spend a dollar or two on themselves occasionally. I know it's tough to be around the ORC kids and to have them always wearing nice clothes, but your folks aren't rich don't take advantage of them. 2) Realize right now that you're just a fourteen year old kid and only a pretty good player (not fabulous) and put your head back in a smaller hat size. In other words, don't think you're hot stuff you're not. 3) Don't show any emotion when you're playing your matches. Not only is it better for your tennis, you'd be surprised at how much better you'll be liked by the adults and even the other kids. 4) Don't expect anything from anybody for free. I will talk to dad and he'll get you two rackets (with ADA racket covers use those and not Head covers. The reason ADA will give you rackets isn't because you're Bobby Blair, it's to get the name advertised at tournaments. And talk up the ADA racket. Tell people who ask that it's as good as a Head Pro and a lot cheaper, etc., etc.) And be loyal to people who have taken care of you in the past. How do you think I feel when I've given you rackets, strings, and hours of my time when you have written me once in two months? I think, "well, I guess since he doesn't need me anymore, he doesn't bother to write." Only be nice to the person if they can do something for me! After the interest I took in you like a big brother don't you think you should write me at least once a week to tell me how you're doing? Don't you think you have at least a moral obligation to keep in touch with me? Face up to your responsibilities. Don't call Dr. Wood any more. I'll be home for Christmas in about 6 weeks and I'll show you how to volley then. Please don't let any other jokers tell you how to do stuff (like Rick Day telling you how to play Joey Perry? He knows what he's doing doesn't he? How bad did you lose? 2 and three, wasn't it? Just work on your own and I'll straighten you out when I get home.) For trouble on your serve, see Roger Pharr politely ask him if (not when) he can help you and thank him for his efforts. Now - I've gotta go study - this has turned out to 27 *be a real long lecture I guess.*

Now you can do one of two things: you can think, well, he doesn't know what's going on, anyway; or you can think, maybe Jim's telling the truth. I know it's really hard for anyone to admit that they are wrong; if you do it, that's a big step toward becoming a real man! I'm sure I'm not the only one who has told you you're not sticking to the straight and narrow, and you've probably thought "What do they know?" After all the work I've done with you, I think you realize that I am interested in how you turn out as a tennis player, and more importantly, as a human being. So right now you can do one of two things:

1) Say "Forget it, Jim Kelaher, you're so crazy as the rest of the world and I don't need to pay attention to you either."

Or 2) Swallow your pride and become a man and admit that maybe Jim's right and you need to really clean up your act and take on some responsibility in the world.

Read this letter a couple of times; write me if you pick answer #2 above. If I don't hear from you within a week I know you picked #1 and then I know that I don't need to worry about Bobby Blair anymore because he won't make it as a tennis player or a person.

Jim

I can honestly say I've probably read and re-read that letter at least 10 times every year for the past 25 years! I'm so grateful to Jim for writing it. For the record, I did choose option #2. And it changed me forever. Jim's letter influenced the player I became, the coach I became, and the human being I became. There has been no shortage of times when I felt my life and actions drifting from my desired path, only to reread Jim's letter and be brought back to what is most important in life for myself and how I conduct myself in concert with others.

Jim, and his letter, also filled an important void in my life, the void where my father should have been. All my life, I waited for my dad to step up. He never really did. I was going to have to be the breadwinner. I was going to have to try to hold the family together when all the while my dad seemed to be doing his best to rip it apart. Jim's letter helped give me the strength and resolution to do it.

CHAPTER

5

SEEMED BELOW WHAT GOD WOULD DO

My coach's letter could not have come at a better time. From my earliest memories of grandmother and mother fawning over me like I was the chosen child, I had slowly been developing an aura about me that I was special. Throw in a few quality tennis results in my early years and that sense of being different or better than others was not totally an illusion. I was learning that winning matches and tournaments and being ranked in the top 10 in the entire state of Florida can have a positive effect on someone's sense of self-esteem. I was also learning that the operative word in self-esteem was self, and people seemed to like me more when I kept my esteem there.

I was still a couple years away from being one of the top junior tennis players in the world, but in the smaller confines of the Orlando tennis scene, I was making a name for myself as everyone was learning who I was. They knew I was very good, a really hard worker who seemingly had all the right stuff to be successful. People wanted to help the up and coming me. As an impressionable youth, I loved that energy; people noticing me, recognizing me, staring at me, wanting to get close to me to find out what drove me. I loved that they wanted to find out what they could do to be a part of what was quickly becoming my crash course with success.

So Jim's letter came at a good time. My tennis was starting to really gel, but at my new club I had a little learning to do. Murray Hough took over where Jim had left off. (Dr. Lex Wood, whom Jim alluded to in his letter, was the volley guru I never had and never would.) When I wasn't on the court with Murray, I practiced hours with Rolph Bonnell, Stan Carpenter, Mary Dinneen, Robert Sojo, and my favorite, Alice Reen. She was a top ranked player in Florida with a great deal of potential. Many in the tennis world predicted she could be the next Chris Evert. Alice and I were all about the dream, about becoming great, when tragedy struck. Playing future top 10 in the world player Kathy Rinaldi in a major Florida junior event, her father passed away from a major heart attack watching her compete. With my mom sick, we made a pact to be part of each other's extended family. We vowed to support each other through our tough times, for it appeared tragedy was to be a part of our growing up experience. After her father's funeral, Alice and I went out to hit some balls. That's just all we really knew. It was the place we felt safe, where we felt most connected. My deep connection to the tennis world was growing. And as much as my love for tennis was growing, that love was coming back to me from all the great people I was meeting, and that felt good.

My first coach, Jim Kelaher, was kind enough to teach me for free when I was just a beginner. My new coach, Murray Hough, was also sensitive to my family's finances, offering to coach me pro bono also. Now that I was highly ranked and going places, in my young mind I couldn't understand why all the other coaches wouldn't want to teach me for free also. Despite being told no several times, I kept bugging the head pro at the Orlando Racquet Club to help me with my serve. Despite being told no several times, I kept bugging the Assistant Pro to help me with my volleys. I kept bugging my primary coach to hit with me more often despite the fact that he was already helping me. I started to see the pros at the Orlando Racquet Club were consummate professionals; as much as they wanted to help me, coaching was their profession, not a charity. My parents found a way to make it work, affording me lessons with the likes of Betty Pratt, a former world top 10 and Wimbledon semifinalist, and my game really started to take off.

As I tried to follow Jim's advice and dial my tennis histrionics back a bunch around my club, a different kind of attention was starting to come my way. Or maybe I should say I just started noticing a different kind of attention coming my way. My sexuality and all its confusion was beginning to kick in full steam. I was 14 with a dark Florida tan, full flowing hair, a toned tennis body, a warm infectious smile, and to top it off, a positive personality. Translation: People were attracted to me. All kinds of people. The girls my age started to chase me around a good bit. The boys my age wanted to be my friend and hang out all the time. From the outside, as adolescent socialization goes, all indications were I was developing quite normally. But in my heart, I knew early on something was amiss.

Direct interactions with others were reserved strictly for my age group. As young boys will be young boys, a female could not walk by without my whole new gang of friends chiming in about what she rated and what was working for them and what was not, and all the lurid things they wanted to do with the girls if they could just get them alone. What I do remember well in those moments was not feeling all the excitement for the girls that my friends said they were feeling. It was not because they were not attractive, they were the cutest young Florida girls you could find. For some reason they just weren't doing it for me. Maybe I was behind my friends a bit developmentally, or maybe my tastes in the opposite sex were different than theirs. I remember telling myself in all the emerging confusion to just be patient. The right girl would appear for me in time.

Also showing me a great deal of attention were the adult males at my club. Married, single, older, younger, there were quite a few of them. I would see them looking my way. Most would acknowledge me and look away. Others would acknowledge me and not look away. They would stare intently at me, not saying a thing. I would feel the glares upon me as I walked by their fields of vision. It should have made me uncomfortable, them checking me out so. But that's not what happened. I would hold their stares long enough to let them know I knew they were sizing me up. I liked that attention. No, I loved that attention, but I hated myself for loving it, for encouraging it, for I didn't know much, but I knew same sex attraction was wrong and not normal and I shouldn't be doing what I was doing. I would fight the urges to strut by where I knew everybody was congregating. I would be strong and stay away, but I could not stay away forever. I began to love the attention, the energy, the excitement of being checked out, checked out for more than just my tennis. It felt empowering, like I had a new weapon, being able to capture everyone's focus, regardless of the how and why of it and I remember liking it a lot.

Before long, one of the guys my age in our group always seemed to be showing up with a different dirty magazine every day. *Playboy* and *Penthouse* were all the rage back then. My friends would whip open to the centerfolds and the oohing and aahing would commence. Some friends would get visibly 31 excited at the provocative layouts. Again, I was not among them. What was happening was that I began to get excited by seeing my guy friends getting excited, and boy did I learn quickly not to let anyone discover the source of my arousal. I was all of 14, a virgin through and through who didn't know jack about sexuality at the time. But what I could tell right from the start was that I was having far different reactions to the normal stimuli than that of my peer group of pals.

As survival tactics go, I could have made it a point to avoid such potentially embarrassing scenes with my sexually coming of age friends. I chose the opposite tactic. To avoid humiliation or detection, I would attach myself closer and closer to my friends. If I wasn't feeling what they were feeling, I learned the mannerisms and verbiage of what a sexually aroused young boy acted and sounded like. I was going to have to fake it until I started feeling it, so I stuck even closer, learned what to say and how to say it and when to laugh and when to ooh and when to aah just like they did. I learned fast and was able to avoid any detection from my peers.

Over time, what was beginning to become obvious to me was that I wasn't feeling what they were feeling and I began to feel like I was different. There were only two sexual orientations I was aware of, a normal healthy dominant straight one that everybody I knew, boy and girl, seemed aligned with, and another odd, strange, not straight orientation. The not straight orientation I had been hearing about from my earliest memories was deviant, wrong, a mental illness according to some, a damnable sin in the eyes of God before many others. I didn't care what it took, that was not going to be me no matter what I had to do, and I was 14 years old and already steeped in a whole mess of sexual confusion.

So I went along with the boys and learned how to play nice to the girls and before long I had my first girlfriend and my first sexual encounter and it was cool and fun and I liked her and I liked having sexual contact with her. Hell, I was 14 and I was getting some, how bad could it be?

My feelings didn't seem to compute or measure up to my friends and peers but I kept that to myself. Right about this time one of my tennis friends at my club, an exceptionally cool older guy who I watched and looked up to so I could learn and imitate how he interacted with his girlfriends, invited me back to his house one afternoon to hang out. I ended up spending the night and we talked and goofed around the house and joked and laughed and he was the coolest guy and he thought the same of me. And before long we were watching movies and without any plan or premeditation I had my first homosexual experience. He obviously had some experience and I did not, but it was pretty intense and we stayed up all night and finally I was feeling all those feelings that all my friends had been talking about, except mine were for this young boy before me and in my heart I was loving it and in my head I knew I was screwed.

When we got up in the morning and rode our bikes to the club to play in the workout, I just could not have felt more dirty and wrong and flawed. My stomach turned at the thought of what I had just engaged in, yet it also turned in excitement over what had just happened. I had never felt like this with the girls I had been with before, so what did all this mean for me?

I tried to play my best tennis that day but I was obviously not myself and my coaches and peers could tell something was up and they asked what was wrong. For the first time in what would become a long pattern of mine, I lied to them about what I had done the night before and with whom I had done it. I am near certain that, at that time in my young life, if I had told everybody I had spent the night with one of the hot Florida cuties who were throwing themselves at me, I would have been given a hero's welcome and would have been deemed the coolest kid ever at the club. It was a time in my young life where recognition like that really mattered to me. But that was not how it was going to be for me apparently. Nobody needed to tell me how to handle this situation, nobody needed to tell me to keep this to myself, to go in the proverbial closet.

Nobody had to sit me down and explain to me what my life would be like if I was open about my evolving sexuality. I knew that if I told them the truth, that I had just had my first sexual encounter with a member of my own sex, it would have been the end of everything for me in Orlando. If word got out about this, I would be kicked out of the club and dumped by my coach and by the time my parents had found out, I would have already been half way across the country on my way to running away. Because to stay would have meant being thrown out of the house for good, and all my dreams of becoming a great tennis player would have been shot dead right then and there, because I could hear it coming already. Nobody was going to let their kids play tennis with the faggot kid or want the faggot kid around their house at all. Even though we were already the best of friends and I spent the night all the time. It was with this existential dread that I intuitively knew I was absolutely screwed if I told anybody the truth about my activities and just as screwed if 33 people were to find out.

What I did have going for me was that the boy who I was just with faced the same consequences if we were to be discovered. So I learned early how to lie about what I was doing and how I felt about what I was doing and the people I was doing it with. I hated myself for that, but hated myself even more for taking such a risk and engaging in such behavior at my club; risking everything. How could something that felt so good and natural to me be deemed so wrong by everyone and God too, and why would a God make something so wrong that felt so right? It just seemed so below what a God would do. My angst and confusion mounted by the hour and I swore I would never do it again. All the while a little voice in the back of my head said that what I felt that night felt right and real and raw, not contrived or faked or mimicked. Very likely I was a gay male and the power of knowing I couldn't risk acting so again was only matched by the power of the feeling that I couldn't wait to do it all again. I was 14 years old, already in a heap of confusion, eager to run away and be rid of all this angst, when I heard that there was a coach named Nick Bollettieri opening a new full-time tennis academy in Bradenton just a couple hours up the road and that it might be a perfect fit for me.

CHAPTER

6

WELCOME TO THE NBTA

The year was 1980. The American tennis boom was in full effect.

Every facet of the sport was undergoing major change. The Open era was flourishing, with the men's and women's tours proving to be great revenue generating engines. The United States Tennis Association outgrew and eventually abandoned the venerable Forest Hills in favor of a massive National Tennis Center as the site of the U.S Open. The game was being played better and better by ever younger phenoms as the world started producing colorful champions one after another. The proliferation of new stars at the top filtered down to the recreational players at the bottom as an ever-expanding economy created a middle class that could partake in activities once reserved for only the wealthiest. With this surge in recreational players came a tennis club-building explosion rarely to be seen again; just add water and another 20 court mega-facility would rise in a city near you as another tennis hotbed was born.

Styles of play became just as diverse as the personalities that possessed them. Serve and volley now had the power baseline game to contend with, as well as the widespread adoption of topspin and two-handed strokes and a far more patient higher percentage baseline game. Younger stars began to dominate the world stage in their teenage years. In California there was word of a club where everybody would come to play, the Jack Kramer Club, the club of champions. The Open era's first super coach and child prodigy had emerged   35 together; Robert Lansdorp and Tracy Austin. They showed the tennis world that with some solid fundamentals and a driving work ethic, one could reach world dominance and acquire great riches well before they adulthood. And to the hard courts of Southern California America's talent came, as families pulled up their stakes from their wintry suburban homes and came to where the sun shone all the year round. The tennis world had never seen such a concentrated cluster of talent. But that was soon to change.

I had swung my way with tenacity and hard work to the Nick Bollettieri Tennis Academy.

My home state of Florida had its own great heritage of spawning world class players and no shortage of great weather to play in. The concept of concentrating a slew of talented kids in the same general confines to train together was not new. Prep schools, college tennis programs, summer tennis camps and military boot camps all independently employed similar models to some degree. But what if someone took the best aspects of each of those and created a full-time, live-in tennis academy for junior tennis players run with the rigidity and strictness of a military camp? Enter Nick Bollettieri.

Nick Bollettieri had a vision. When I state that every aspect of the sport was booming, the high performance coaching and training businesses were no exception. Nick parlayed his early success at the Colony Beach and Tennis Resort into purchasing a 40-acre plot of land in an unincorporated area of

Florida near Bradenton. With a lot of hard work and innovation, the first full-time, live-in, year- round junior tennis academy was born. But not just any type of tennis academy; the Nick Bollettieri Tennis Academy (NBTA) was for the best of the best junior players in the world. The facility had only been open a year but I knew the names of all the nationally ranked kids flocking to Florida to train in nearby Bradenton. The reputation of the NBTA grew quickly as the place to live and train on the East Coast if you had aspirations of becoming a great tennis player.

So it was with great excitement when a Dr. Richard Nazareth, a long-time supporter of mine from my early days at the OTC, stepped up to mention he could arrange a tryout for me at the developing NBTA. A seriously successful plastic surgeon, Dr. Nazareth was one of the kindest people from my old club. He knew everything that was happening with me at home with my mom and the troubles my father had with his alcoholism. He knew I had little margin for error at home; both of my parents were in poor health. A setback for my mother or a relapse from my dad and my chance of playing great tennis on a world stage would be severely handicapped. He saw the NBTA as a golden opportunity for me to prosper as a young person and as a young player. But he also saw it as another opportunity. As stated, tennis was booming and everyone wanted to get in on the action. Dr. Nazareth was a smart guy who knew tennis as well as anyone in Orlando. He had seen me play in some tournaments and recognized that I wasn't being outclassed by those that were getting the better of me, just that I needed a little more maturity and a more sophisticated training regimen. The NBTA seemed to be offering all of that. Dr. Nazareth wanted to be a part of my success. A big part. Like a 20 percent part of it. It being everything I was ever going to make from tennis throughout my lifetime. In return, he would pay my expenses to attend the NBTA full time and whatever travel expenses I needed until I was in the black as a professional tennis player on the ATP tour.

At 15, this all sounded exciting to me. He apparently felt there was going to be quite a bit of something to take 20 percent from. With nothing else to compare his contract to, I thought his offer was the greatest thing ever, that a person of his stature and wealth wanted to invest in me and my life and my tennis. But after the excitement of the initial offer wore off, the reality of what going to the NBTA meant began to set in.

Attending the Nick Bollettieri Tennis Academy meant moving away from   37 home at 15 years old, away from my sick mother and struggling father and leaving my little brother alone to deal with everything without me. For the record, this was 1980, before all the modern inventions of home schooling and USTA Player Development sites and private tennis academies now littering the country were prevalent. The model at the Nick Bollettieri Tennis Academy was vastly unproven. The thought of having dozens of teenage kids from all around the world living away from home for the first time; practicing and training together on the same courts six to seven hours a day; going to the same school and taking the same classes; trying to beat each other's brains in on the weekends in tournaments; and then coming home to live mere feet from each other in the same dormitories: I mean, what could possibly go wrong?

My Number One fan and supporter — my mother Margaret: Just look at her fierce love and pride as she looks into my eyes. I can only imagine how hard it was for my mom to watch me leave home for good at 15 years old

My tryout was arranged at the Colony Beach and Tennis Resort Courts, where Nick Bollettieri was already training players. Mom was pretty quiet the day of my tryout; I'm sure she had mixed feelings no matter the outcome. I met Nick's assistant, Julio Moros, who took me to the court to see if I was academy material. The workout was to last an hour. As nervous as I was, being on the first court with all the eyes upon me motivated me to do my best. I felt I was doing well, when half way through my tryout, Julio informed me I had qualified for the academy. I was scared telling my mom, afraid she would not want me to move away from home at such a young age. But we had both known for some time now that prosperity and success lay outside the dusty dirt road we lived on in Orlando. Tennis was to be the delivery system by which all prosperity would come. It meant being associated with people and athletes of a different breed; either the wealth of the OTC or the ORC or the great athletes I was facing every weekend in tournaments throughout greater Florida. The academy would have me permanently embedded with these types of families and players, people Nick would make very clear were the winners in life and if you wanted to be successful in life, find out who the winners were and stick close.

My mom believed this theory too, as did Dr Nazareth, and coach Hough and coach Pratt from ORC and my former coach and mentor Jim, all of whom in their own ways told me that the sign of a successful person is one who never regrets taking chances, only not taking them. And what lay before me was an opportunity very few aspiring young tennis players ever got the chance to take. All was quiet on the homefront for once. Mom was in remission from her cancer, dad was going to Alcoholics Anonymous and doing the best he could to love and provide for my mother through her illness while taking care of himself. My brother was cool, and frankly, I was more than alright with the whole idea of moving away from home at such a young age.

Most importantly of all, those who knew me best and wanted the best for me were on board too, especially my mom. So without even the slightest bit of drama, I accepted my offer to attend the NBTA to begin in the fall of 1980 as a full-time, live-in attendee of what was soon to become the greatest and most famous tennis academy the world will ever know. If I was ever going to make it in tennis, the NBTA was the place to be. I was 15 years old, preparing to move away from home for good. Life was setting up perfectly before me to succeed. All that remained was for me to execute.

CHAPTER

7

TRAINING WITH THE BEST

I enrolled at the NBTA on Labor Day of 1980, with two rackets, a couple pair of Kmart shoes, and 10 bucks to my name. Many a great tennis mind has worked tirelessly trying to concoct the perfect training routine. In the 30-plus years I have been away from the academy, high performance tennis training has come a long way. For myself and the dozens of other talented teens who descended upon Bradenton back then, we were not these perfectly polished finished products. We all had a great deal of upside still to go before we reached that plateau in tennis where a player has to work unimaginably hard just to get a little better. What Nick did, whether by master plan or just idiot savant, was throw a bunch of hungry talented teens together and have us compete with each other all day every day in essentially every area of life. We competed with each other academically, socially, on the court competitively and most importantly, for Nick's attention. If you got picked to be on Nick's court, that meant he saw something special in you, that you had what it took to be a winner, for that was what Nick was all about and stressed from day one. To be a winner, act like a winner, train like a winner, hang around the winners and guess what? You'll soon be a winner yourself.

From a strictly tennis perspective, we were all pretty successful players already, with techniques and styles of play pretty well ingrained. The NBTA was not so much about technique as it was about training. There was very little overhauling of players' games when you got to our level of play; the cost benefit analysis of making major changes was just not favorable. What NBTA   41 provided for us was an opportunity to groove our respective styles through hours and hours of daily repetitions, but all in a hierarchical court structure with the pinnacle achievement being trying to capture Nick's eye and get chosen to be on the desired first court with him.

Dani Leal, one of the best juniors in the United States, with future top-30 singles player in the world (as well as my childhood friend) Patricia Hy and myself as we relax poolside after study hall.

I walked into a Who's Who of junior and future professional tennis players: Jimmy Arias, Mike DePalmer, Eric Korita, Carling Bassett, Pam Casale, Pablo Arraya, Kathleen Horvath, Cary Cohenour and so many others. These were my new best friends. I wanted to be just like them, which for me at that time meant to train like them. This proved to not be difficult. There were no individual programs at the NBTA. We all got up at up at 6:30, had breakfast at 7, bus at 7:30, school from 7:45 to 11:45, lunch at the academy 12 to 12:30, on the court from 12:30 to 6, shower, dinner, a no talking study hall from 7 to 9, from 9 to 10 poolside relaxation, 10:30 lights out. Get up the next day and repeat. This was my life. If I wanted to be successful at tennis, I was in the perfect place. Off the courts Julio Moros along with Carolina Bolivar-Murphy, who managed the dorms and was our go-to person for any problems, took such great care of me, making sure I was doing OK.

The Bradenton Academy, where I went to school each morning, was founded by Dr. Murray Gerber and his wife Lois. The Gerbers, along with their daughter Susan, an English teacher, knew of my very fragile upbringing and showed an amazing amount of love and support. Mrs. Gerber and Susan in particular provided me with a great deal of encouragement, made me feel special and always reminded me I would do great things in life. Their impact on my life was a game-changer, a defining moment, and I am clearly in a better place in my life today due to their impact on me at a very important time in my development. To this day we are still family although sadly Dr. Gerber has passed away.

One area of life I was already successful at was getting attention. Not always the kind I wanted, like from the adults at my club, but on a tennis court I knew how to catch your eye. It wasn't long before Nick figured out who the overly hard-working enthusiastic new kid was. Soon I would get the first of many acknowledgements to come from Nick that I had the right stuff to make it as a tennis player. I played with a chip on my shoulder; like I had something to prove. I was going to be tougher and work harder and compete until the last ball was hit. Nick loved this and it couldn't have been more than a couple weeks of being in attendance at the academy before Nick sat down with me to learn more about my life and circumstances. When I explained my family's financial hardships to him and the lifetime deal I had made with Dr. Nazareth just to be able to attend the NBTA, Nick did the first of what would become many magnanimous deeds.

He took my lifetime contract with Dr. Nazareth and he ripped it in half. He took my half scholarship to attend the NBTA and he made it a full ride. Carolina had played a major role in helping Nick to better understand my difficult home life and her desire for me to be able to stay at the Academy and suggested to Nick I receive a full scholarship. Nick became the coach and father figure I never had but always wanted. And it could not have come at a better time. Practicing every day for hours on end with the best junior players the United States could produce was paying off. At the NBTA, if you were a good enough athlete with a good head and a strong work ethic you were going to get better, and get better quickly. And I did. Within a year of being at the NBTA I had gone from being number 10 in Florida to a top-15 junior player in the United States, suddenly thrusting me among the best players in the country and all that entailed. Frankly, nobody from the Blair family or anyone from my old neighborhood knew the first thing about being great at tennis, but Nick did, and I was very fortunate to be under his guidance and tutelage at such an important developmental period in my life.

And so I had arrived at last that competitive stage I had worked so hard to attain. It was June of 1981 and I was competing in the State junior championship tournament in the boys' 16-and-under division. And I had reached the final. I would I face my long-time great friend Robert Green. It was to be a defining moment.

Leaving home left me so excited for the future. But I was so worried about my mother and my brother and best friend, Joe, as I began to compete around the world.

Robert and I had gone to the same school since the first grade at St. Charles in Orlando. The Green family was tennis royalty in Florida tennis in the late 70s and early 80s. Robert's mom was the president of the Florida Tennis Association and Robert had several siblings who had paved the way for him on the Florida junior tennis circuit in earlier years. His brothers Raymond and Chris and his sister Peggy all played competitive junior tennis and did it very well. The Greens were also quite affluent and always contributed to organizations and others at all times. Mrs. Green took a liking to me and was instrumental in helping me with funding for tournaments and equipment by having the Central Florida Tennis Confederation sponsor me.

44   The Greens were at the heart of an extraordinary support network of indi-

viduals who supported me back then, financially, emotionally and morally. As I look back now, I am filled with gratitude toward them.

I remember Jan and Bill Enos, who stepped up and guided me as I grew into a young man. They always encouraged me to remember the importance of my on-court behavior and of being a role model.

Mary Ann Plante would always encourage me and helped me financially from time to time, which meant so much to me. I recently spent an incredible evening with Mary Ann for her 80th birthday with my longtime fried T.J. Jones. I will never forget Mary Ann and her love and support for me in the early years, and I must say she was a heck of a mixed doubles partner.

A wonderful woman named June Fry, who shopped at Match Point Tennis shop on Highway 17-92, really made a huge difference for my parents as she provided thousands of dollars towards my tennis when I needed it most as I entered my early teen years. I often wonder where Mrs Fry is today so I can give her a big hug and say, "Thank you."

On the Florida junior tennis circuit I had the incredible love and support from the most important person running and organizing junior tennis in Florida, Bobby Curtis. He loved me and I loved him and still do to this day. He was always in my corner and always made mom and me so comfortable even though we stuck out like a sore thumb.

Mr. Sojo, my great friend and competitor Robert's dad, always gave me support and from time to time would buy a nice warmup suit for me or something else I may have needed for my tennis and would say to me, "Do not tell Robert, but I think you are great and you are going to make it in life one day on and off the courts." You have no idea how that made me feel at 12 and 13 years old.

And of course none of this would have been possible without Jim Kelaher picking me out of a big crowd a few summers earlier and taking my fragile life under his wing.

And now I had arrived at that game-changing moment. There was Robert Green across the net from me, a familiar face but in a very new environment. We were shaking hands. I had just won the most coveted tournament in Florida, the State Closed Junior Championships for the boys' 16-and-under division. I was the Florida boys' 16 champion. I had arrived.

I knew that although I was alone on the court, I had would not have gotten to this point without the incredible contributions of all those generous 45 people. And I also knew I was never going to allow where I came from, what my home looked like, how much money my parents had, or what kind of car we drove or the clothes I wore ever again to affect my ability to perform on the court at the highest level. And I would expect the best result every time I walked on the court.

For many years I had used my circumstances as an excuse for losing matches or acting out in a negative way, to feel sorry for myself. After this day, this victory, I was determined to create my own destiny with every result and every action on and off the court. I had arrived on this day and I was there to stay. Mom and I left that tournament that day with the winner's trophy. Looking at each other, we smiled and shared a good cry, realizing that our efforts as a team were beginning to pay off. I will never forget the car ride home as my mom kept bringing up story after story of all the people who had helped us. She pulled over outside Orlando before we arrived home and asked me to make a promise to her.

I said, "Absolutely."

She said, "Bobby, never forget all the people who helped you. And from this day forward, do something for someone else every chance you can. Just step up and do it, even if it's not easy".

I said I would. I left that moment feeling indebted to so many. I felt an obligation to show them their time and investment on my behalf was good and well deserved by conducting myself on and off the court in the most professional and respectful manner. The first nine months at the Nick Bollettieri Tennis Academy had improved my game so much, making this moment possible. Again, it was Nick who was instrumental not only in my win on court, but in a life-changing moment.

8

FALLING IN LOVE:
THE WORST THAT COULD HAPPEN

Nick and the NBTA were providing me with a platform on which to thrive. I had a whole new group of great guy friends to whom I was able to be as close as one could be without the awkwardness of my hidden sexuality affecting my ability to live comfortably. The girls loved me and I was able to secure a girlfriend there early, helping keep my secret under wraps and avoiding detection. Everything was still quiet on the home front. Mom's cancer was in remission and Dad was sober and working his AA program. I was working super hard on my tennis and enjoying the fruits of my efforts. I was as happy as I had ever been in my young life.

And then it happened. At the age of 17, I had my first serious crush.

His name was Dani Leal. We were already friends when I played him in the finals of the Bollettieri International Junior Championships at Christmas of 1981. During our match I was having a hard time competing against him as intensely as I normally did. Maybe I was tired or just had a bad day, but I remember the feeling distinctly. After the event, Nick offered Dani a full ride to come to the Academy, which he accepted. Within a week of his arrival we were inseparable.

My every thought was soon consumed with him, with where he was, what he was doing, who he was talking to. We were the best of friends; hung out all the time together, he oblivious to the obsession he had become in my young life.   47

I was alone in a love meant for two. Little did I know then that falling in love was the worst thing that could ever happen to a young gay male like myself.

I knew I couldn't risk expressing how I felt. Too much to lose. I would chastise myself for allowing myself to have such strong feelings for him. He was a close friend but also a close competitor of mine, someone I needed to keep a competitive advantage over anyway I could. The whole ordeal was torturous. I would admonish myself every day to knock it off, to stop feeling this way, like somehow I had some control over how I felt about him, for it's been said you can choose who you like but not who you love, and it might have been easier for me if he wasn't right in front of me all day.

Every day I would struggle with my feelings. We were the best of friends so I was not being denied his attention and affection. Our connection was everything I could have hoped it to be short of him knowing how I really felt. At times I would find a place of comfort regarding him. The strong feelings I felt for him would abate to where I could be around him as just a friend. Then something would trigger me. We would often play each other on the court at the academy. I would get so mad with myself for not treating him just like any other tennis competitor. I just couldn't beat him, and it had little to do with him being a better player than myself. I just couldn't don my normal game face with him, that killer instinct, leave it all out there, win no matter what intensity that was becoming my trademark.

My feelings for him were just too strong. I would give him every close call, every benefit of the doubt. I tried so much harder at not alienating him than I did at trying to defeat him, it would leave me so angry at myself for being weak on the tennis court, for not having my priorities in line of being the best player I could be every day.

At times he would have a girlfriend. I would see them together and literally get physically sick. I would retreat to my dorm alone and just stew with inner turmoil. People would sometimes see me in my distressed state and ask me what was up, if I was feeling OK? After a particularly tough evening of seeing him all about with his new girlfriend, he came back to the dormitories to see why I was hanging out alone when all the girls at the academy adored me. And then he asked me which girl I liked. I so wanted to look him right in the eye and say "You..I love you...I love everything about you. I can't think, I can't sleep. I can't eat. I'm in this perpetual state of distraction when you are in the same room as me .When I see you talk to other people or start to flirt around with another girl I get literally sick to my stomach and I feel like I'm going to go crazy if I don't tell you this now."

I absolutely knew I could never say those words to him no matter how many times I rehearsed them. I would have the most vivid dreams of us being together only to wake up in shock and deeply saddened that my dreams were merely that. Other times the dreams were devastating, with me humiliated and the friendship destroyed. The message I was getting from these visions was that I needed to continue to hide who I was and hide it really good. There was nowhere to go with what I was feeling. Nobody to talk to, nobody I could trust who would handle my feelings with the care they needed. It was a loneliness at times that I can barely describe, even today.

I cringe now at the thought of what it would have been like to have tried to have come out back then. What would they have done with me at the academy if I had? It would have been pandemonium. My ability to hide who I was from a very early age was a survival skill I needed, but it became a temporary solution to a long-term problem. A problem that grew every day, with every encounter I had in those young years. I was not being honest and I was not being true to myself. And if I could get away with this behavior without being caught, then I could repeat it, over and over. If my transgressions weren't exposed, in my mind it was only a lie if I got caught. I would rationalize my actions away that I would straighten all this gay stuff out another day, some future day. Or I would try to pray it all away. Maybe I would just grow out of it. Or else some day I'd tell everybody, just not today. Or so I would tell myself. Everything was beginning to be put off to some future vague date that I convinced myself would come.

I now know those future projections were just a method of dealing with the anxiety that I was different from my friends. I was becoming aware that I was part of a minority in our society that was horribly misunderstood. That I possessed a sexual orientation that was demonized and stigmatized by powerful social forces way beyond the scope of my control. Those social forces had been telling lies about my makeup for some time now, that gay men like me were mentally ill, that we were all sex crazed pedophiles going straight to hell to burn in perpetuity. And it was just all so confusing, for all I knew myself to be was a young guy without the language or reasoning skills to fully explain why I felt the way I felt, and why I loved the people that I did, other than it was all I knew and that it was hardly a matter of choice.   49

It was right about this time that I was becoming socially and politically aware of what it meant to be gay. I sought to better understand why I was different from all the other kids at the academy and if there was anything I could do about it. I didn't sign on to feel stressful, difficult, isolated, lonely, not understood, and unable to express how I felt to anyone. I wasn't much for school and our assigned textbooks back then, but I was developing a thirst for learning what all the feelings I was having were really all about. Those days were the pre-internet days, well before our modern times of having the entire history of human thought in the palm of our hand. My education was going to take some hard work. I was afraid to go to the library and check out gay related books and certainly I wasn't going to be caught dead reading one in the stacks by anyone I knew. So I had to look around in book stores and magazine shops. One day at the magazine racks I found a long essay about a pivotal news story I remembered from a few years earlier and I began eagerly to read it.

The article was about Harvey Milk, the first openly gay politician in America. I had never forgotten the moment in 1978 when we were watching TV at home. Suddenly, the show was interrupted for a breaking news report. California Senator Dianne Feinstein appeared on the screen. Cameras and microphones were thrust in her face as she waited for the crowd to quiet before she spoke. Two politicians in San Francisco had been shot dead, Mayor George Moscone and Harvey Milk. It was shattering news, but of course I said nothing to my family.

Now I began to read the magazine article with increased interest. It recounted Milk's strong belief that every gay person should

just come out, just get it over with, just come out to our parents, to our friends, to our employers, to our neighbors. I remember thinking how insane that sounded back then; yet how right that sounds today. If we all came out today in unison, the whole struggle for gay rights would be over. So many straight people would learn that their children were gay and their brothers were gay and their sisters were gay and their closest of friends and most trusted confidants were gay and that the boy scout leaders and military personnel and clergy and yes, even aspiring professional tennis players like myself were gay. If you loved us before, you would love us even more now, knowing the burden we carried.

I read on as Milk made it sound so simple to come out. Just say those three simple words: I am gay. But what he implored all of us in the gay community to do was being said completely in the abstract. It would be so much more complicated for each of us to do in our personal lives, yet he was so right, that it was just three simple little words to say. Yet he seemed oblivious to the reality that the shortest distance between two points was often unbearable. Three little words. I am gay. I cannot tell you how many times I stood in front of my mirror rehearsing those three little words. I would even pull out a stop watch and time how long it would take. If I said it quickly, three tenths of a second, if I drew it out, maybe a whole second.

Three words it would take me 30 years to finally utter to my straight tennis friends. People out there in straight world 2014 likely shake their heads in disbelief that something so seemingly simple could be so hard to say; but that was my reality, and that of countless others, back then. I continued to scour the magazine for more about how Milk had started to make such a difference in San Francisco politics. I recall how moving it was to realize that maybe, because of Milk, there might be a place in the future at society's table for people like me. Harvey Milk had been out and talking about it and he hadn't sacrificed one bit of who he was, all the while encouraging us all to come out in nearly every sentence in which he was quoted.

I remember thinking more and more about him, dying inside to have a mentor or guide like him to talk to about what I was experiencing. If only I could have asked him: Would it better to be out of the closet and work on managing the reactions around me now, or was it better to just put off my coming out to a day when hopefully I was more mature to handle the matter?

Then I came to the part of the essay where he was shot dead by a deranged gunman. As I was reminded of that terrible moment, my heart sank like I had lost a very close friend.

Was this what it was going to be like for me if I came out in a sports world where there was nobody else out? I knew enough from my reading that there had to be other male athletes in competition oriented just like me, but was professional sports ready for an out of the closet gay male athlete like myself? Is this what it would be like, to be in fear for my life? What about all my athletic aspirations and everything I had worked so hard for and my mother had sacrificed so much for? Should I just forget about all my dreams because apparently the times were not safe for coming out. Not even close. I kept reading. The article vividly described how the gay and lesbian community, accompanied by thousands of straight marchers from their extended community, performed one of the most elegant responses to senseless violence in civil rights history, a silent candlelight vigil through the darkened streets of a San Francisco night. And I wondered then as I wonder right now if I could have remained that calm in the face of such evil because something was just so wrong about how Harvey Milk's life was taken.

But as I read on, my spirits were buoyed by such a courageous statement by my distant brothers and sisters that maybe someday there will be a seat at America's table for people wired like me. I was a long way away in space and place from the marchers on that dreadfully sad night in San Francisco, but their courage in mourning touched me deeply and forever and I knew that some day I would be a part of future marches. I committed right then and there to grow up to be just like them in their fight against injustice. I would fight someday for my fellow brothers and sisters. There was much work to be done and I was going to need to be more brave than coward. I would do everything in my power to never have to hold a candle for another slain brother, even if that meant being the person they were holding the candle for. But I was soon to learn that every time I felt I could step forward, that candle of hope was being snuffed out for me.

9

NEW AWAKENINGS, COLLEGE DECISIONS

Summer of 1982. I was a teenager living away from home. Be careful what you wish for. I loved my new environs at the NBTA with all my great new tennis friends, but crazy as my home life could be at times, I missed my family. Sure, my immediate living conditions improved from a case of addition by subtraction; not being around my father's alcoholism was good for my serenity, but I worried daily about my family. Maybe I had a little case of survivor's guilt. I worried about my brother and how he was dealing with everything, I worried about my Dad and his sobriety and his ability to take care of my mom and brother. And, of course, I was worried sick about my mom and her cancer and that impending doom that hung over us if it was ever to return. We youngsters grow up quickly in this tennis life. Someone puts a racket in your hand one day. Take a couple of lessons, a workout or two. Then someone gets a funny idea that you should play a tournament. You take a couple of beatings, stick to it a bit and before long you're driving home with your first trophy clenched to your breast. It's not for everyone. Let me state clearly, there are much less demanding ways to go through childhood than training to be a an athlete. Having to eat, drink, sleep a sport from a very early age to have any chance of success is probably not the most normal way to grow up. But it was the life I chose and loved from day one.

I was growing up in tennis' golden era. The names and personalities on TV will always be part of our sport's history as professional tennis surged into the sporting mainstream. We all had our heroes, players we put on pedestals, whose panache and ability seemed safe to admire. No real worry about conceding a competitive advantage to those guys; they deserved one. But we start growing up. The players a little older than me seemed so much better and out of reach; best to concern myself with my own age group.

A couple more years, a few more inches, 20 more pounds or so, all of a sudden my serves are popping a few feet up the fence, just like all the guys I looked up to, and my kicker is starting to really jump, up high and away, just like all the guys I look up to. I'm running shots down I never ran down before, serves I used to just wave at I'm cracking back deep and with malice, my ground strokes and passing shots are getting pretty heavy and then the guys I looked up to all those years want to hit a few, and we do, and I can more than hold my own. Hell, I even push them around a good deal. It's natural to minimize it, say it's only practice, don't read too much in to it as the guy I was just pushing around goes off to play the tour. Then one morning I pick up the sports page and there it is, the guy I was just pushing around just beat one of my idols, and I get a little nervous thinking wow, maybe, just maybe, some day that could be me.

But I'm still an amateur, a few hard years away from pulling down a paycheck for my tennis exploits. Tennis does have ways of rewarding its non-professional ranks, though. A couple of good results and it's all about rankings and getting free stuff. Rackets, shoes, clothes. Nothing cooler than being a kid and getting a huge box in the mail from Nike or Prince, full of the latest models and the latest lines. Just made me want to get out there and work even harder. As I get a little older, more free stuff, 16, 17 I'm still going at it hard. I got my full ride to the NBTA more out of need than merit, but let the record be clear, having the top ranked kids at your academy is good for business. As we junior tennis phenoms keep progressing, the awards start to grow. In 1982, my first year in the 18-and-unders, I get invited to try out for the US Junior Davis Cup (JDC) team in California. Brutal, all-expenses-paid, two-week trip against the nation's best. Make the team and it's an all expenses paid summer of travel and tennis with the best the United States Tennis Association has to offer.

I didn't make JDC my first year but saw I could more than hang with the best. After those tryouts in 1982, I hit the road out west to play a couple of the hard court nationals. First one in Burlingame went alright; the second one in Belvedere I made my first national final on the hard courts, beating some of

the top players in the country along the way. Feeling pretty good about myself and how I was playing, it was off to Louisville for the National Clay Court Championships on my favorite surface. My flight arrived at the Louisville National Airport, and upon grabbing my luggage I was greeted by a rather gregarious man representing the tournament holding up the tournament housing card.

Traveling the world on U.S. Junior Team to Costa Rica: Marc Fishman (top right); Dan Granot (top left); Dani Leal (middle right); myself (middle left); Joven Cizek (back left)

"Well hello there young man, my name is Jim Baird and I am in charge of the housing this week, and let me help you with your bags, because you are staying with me."

OK. I was riding pretty high then I recall, felt I had it going on. I was feeling really good when Jim grabbed my bags and walked us out to his brand new Mercedes and drove us to his beautiful mansion in the Louisville suburbs. I could get used to this life real quickly, I remember thinking. A couple of things I knew I liked was getting a lot of attention and being around wealthy, successful people. Jim was both. We hit it off well from the moment we met; he just could not have been any nicer to me. He escorted me around town that whole week, gave me some extra spending money to take my friends out, took me shopping and to dinner, and within a week he knew everything about me and my family and what my young tennis life was like and I felt I had made myself a great new friend.

Front row: Aaron Krickstein and me; Back row: (left) John Powless, (right) Gene Scott, as we won the International Senior and Junior World Team Championships

I remember wondering that first year in 1982 when I was 17 if Jim was gay; if he had picked up on some energy of mine or if I was just being a bit paranoid. Either way, I had a good tournament and as we parted, we traded numbers and addresses and promised to keep in touch throughout the next year, where hopefully he would house me again the following year. Call me naive at that age but I was not the only young man staying at Jim's house that week in Louisville. A young boy named Gene was there the whole time. Jim and he seemed oddly close for two people with 30 years difference between them. They both always seemed to have a beer in their hands and the smell of pot hung heavily in every room they occupied. At other times they would disappear for chunks of time together. At first I thought little of it until near the end of the week when early one morning I saw them both emerge from Jim's bedroom.

My best friends and I wrapped up our life-changing times at the NBTA by winning the
State High School Tennis Team Championships. (Left to right) Tony Zanoni, Cary Cohenour, me,
Mike Gustafson, Dani Leal, Shawn Cartwright, Darren Herman

My reaction was one part disbelief, another part intrigue. How did that
ever come to be? What kind of arrangement did they have? Everything about
that first week with Jim Baird seemed idyllic. He literally was the nicest most
generous person I had ever met. His demeanor and mood never altered from
the moment he set eyes upon me at the airport. In retrospect, I knew what that
first look he gave me at the airport meant from my days at the Orlando Racquet Club when I would catch the older guys checking me out. But I was in
Louisville to play tennis and just wasn't going to go there. Before I left, I sat
down with Gene, the 15-year-old boy, and asked him some questions.

He told me he had fallen on really hard times, was struggling some, when
Jim rolled up in his brand new Mercedes and told Gene he was coming home
with him. Jim took him in, helped him clean out and clean up and was training
him to become part of his sales force. If he could stay clean, Jim would get
him a car and a job and set him up good. I couldn't help but ask what he had to
do for all that and Gene hesitated, a little shy, a little ashamed, and said he let
him have his way with him. He never had to touch him but he let Jim go down
on him when he wanted to and for that he had a home and a life and a chance
at a great life and that he wasn't gay but he felt somehow that he owed Jim
that for all he was doing for him. And as long as he didn't have to do anything 57

to Jim he could deal with it, but he was torn because he knew it didn't feel right. He also felt a huge obligation to this most complex of men who would do virtually anything for him for just a little bit of play each week. Hmmm, I thought to myself, as it was becoming apparent to me that I too could have such a set up life with my new friend if I so desired. I left Louisville that year in 1982 in a good place. Jim and I stayed in touch throughout the next few months, with us promising to have a lot of fun together the next year when I came back to Louisville.

Fall of 1982, I'm back at the NBTA for my senior year of high school. I was one of the top two or three recruits in the country for college the next year. The payoffs from the hard work were about to multiply. Free stuff was great, free trips and tryouts were better, but a four-year all-expenses-paid full scholarship to the university of my choosing was pretty cool. My best friend and first crush was heading out to Malibu, California to play for the esteemed Dr. Allen Fox at Pepperdine University. In my readings up on gay culture, Southern California, and in particular West Hollywood, was akin to gay Disneyland. I often wondered then and now if my young life would have been different if I had had young gay friends like me, young gay men that were positive role models and living proud openly gay lives. When I read up further on Malibu, I saw that Olympic diver Greg Louganis lived there. I had a thing for Hollywood and celebrity at this time in my life; I wondered if I got accepted to Pepperdine maybe I could have gay friends, maybe even a gay boyfriend. Maybe even a famous gay boyfriend like Greg Louganis, whom I could fall in love with and, oh, the crazy dreamy young mind I once had.

But Nick had other plans for me. Nick had a great working relationship with the head coach at the University of Arkansas. This was Tom Pucci's top 10 nationally ranked program. He arranged a recruiting trip for me to go to Fayetteville and visit the school (another perk of being highly ranked, back in my day incoming recruits had up to six free trips to all the schools that would have them). From the first moment I met coach Pucci, I knew he was the right coach for me and I would be attending Arkansas the following fall. He said all the right things to me from the start; that he wanted me to be a leader and that he would treat me and all his other players like his own sons. Plus this was about as middle America as one could find. Considering what my emotional maturity was back then, it was likely best I chose a school with no semblance

or proximity to anything resembling gay culture. I was thriving as a tennis player keeping my sexuality in the closet as I had at the NBTA; this was no time to put my tennis future at risk. To whom much is given, much is expected. A lot was being given to me to attend the U of A on scholarship, a lot was going to be expected. This was no time for experimentation and distractions. There would be time for all that down the road. It was going to be time to play tennis and get an education. With great pride and joy I accepted my four-year full scholarship offer to U of Arkansas early, getting that stressful decision out of the way.

CHAPTER

10

LOSING MOM

Back at the academy, I got a letter from my mom. When cancer enters your life it changes everything. You know it could come back any time, you know you can never fully relax, you know it's random, aggressive, life changing, deadly. You try to act like everything is okay but tension always hangs in the air between you and the afflicted. I worried every day when I was at the NBTA that I would get that letter from my mom saying the cancer was back. This was that day.

I opened the letter and there it was. Her cancer was back and it was bad. I started crying immediately. The people at the academy were unbelievably consoling. I got to the phone to call my mom but we didn't say much. It was such a profoundly sad moment for us, she couldn't even give me the hollow assurances that she would be okay. She was back in chemotherapy and radiation treatments and very weak and very sick. She implored me through the tears to be strong, that she was fighting as hard as she could and that I should too, with head up and shoulders back, and not to let her illness affect my dreams to be the best. She told me that God knew what he was doing and who were we to question His master plan, that I was her son, and to keep making her proud every day. She said she would defeat this cancer but only if we both stayed strong and fought. But she was not going to be fine. Her cancer was pretty advanced when they found it, but my mom didn't want to share that with me. Summer of 1983, I have my full ride in hand. I seriously debated taking the summer off to go home and be with my mother. Her treatments were not going well and the word came down that she was terminal and it was just a matter of time. But mom would have nothing of this. In one of the last and most fiery conversations I had with her she implored me to go out and play with a mission, a higher purpose, that though her time here on earth was coming to a close, she believed strongly in the afterlife and we would meet again on the other side and rejoice in all the great tennis memories I would accrue that summer.

What are you supposed to say to that? My mother's dying wish was for me to go out and play my heart out for her, who gave me everything. And I did.

The summer began with the JDC tryouts. A year older, a year wiser and playing with a sense of purpose that was hard to explain or quantify. I just felt like I couldn't lose and I wouldn't lose, and I didn't. I swept through the grueling tryouts of America's top 36 juniors in style, winning my division and cruising in to a position on the elite Junior Davis Cup team. Summer was shaping up well for me as I got off to a great start and headed in to Louisville once again, dreaming of becoming a national junior champion.

I was excited to see my new friend Jim. He had been so kind to me and my family from the first moment of hearing about my mom's illness. But this year I did not travel alone. I had made the US JDC team, meaning I was part of a dozen traveling players flying around the country with coaching staff in tow. I usually roomed in hotels with one of my teammates but Jim had arranged for me to stay with him when I came to town. One other thing I brought with me to Louisville that summer was a girlfriend, Mary Clare O'Brien, whom I had met in Dallas at the National Indoors the past November.

I was nervous about showing up to Jim's. The look on his face when he saw who I showed up with was intense. He was not happy. I picked up on the vibe but he kept his cool and graciously welcomed us to his home. That night he took us to dinner, his focus laser sharp on me, barely even acknowledging my girlfriend at the table. My girlfriend and I retired to our room for the night and did what young lovers do when they hadn't seen each other in a while.

The next morning Jim was tense. He pulled me aside and told me she can't stay at his house any longer and he had arranged for a hotel for her to stay in. He said that if the JDC coach found out what had happened the night before with us making all that noise in his house, I would be thrown off the team. He was promised to keep the whole ordeal quiet as long as she just moved over to the hotel.

Confused, we agreed. I asked about Gene's whereabouts. Jim said they had had a falling out just last week. I said that seemed odd. I had just spoken to him last week, which he was surprised to hear.

"What did he tell you?"

"Not much, said you guys were all cool."

"Well, don't worry yourself with such matters. You're here to play tennis and win a national tournament and I am your host and it's just the two of us and let's have a great fun week like we spoke about. Do you need anything? Here is some money to get you through the week in case I don't see you during the day with everything going on this week."

The week commenced. I was playing well and had a good chance of making a deep run on my best surface, the green clay. After the matches, I would come back to my housing to this giant house all alone with Jim. We would talk about life and the future and mom and her struggles and all the ways he could help my career. If I kept improving and if we stayed in touch he made it clear he would help me. We talked about all the great places we would travel and great things we would do, and how I would need a car at college and maybe we could go car shopping after the tournament was over. It all felt so positive and supportive, like he was already one of my best friends.

I won my early rounds handily, played a couple of tough matches and then had a big win in the quarterfinals. I rushed to the phone to call my mom and give her the great news but the conversation never got going. She was hurting badly and I instantly got scared her end may be near. I debated defaulting and going home to be with her, but again she would have nothing to do with that. I was crying as we hung up, her last weakened words to me were, "Head up, Shoulders back."

I hung up crying. Jim walked in and saw me and told me to relax and he would see what he could do. I was upset, Jim was consoling me. He talked again about the truck he wanted to get me as he started to rub my cramping legs. I laid back, having already decided in my mind if he wanted to be with me I would let him. This was my introduction to the hustling life. Somehow in my young immature mind I felt a sense of obligation to this complex man. I was too young to know what was really going on here, not just with me but with Gene and likely countless other teenage boys like myself who had been whisked away in his new Mercedes to his beautiful home. It was such a confusing time. He couldn't stop gushing about how proud he was of me for making the JDC team and how courageous I was being in the face of my mom's illness and how I just needed to lay back and relax and everything would be alright. And I had a big match to prepare for the next day and that's when his sports massage of my legs veered out of bounds as I didn't resist and just let him do what he wanted to while I just lay there.

Next day, biggest match of my life and I'm dying. My legs are tired, my mind and emotions are fried and confused and I'm playing a beast of a junior in Luke Jensen. I got off to a terrible start and was pretty much getting my butt kicked. I was down a set and a break and nothing was going well. I was at the back of the court trying to gather myself on a scorching hot Kentucky morning when I hear a woman's voice yell right to me, "Head up, Shoulders back and come on now!!!"

It was my mom, being escorted in by Jim. He had called her the night before and made arrangements for her to fly in that morning to see me play my semifinal. I almost lost it right there on the court. It took me a couple of moments to process what was going on, but before long, I dug in. The sight of her being there triggered every coaching tip she had ever given me: One point at a time, never give up, embrace the pressure, make your opponent beat you, wait for the right time to exert your will on your opponent and then go for the win. And with each point I won, my mom let me and everyone know she was there and whom she was rooting for. My mom had never seen me play outside of the state of Florida, yet here she was, being escorted in to the front row to watch me play the biggest match of my life in front of a packed crowd. I got going pretty good upon her arrival. Evened up the second set, eked out a tight second tiebreaker to put it in to a third, got behind again in the third, started cramping. But I never gave up, hung in there, hung in some more and in well over three hours pulled off a 7-5 victory in the third, a marathon comeback over one of the best juniors in the USA.

I guess we all have those moments in our lives that if the cameras were rolling, it would make great entertainment. This was mine. It's hard to write this without getting overly emotional about it all even 30 years later, but it was all that. I cramped up terribly after the match as my mom did everything she could to help me, both of us sobbing uncontrollably. But as tennis goes, my work in Louisville was not done. I had 24 hours to pull it together and play for my first national title against soon to be famous Aaron Krickstein. That evening Jim was hosting a dinner for my JDC team and all our friends and family. I recall sitting down at the table, looking at my girlfriend, at my JDC coach Brad Louderback, at Jim and at my mom and thinking how crazy my young life had become already. I just have to believe that Federer and Nadal didn't have to go through evenings like this the night before their first big title match. I was the center of so many people's attention that night, and as I said, I loved the attention, but this was a bit much. I just could not wait to get the dinner over quickly and get away from everyone.

Big match the next day. My mom is on fire rooting as hard as she ever has for me as I played the match of my life. Nick flew in for the event but chose to sit with the Krickstein camp, something that didn't thrill me, but this was no time for resentments. We fought for hours, I'm hanging tough, it was 3-3 in the third and I got my introduction to the tennis big time. Aaron started raining winners down on me one after another. Huge forehand after huge forehand and I remember thinking I can hang with these guys but the great ones have another level. Aaron took me out 6-3 in the third for the National Clay Court title.

Moments after our National Championship match, my respect and admiration for Aaron is immense.

(Left to right) Me, Nick Bollettieri and Aaron Krickstein, moments after our marathon three-set final.

Exhausted, right after shaking hands with my opponent, I hobbled over to my crying mom and just put my arms around her and held her as tight as I could. It was the most heartfelt moment you could ever imagine and I just don't think I could possibly have felt more love for another person than I did in that moment of embrace. We did it, mom and I. From a dirt road home in the Orlando suburbs to my first ball hit with her on some scratchy public court, here we were, on the national stage, we had made it, her boy and herself. We were both so overcome with emotion, me just holding her there as long as I could until she whispered in my ear, "I'll be watching over you from heaven soon, my son. Go out in the world and make a difference. You have made my life the best any mother could dream of."

I feared this would be the last time I would see my mother alive. She would lose her battle to cancer five weeks later. Her funeral was tough. I walked away from my mother's grave alone to have a moment to myself. I was profoundly sad. Yeah, she was my mom, but she was my best friend too and taught me everything about life a person could in our way too short time together.

I was an adult now, off to college and the big time. But a part of me died that day too, my innocence and my ideas about life being fair, and I learned that bad things can happen to good people.

I realized that day that people leave a legacy behind; my mom had raised her two boys almost to adulthood and she was a part of us and just because she was gone now did not mean everything was forgotten. The values she drove in to me from my earliest memories were just the kind of strong ethics a person like me was going to need as I began to come of age in a world that was not going to be very welcoming to people like me. I tried to apply her favorite words and rejoin the crowd, Head up, Shoulders back, but I just couldn't do it quite yet as the waves of sadness overcame me again.

Here was a woman who had lived her entire life for her children and her concept of God. And so we convened at her funeral, hundreds upon hundreds of people, to celebrate the woman my mother was and the life she lived. It's amazing how in tragedy like this one can see the silver linings of it all, for as profoundly sad as I was that day, the respect and turnout for my mother by all the people she had touched, many of whom I had never met, was amazing. People walked up to me and shared beautiful anecdote after beautiful anec- dote about how my mother had touched their lives in such a graceful way. And as sad as I was, I caught myself for a moment thinking how incredibly lucky I was to have been born to such a wonderful woman.

Last picture of my mother and I, taken the morning of the
biggest match of my life. Playing for the Number One U.S. Junior National ranking in Louisville, KY

My friend Alice, whose father had passed five years earlier, and who I comforted by going out on a court with her to hit some balls, came to my 67 mother's funeral. She and I repeated the same ritual when it ended with her dragging me out to the court to comfort me in my time of grief.

My mother's work with me was done. Maybe it was our tough conditions that created the urgency in her parenting, but she lived for one thing, her children and that we would have a chance at a better life than she had. I eventually composed myself enough to rejoin the group, head up, shoulders back, just the way she would have liked to have seen me. My head could have been higher, my shoulders more back, and I think my mom would have understood that a part of me died the day she passed and even now 30 years later, I miss her every day.

CHAPTER

11

HIDING IN PLAIN SIGHT

Fall of 1983, I arrived at the University of Arkansas, a nervous but excited freshman. I was still filled with grief over my mother and at first I just kept to myself. But soon I realized I was in the best place I could be. The structured days of the NBTA were behind me and I was, in a sense, freer to run my own life. But I had a team now, and they were a great group of guys.

I felt comfortable, supported, happy. My new roommate, Richard Schmidt, was sympathetic to me in my grief. He became a lifelong friend.

Like any freshman, I was nervous about my classes and how I would keep up with the academics. I'd had a good education at Bradenton Academy but my focus had been on tennis. College classes filled me with trepidation.

I missed my mom terribly my first month away at school, and my struggles were becoming apparent.I knew I just needed to let go, move forward, and to live my life in my mother's honor.

But it was hard. My emotional roller coaster reached a head during an important challenge match against teammate Bobby Banck, a player I needed to beat to secure a high spot on the roster my freshman year. I started slowly, showing little fight or game when my emotional levee suddenly broke. I broke down crying right there on the court in the middle of the match. I was in so much pain and just didn't have the skills to navigate my way out. I lost the match meekly, and coach Pucci immediately called me in to his office to talk. There was no conversation in our "talk." Coach was at the end of his rope with my temperamental self. He had a team to run and matches to prepare for and 69

I had two choices. Toughen up or go home. Period.

Coach Pucci's bedside manner sucked; his ultimatum just made me cry more that pivotal day. But tough love isn't supposed to be a soothing, nurturing event, that's why it's called tough. And rarely are there style points awarded when you tell a young man in grief what he needs to hear over what he wants to hear. What mattered was after my tears stopped, I understood clearly what coach wanted from me. My mother's passing was either going to be a crutch for me to use for the years to come or it was going to be my wakeup call to toughen up and grow up and live the life she would have taken great pride in me living.

I quickly grew to love my new home. I loved the tennis. I loved my team. I loved my coach. The University of Arkansas was the perfect place for me to be. Though it took a bit of getting used to, team practices were great and I was improving quickly. Practices were shorter but more intense. Now it was just two players to a court, no waiting in line, no more fed balls, just two grown adults hitting pro balls at each other for as long as we could stay out there. Plus college tennis was all hard courts, which also took some adjusting to. I was hungry to get better and my improvement curve was still pretty steep. I still looked to tennis as my ticket to success. I knew I was just a couple levels of improvement away from being able to compete on the professional tour. I had just turned 19, was in my freshman year and was in the running for a high spot on our roster. Coach Pucci's tough love had worked. I was in the best shape of my life and playing my best tennis ever; all I had to do now was stay healthy, stay out of trouble, and pass a few classes and my next four years were looking great.

Yeah, those classes. I remember in freshman orientation the counselor spoke of keeping our triangle in balance. Being student athletes, the three legs of our triangle were athletic, academic, and social. Too much or too little of any of the legs and our triangle would get dangerously out of balance. I could tell from the outset that school was going to be a problem. I was at the NBTA to play tennis and pretty much cruised through high school. And sure, the University of Arkansas was not Stanford or an Ivy League school, but all the professors had PhDs and knew way more than me, and all the writers of my text books had PhDs and knew way more than me. All the students I was competing with in class were not practicing twice a day for five hours with an hour

of conditioning thrown in, plus being gone every other weekend traveling for matches. So yeah, school was going to be a problem. Like so many freshman athletes trying to get settled at a school of higher education, I chose the major of eligibility. Just stay eligible so I could keep playing ball and maybe come my junior/senior years the whole education concept would make more sense to me.

Compounding the complexities of school life was that third leg of the triangle, the social. Being a good looking kid with some sports genes continued to make me attractive to the opposite sex, which allowed me to keep my orientation safely hidden away in the closet. I knew my dating women was a short-term solution to my much larger long-term problem. But as with most teenagers, none of us tried to secure a life partner to live with happily ever after. We were all curious, experimental and desirous. It was not hard for me to fit right in to the hetero world that was my young college life. I had made it through the summer of 1983 on the JDC team undetected by any of my tennis peers; no small feat considering I was embedded with these guys 24/7, on the courts, traveling together, housing together and living life together. My self-imposed discipline at the NBTA during the couple of years I had to hide my crush from everyone taught me how to not just be in the closet, but be in the closet with lock and key with the secret combination safely secured away. Or so I thought.

Jim Baird in Louisville had hundreds of young good looking tennis players to choose from. Why did he pick me? Did he pick up on my energy? I ran our first encounter through my head a hundred times. Why out of the sea of people coming down a crowded escalator did this older gentleman lock onto me? Was I tipping my sexuality off? If he could figure me out so quickly, who else was on to my scent? The only people who would care about such a thing were those who were oriented like myself, which was fine by me. But I was in Arkansas in 1983, not the most socially evolved of times and places. The men's tennis world that I was deeply immersed in was not ready for an out-in-the-open gay male competing for its highest awards. I was on a full scholarship to play tennis, which could be pulled from me at any time for any variety of reasons. Fayetteville was just not the place for me to be poking around at night to see what was going on.

Statistically, I was by no means alone. If you run the numbers, there were 15,000 students at U of Arkansas, half men, 5-10 percent of that is around 500 young gay males all hiding in plain sight all around me on the sprawling campus. They weren't looking for me and I had a lot to lose looking for them. 71

If any seeking or experimenting was going to happen for me in my early college experience, it was going to be far, far from the campus I would call home these next few years. I survived my first season mourning my mom's passing without much going on. Starting my sophomore year, I was dealt another blow. My reason for going to the University of Arkansas left. Coach Pucci took a job as an athletic director at a small school in California. I remember thinking, "Does everything good in my life have to leave?" Enter Ron Hightower, a great player in his own right and one of the best tennis minds I had ever met. I took to him instantly, squashing any thoughts of transferring to the west coast schools of Los Angeles, a city in which I had always dreamed of living. But I got to go to LA all the same.

Practicing at UCLA in 1985 before the semi-finals of All American Classic against Ricky Leach from USC.

Early in my sophomore year, my first trip away from Fayetteville was to Los Angeles to compete in the ITA fall classic. We were playing on the UCLA campus in Westwood. The tournament hotel was a Holiday Inn, a tall cylindri-

cal tower at the corner of Sunset Boulevard and the famous 405 freeway. Up to this point in my life, my few experiences in the gay lifestyle had not been particularly positive. That was soon about to change. I knew about a couple of the gay-friendly enclaves in the United States at that time, The Castro in San Francisco, South Beach in my native Florida, and West Hollywood, a mere cab ride down the street from my hotel and a community dominated by out-in-the-open gay men. I couldn't wait to sneak away from the hotel and check out this most intriguing of locales.

So excited to be in Los Angeles, at UCLA in 1985, playing for the top ranking in college tennis.

The players were housed near the top of the hotel. After curfew, I had already decided to sneak out and take a cab down to Santa Monica Boulevard and check out what this West Hollywood place was all about. Not wanting to get caught taking the elevator, I took the 20 or so flights of stairs to the rear exit of the building, and I remember thinking once again, why did seeking out what I knew was natural to me have to be made so difficult to pursue and looked upon as something that needed to be done in secret? Always keeping my true self hidden.

I reached the street, took a cab from Westwood to West Hollywood, and once I started walking down Santa Monica Boulevard, I realized I had arrived. What a place. Gay Disneyland I remember thinking, blocks and blocks of gay males everywhere, beautiful, young, fit, stylish, one after another after another. It's hard to explain the feeling of disbelief I felt walking down the boulevard that first time, being honked at and waved at, and not being afraid to wave back for fear of being noticed. Not that I wasn't afraid. When you're so far in the closet as I was, it does things to your mind. Every encounter can be the one that exposes you for being different, for being part of that other group that straight people are confused and fearful about. So it took me a few honks and a few waves before I loosened up and smiled and waved back. Even then, if I can use an analogy, if you're afraid of flying for a long time, when you overcome that fear and finally get on a plane, you may be able to fly but you're not comfortable at all that first time. That is how I can best sum up my experience, but that was not all that was making me uncomfortable.

This was my first foray into "out" culture. So this was what it was like to be out...this is what it looked like to have pride in who you were, pride in being gay. It felt so liberating to be able to just relax and take the tension out of my shoulders and face and smile at all the beautiful boys and men who honked and waved at me. It was also going to take some getting used to. This wasn't some private party or gated community. I was standing on the corner of Santa Monica and Crescent Heights. On one level, I was watching the world go by. On another level, I felt a heaviness overtake me. This is when I began to think, what is my life really all about? Nobody really knew me and I had an awful lot to learn about myself. Could I have an open gay life like all these people? Could I have gay friends too? Maybe even a beautiful boyfriend that looked like one of these guys. All these swirling thoughts were exhilarating as I stood there a bit longer on the corner.

I had a match that next morning. I had to get back. To my hotel. To my tennis life. To my closeted gay life. And it struck me how beautiful this West Hollywood place was and just how far away I was from ever being able to
experience the free and open pride all these lovely gay young men were dis-

playing on this most seminal of nights for me. I thought about my tennis and university life, how I always had felt it was my ticket out from my circumstances. But was it really? Was it a ticket out, or a trap, keeping me hidden inside the baselines of a tennis court and away from realizing who my true self was? I sat a little longer reflecting on how far apart my tennis world was from this new exciting, out in the open and proud gay life. How do you get from where I was to where all these people were as they drove around West Hollywood waving at me?

My head spun with excitement and confusion as I started my trek back to the hotel. As I said, I was nervous as all could be about being out on the street in an openly gay community. Compounding my nervousness was my desire to hook up with someone. At the same time I was scared stiff about this plague called AIDS that seemed to be targeting the gay communities around this time. My fears of exposure, personally and sexually, kept my outgoing personality in check on my first trek to this most intriguing of gay locales. But on my late night cab drive home to my tennis world, I knew I would be back to West Hollywood, a little more emboldened next time. I spoke to nobody that first night out. Yet at the same time, I could tell by how they carried themselves, they all had something I wanted — that inner freedom and pride in who they were without the fear of letting people know who they really were. I had no concept then of how long it would take me to reach that same place internally and within the gay community. All I knew was that I would be back here again soon, because they had something I didn't. These young men and women were out of the closet, living openly gay authentic lives and I wanted what they had. I would be back, for I knew these people had something to teach me.

CHAPTER

12

A WHOLE LOT OF FIRSTS

Back from Los Angeles, the college tennis season hit the ground running. I secured the top spot on coach Hightower's Arkansas Razorback roster among the finest group of teammates a college athlete could ever want. With our team solidly in the top 10 in the collegiate team rankings, we seemed to play a match every day against amazing competition.

The early to mid-1980s may have been the golden era of men's college tennis with future world-class professionals up and down every NCAA lineup. It was becoming apparent that the California schools had teams that were just a little deeper than we were in Fayetteville, making it difficult for our team to beat them consistently. Because I secured the top spot on our squad. I was assured of playing all the other teams' best players; which meant the best players in the nation. If I was ever going to make this next breakthrough in tennis, I could not have been in a better position to do so.

And I did.

After a successful sophomore year, me and the hundreds of other hungry and capable college players spanned the globe to try our hands at the experience of the professional tour. I remember the process of deciding where to go.

These were the pre-internet days. We aspiring players would write to the USTA or the ITF and get the schedules of futures and satellite events taking place all around the world. I would spend nights reading the schedules, looking at all the exotic places my tennis could take me, and my thoughts   77 would invariably drift toward my mom. She was right. All the hard work and sacrifice had paid off. I would think about those trips we used to take to the Orlando Airport to watch the planes take off and her encouragement to work hard at my tennis so that someday I would be on one of those planes heading to a pro tournament. How prescient those moments seemed now as I scanned the schedules to see to what far distant land my tennis was to take me.

Not quite ready to challenge myself with an exotic cosmopolitan culture, I played it safe and chose the Canadian satellite tour the summer of 1985. My grandmother lived just outside of Toronto, so I had a relative home base and security to go to if life on the road with my tennis brethren began to wear upon me. The first event was in Kitchener, Ontario. Many players can spend a lifetime chasing their first ATP point and that elusive world ranking. I was fortunate and played super in my first event, qualifying and winning the tournament, defeating my childhood junior idol, Todd Witsken. My first ATP point, my first world ranking and my first paycheck. I remember coming to my hotel room and counting out the money from the week. I won $1,350. It wasn't a lot, but it was more than I had ever had to myself at that point.

Tennis players are a funny breed with money. Living lives of relative privilege, the value of a dollar often evades us. We are not hourly wage-earning types; much of value has been given to us our whole playing lives. Many of my peers who went on to have successful professional careers took their first big paycheck and bought Porsches or BMWs. Which I guess is cool if you're trying to live up to the image of the cosmopolitan tennis pro. I on the other hand had a different relationship with money. I just could not imagine buying a depreciating asset with my first chunk of income that could be invested. And in my heart, that 1,350 bucks was not really mine to spend. It belonged to all the people along my tennis path who gave to me and my tennis. Jim Kelaher, Nick Bollettieri, Jim Baird, The U of Arkansas, Dr. Nazareth, all the people from Orlando who helped my tennis progress, and of course my mom. It would have been great to have been able to see her coming away from the tournament site with my prize money check in hand, but I did the next best thing I could do. I drove to Thunder Beach, 70 miles outside of Toronto, to see my mom's mom, my grandmother Nana. I took her to lunch to celebrate. As exciting as it was to now have a world ranking and some money in my pocket from playing good tennis, the highlight of that week was being able to see the look of appreciation on my Nana's face as I picked her up, took her to lunch and paid the check. I was growing up and it felt good.

The tour. The satellites are where it begins for all of us. Only those who go deep into tournaments are playing on the weekends and there is only so much practicing a player can do. Translation; there is a lot of down time. After my West Hollywood experience, I knew the larger cities had gay-friendly neighborhoods that were just the kind of places I wanted to explore. The problem was the tour I was on was not New York, London, Paris. This first week was in Kitchener Ontario, not exactly a landmark cultural hotbed. It was going to take a little research on my part to find out where the action was. On the plus side for me, I was in Canada on my own, unsupervised, my own man, growing up, in control of my own circumstances. I didn't have a curfew or anyone to answer to. But I was traveling with several life-time tennis friends who knew nothing about my secret life and it had to remain that way.

My great friend Robbie Weiss and I touring the Canadian Tennis Circuit together in the summer of 1985.

Not getting caught became a preoccupation of mine. This was different than sneaking out after curfew to catch a 20-minute cab ride like I did in Los Angeles, where I knew nobody knew me. This was small-town Canada. The pro tennis tournament in town was a major attraction and my doing well that week meant a lot of people in Kitchener knew who Bobby Blair the tennis player was. Which was fine, if I was at the tennis club playing tennis. It would 79 not have been fine if I was seen cruising the gay part of town or coming in or out of a gay club, or worse yet, once inside the club, to have met someone there from the tournament. That would have been devastating to my young, firmly in-the-closet self.

And here began the onset of my double tennis life, where I could be one person by day to all my tennis peers and someone completely different by night. This was the beginning of having to mislead and outright lie to some of my closest friends about what I was doing at night. Or why I was always going out alone, or driving ahead to the next town by myself a couple days early. I would give one answer to my tennis friends, why I was going ahead early and alone, but the truth was, I wanted to scope out the next town ahead to see where the action was and learn my way around. Or maybe I was doubling back to a town I had already been in to see someone that I had hit it off with. It wasn't hard to keep my tennis friends away from my secret; at our young age it was likely the last thing they would ever have expected from me. But thus began the slow and gradual re-prioritization of my life; where my monomaniacal obsession to become the best tennis player I could be began to give way to self-exploration. As I began to mature, I realized

I was more than just a tennis player and that there was a great big world out there I wanted to explore.

I had a lot to learn about the gay life. I would meet men at the various locales. They would ask my name, where I was from, and what I was doing in town. "I'm Bobby Blair from the University of Arkansas and I'm a tennis player here in town for the local pro event," was said to nobody ever at a gay bar. I learned the value of having an alias. I would be Mark from Florida, in town to visit my grandmother. Implicit in my use of aliases as I traveled around playing tennis was this intense shame about being Bobby Blair, a gay tennis player. Always in the back of mind I was calculating. What was the cost/benefit analysis of letting these virtual strangers know who I really was?

I knew I was just in town for a short time; this was maybe the only time I would ever meet this person. I wasn't looking for a boyfriend or someone to travel with me. I was just trying to learn my way around communities that I was becoming aware dotted all the major cities I would be traveling to in the years to come as I pursued my tennis goals. Also, I must be honest.

Wherever I went and walked in, I was the new kid in town and the object

of much attention. One would think that conversations among the people I met would have been deeper and more soul searching about what it meant trying to find one's way as a gay man in a straight world. But they were not. Before my seat was warm and my beer half gone, the questions I would be asked were: "Where are you staying?" "Where is your hotel?" "Are you staying alone?" And "how long are you in town?" The locals were trying to close the deal with me quickly and that just wasn't my thing. These were my first real excursions into gay culture as an independent young man and I wanted to learn as much as I could about what everyone else's experience was like.

So I would ask my questions. I would meet all types checking out the scene. There were a few like me, in town visiting someone, but most were local kids from the community who were not in the closet like me. I would probe them as to how their outing came about. Either they could not hide it any longer or they got caught, but they were out at a time and place where being out was frowned upon. They wore the heartbreaks from their family rifts in their eyes, the ultimate rejection from those who gave you life and who you hoped would be there for you no matter what. But their families were not there on this most fundamental of areas; quite the opposite, and the pain from the rejection was hard to hide. These new people I met would seek comfort in whatever way they could find. Sadly for the many displaced youths I met back then, they chose to anesthetize themselves with drugs, alcohol and sex.

I found their lives complex. Not all of them. Many of the club owners were older, more successful, involved in seemingly healthy long-term relationships. But the majority of the guys I would meet along the way were not in the best of places, and I found their choices in dealing with their circumstances unhealthy and unsafe, further reinforcing my thoughts about staying in the closet. If this level of pain and rejection was the reward for coming out, no thank you.

But there was a side of me that loved the clubs. I recall being so excited to check out the local clubs in some of the locales; sometimes I would get there a couple hours before they would even open. I recall wondering then if I would have been so excited if I had qualified for the French Open. The answer was likely no, which meant my pursuit of this other world and this other part of myself was starting to become a distraction from my tennis.

But the push and pull of the lifestyle had not begun to have negative effects quite yet. And as much as I didn't adhere to the way everyone else was conducting themselves in the gay bar scene, I loved the attention and the guys, 81 for they were just like me; young, confused, scared and just seeking a little love and understanding compassion. I was still very focused on my tennis and was not into all the drugs and late night partying that seemed to dictate their lives. And this was the 1980s and the age of AIDS was plaguing the gay scene. The combination of being terrified of getting sick and just being very careful about myself and my body led me quite accidentally to adopt the safest of safe sex habits, so I was fortunate there. If I was ever in the company of strangers, I just assumed everybody I met had HIV and conducted myself accordingly. Better safe than sorry never had more meaning than for me and countless other gay youth during that scary time.

Most importantly, my excursions into the gay parts of town were more about companionship. These clubs, for all their faults and questionable lifestyle choices, became safe havens for me and others.

These were places we could go to be accepted, in direct opposition to the rejection we felt outside of the clubs and bars in these little corners about town. And we all implicitly knew this and did our best to treat each other so. We were strangers to each other but on many levels we were not; we were just friends who had not met yet. And in a very short time, I knew I could be a supportive positive influence on these young people's lives just by how I conducted myself with them. I knew I had it better than most of the people I met on my travels; full scholarship, tennis pro, pretty safely in the closet and able to function quite comfortably in the straight world undetected. They would come on to me awkwardly and aggressively, and I learned early how not to hurt anyone's feelings who came on to me but was not my type. I could leave the situation leaving everyone feeling good. I never led guys on nor did I play with anyone's feelings, for I knew their lives were already complicated enough and it just isn't that hard to be kind. But also from a selfish perspective, I had a vested interest in leaving the clubs in a good state, for I knew I wanted to be able to come back to those places the next day and the next year, and these bridges to the gay world were hard enough to find. So I took the greatest care in not burning any of them.

And so it went that summer of 1985. It was a summer of firsts for me.

I accomplished a lot and I learned even more. There was another world out there that I now knew how to navigate and that was exciting to me. On top of that, I felt I had the best of both worlds; this awesome tennis existence that kept getting better year after year, and this new secret life where I could go and explore and meet new friends and learn what it meant to be a young gay man in a straight world. I could seek comfort and connection there, which I enjoyed immensely, but more so, for the first time in my young gay life, I didn't feel so all alone. I was having fun with other young gay guys like myself. Nothing extraordinary, just guys drinking beer, watching sports, shooting pool, and listening to music; but all in the company of like-minded individuals.

And I was pulling it off. I remember getting a charge being able to just internally flip a switch and go from gay Mark at the nightclubs to straight Bobby on the tennis courts, with neither world knowing the first thing about the other and pretty confident that if I watched my step, I could keep it that way. But I also had no illusions about how far apart I was from living an authentic out lifestyle as a young gay man and certainly was not proud about the methods I had to employ to keep my double life a secret. The complexities of trying to lead a secret double life would reach an early crescendo when I came back to Fayetteville for my junior year of school in 1985 and was met at the airport by the loving embrace of my girlfriend at the time, Kim Cain.

CHAPTER

13

THE PUSH, THE PULL

1983: Flying home from my mother's funeral early my freshman year, I had a layover in Dallas/Fort Worth. I wasn't the happiest guy you could imagine; was just staying to myself trying to make sense of it all when this woman sitting next to me started up a conversation. I was mired in my own stuff, and I remember hardly anything about the conversation other than she was just the kindest, most caring woman I had ever met. She knew I was grieving as she let me go on and on about my mom and how unfair the world was for taking her so early. Her gaze never wavered. As we boarded our connecting flights, I discovered she was heading to Fayetteville too. We agreed to continue our conversation upon our landing.

Her name was Kim Cain. She drove the coolest little convertible Mercedes, ran a little business in town, came from a great family; which I always found attractive. She was a bit older than me at 25, which was fine by me. We parted ways at the airport, agreeing to stay in touch. A lunch here and a night on the town there and before either of us had a chance to even ask what we were doing, we were pretty much living together.

She just could not have been a nicer, more nurturing person. After my unrequited first love at the NBTA and my experience with being the prey to the friendly predator in Louisville, I was perfectly content to put all my gay issues on the back burner while trying to get myself settled at school.

So it was with a mix of excitement and fear that I returned to campus for my junior year. I was fired up to play tennis again; had my first world ranking and was slated to play number one for the team. But my fear was the ongoing push and pull between my gay instincts and my need to keep my lifestyle a secret. At home, I would constantly question whether I was really gay or not, or maybe just bisexual. Whatever that meant, I would bargain with myself about whether it wouldn't be just a whole lot easier to keep living the straight life and keep my gay feelings at bay. I was pulling it off. I had the cool girlfriend. I was good at hiding it, which wasn't hard in Fayetteville. Nobody in hyper-straight tennis culture ever suspected me, so hiding the real me proved to be somewhat easy. Hiding the real me from myself was proving to be more troubling and difficult. And so began the push and pull. On my summer travels, it seemed every time I encountered a different slice of gay culture, I just felt more at home there. There were many reasons for me to not explore the scene. Fear of getting caught, fear of getting sick, fear of falling in love again and how distracting that was when not able to pursue those feelings. A refrain I had used for so many years for myself was: I could put this off, I didn't have to have this all figured out now. Yet every chance I had on the road, playing away from home and my friends and my girlfriend, I searched a little more. Couldn't I just put it off a little longer? I had it made at home, I didn't have to take these chances. Why couldn't I just choose the straight life and be done with it? The push. The pull.

Subconsciously, when I was alone and on the road, I wished I would not feel so at home at the clubs. I wished I would not feel the attraction, not feel the connection and affection and compassion I felt for my fellow gays. I remember thinking out loud one time as I was parking my car out back before I entered one of the nondescript out-of-the-way clubs, if I would just have a bad time, seriously, just one bad time, if fights broke out, if the club was raided, if people were cruel or rude or criminal, anything to give me a reason to never come back, I could put this all behind me. But that just never happened.

When I would return to a night club, the owners remembered my name, the bartenders remembered what I drank. I would see many of the same patrons as the evening before, and before my seat was warm I was being asked my name and about my day and if I would like to play pool. A part of me really wanted to have a bad time, but that just wasn't happening. The push. The pull.

I started to dabble a bit more in the lifestyle. I would drink a little more than I should, started to do some of the recreational drugs that were offered

me. I met some very nice young men on my travels, men I was attracted to and men that were attracted to me. I began to explore my sexuality with them. I would go out into the world wanting to learn everything I could about how the gay club scene worked. How to communicate, how to flirt, how to be the center of attention yet not lead anyone on. I made close enough friends to feel at home, yet not too close to risk being outed.

I kept returning to the gay parts of town. As day would turn to night I would sink further into the clubs, often losing track of time. Then it would come, last call would beckon from the bar. Mark from Florida had to switch into his mythical phone booth and return to being Bobby the tennis player; but not before important information was exchanged. Being the new kid in town had its advantages but also its issues. The come-ons from the fellow patrons could be awkward, sometimes aggressive, often sloppy as the drunk crowd spilled out into the night. I took great care in not being rude, in not making people feel badly for my not wanting to go home with them. Enough damage had been done already to their young gay lives; I certainly didn't want to pile it on in any way.

So I would exit out the back, always alone. I viewed my re-emergence from the gay bars back in to straight world as hostile those first few steps out in to the night. Nobody was to be trusted; not my new gay friends, nor the strangers on the street who I did not know but who might know me. I was visiting their town as Bobby the tennis player, my name was in the paper, my picture as well if I was having a good week. They could be from the tournament themselves. I just never knew. So I trusted nobody as I reclaimed my true identity. Only upon driving home, well clear of the gay part of town and seemingly undetected, could I let my shoulders relax and let out a big sigh of relief and laugh to myself about what a great time I just had. Reveling in the thrill of having just gotten away with my secret double life once again.

But did I? An unease would visit me on those drives home. I knew I was being unfaithful to my girlfriend and I knew I was being dishonest to all the people closest to me in my life. I sensed where all this seeking and experimentation was going and I would fight with myself. One minute chastising myself for succumbing to my urges again when I had so much at stake and so much to lose and a great woman who loved me waiting for me at home. All this focus on being discreet, about living in the closet and living a double life. Somewhere between my departure from the clubs the switch would flip and I would go back to being Bobby Blair, yet knowing I was unable to be the real me in my tennis world. The clubs where I just had a great time, where I felt most comfortable in my own skin, I couldn't be the real me there either. Bobby the tennis player had to be Mark from Florida in town to visit his grandmother. How was I ever going to get to know the real me when I refused to let anybody else know? The push. The pull.

Near the end of the summer of 1985 I had an epiphany. I was making friends on my travels. I was starting to see that it was possible to be gay and have a social life; that I had a whole other side of me apart from my tennis I wanted to explore and let other people get to know. These new friends knew nothing about Bobby Blair the tennis player. They would have guessed a place called Nick Bollettieri's was a place to get a great pizza. I just sat as one among the crowd of boys, drinking my drink as the night entertainment would commence. I would struggle with myself on these outings. Was I an outsider checking out the scene, observing to see if this was for me? Or was this who I was? It was at clubs like these along my journey where I was going to learn about the gay life and ultimately about myself and how to make this work.

Not being a local, on my travels I never knew exactly what the clubs I would enter would be all about. Different cities would have different ordinances. Some were just plain old dive bars with the standard TV, jukebox, pool tables, and that stale beer stench you can never locate in space or origin. Guys from all walks of life passing the time and having a mug of comfort and connection. Other locales were far more engaging. Strong drinks, packed dance floors, pulsating stereo set-ups, high tech dance clubs with great light systems, all leading up to some featured midnight performance involving go-go dancers and other assorted singers and performers. I was a young kid from the suburbs who knew his artistic limitations; there was little doubt which side of the line between the entertainers and those being entertained I belonged.

The shows would rage with energy. Depending on where I was seated, I would throw my money to the performers as they danced, their appreciation signaled by the glint in their eyes and the smiles on their faces. The intensity was vibrant as act after act took the stage. My drink always seemed full with a cocktail being sent my way every few minutes, and I was happy as I could ever be, talking and laughing and howling with my new friends at my table. Then on the stage came that awkward time of the night when they ask a person from the crowd to come up and dance for the fired up patrons.

I was the new guy in town, the fun guy, the cute guy, the guy everyone wanted to dance with and dance for, play pool with, buy a beer for, get the phone number from. I was very much in my element, my comfort zone, being the center of attention, all the attention being good.

I was in the spotlight, I loved it, and one night it shone a whole lot brighter. It was a Friday night, late, in a little bar in Shawinigan, Canada. I had already frequented the place several times that week. I had gotten to know the owners, the staff, the DJ. I was hanging with them, and it got later and later and the drinks were flowing. And then I started hearing guys calling out my name...Mark, Mark, Mark. Friday night was cabaret night with male dancers from Montreal, but apparently the dancing wasn't done. The dancers wanted me on stage next. I shook my head, absolutely no way! But they weren't having it. The chants of Mark, Mark, Mark just kept getting louder. I kept shaking them off and then I felt two hands at my back pushing me off my seat and on to my feet. As soon as I stood up the crowd went crazy and there was nothing left to do but slowly, with equal parts hesitation and excitement, work my way up to the stage to pay my dues. The push, the pull.

I climbed up on the stage as the DJ asked me what song to play. "'Penny Lover' by Lionel Ritchie," I said. The energy in the room was great, young guys getting their fun on among their tribe, our tribe, my tribe. Safe, secure, hidden from the harsh judging eyes of straight culture, all their eyes were now upon me. Could I perform?

The song began and what few moves I had I started in on awkwardly. But this wasn't about winning any dance contests. This was some unofficial tribal ritual I was undergoing, partly from cajoling, partly from inside myself wanting to prove to everyone watching that I belonged here, that I was not an observer. These were my people and I could stand before them innocent and vulnerable, and I could learn to trust them and they weren't going to hurt me.

As the song picked up, the lights and the sounds and my head began to swirl as money started flying my way and not just crumpled singles: 5s, 10s, 20s raining down in bunches as the catcalls intensified to take it all off as I undid another button and another button as more green started flying my way; half way through the song my shirt was off, yet they wanted more and more and the money kept coming and the clothes kept falling and when the music stopped and the lights came back on there I was, innocent, vulnerable and feeling as exhilarated and embarrassed as I possibly could. I picked up close to $450 from the dance floor around me. The push. The pull

Internally I had already accepted them. That night on the dance floor was their way of showing their acceptance of me. The gay me. If there were ever any remaining doubts about my gayness, they were eliminated that defining evening.

So coming home to my girlfriend at the end of that summer was complicated. Our circle of friends was getting serious. Couples that used to hang out were making commitments to each other, people who used to sleep over were now moving in together, houses started to become homes and investments, rings began to appear, weddings were being planned, a girl in our immediate circle was pregnant and really excited about becoming a mom.

All our youthful and carefree flings and hook ups were starting to get real. And with each announcement from our friends, the pressure ratcheted up a bit on me and my girlfriend to get more serious, but I just couldn't. It was just not where my heart was and I hated to have to lie to her, for she had been so good to me and deserved better. It was in that moment that I began to realize how insidious living in the closet can be as it suffocated the integrity out of decent people like myself.

I didn't really know what I wanted other than I didn't want to keep living the lie that I was living. Young gay men like me only had a few choices and none of them were good. I could choose a life in the clergy and swear off all issues of sexuality through lifetime vows of celibacy. I could choose to come out to my friends and family and let the bigotry chips fall where they may. Or I could live the push and pull life of a gay man in the closet, securing girlfriends at times in my life where it would be advantageous for myself career-wise or when I felt the pressure building around me that someone might be on to my secret.

Yet that involved another person; a trusting unsuspecting person who deserved better than what I was bringing. As the burden of my gay shame grew, I would seek comfort in heterosexual relationships. As the burden of my guilt grew, I would be overcome with a deeply grounded sense of what was right or wrong and exit from said relationships. It just couldn't be all about me all the time when other people's feelings were involved. I knew that. I knew how important that was. Yet I just could not honor those words with action. And so began a pattern in my young adult life, the push, the pull, of hiding and escaping in and out of the comforting arms of a female other.

CHAPTER

14

FOREST HILLS

I had an excellent junior year campaign playing for my school, and for the second time in my career won the attention and support of the USTA Player Development program. Player Development was not as extensive and involved back then as it is today with its full-time coaching staffs and permanent training facilities. The JDC teams did help us with expenses, also assisting us with wild cards for entry in to bigger tournaments that we may not have qualified for on our own. I received a wild card in to the US Open Men's Clay Court Championships that summer. I invited my father to watch, buying him a ticket. I was ambivalent about him coming. My desire to have a strong father figure in my life still burned brightly. Unfortunately my father was just not made of the right stuff to be that guy. I played the number 27 player in the world, Pablo Arraya, in the first round on the stadium court, giving him all he could handle in a long three-set loss.

Walking off the court, my dad waited awkwardly. As I greeted him, he said, "Geez, I never knew you were this good." He probably didn't mean anything critical by that; he was out of his element being in my tennis world. I had a choice to focus on the "how good I was" part of his comment, or the "he never knew" part. I focused on the latter for it reinforced all the feelings of neglect and abandonment I had been feeling from him my whole life. As we parted I felt a profound sadness that my relationship with my dad was never going to be that storybook type of bond. His well of love and support for me had run dry some time ago. Leaving Indianapolis, I secured another wild card into the qualifying of the Tournament of Champions in Forest Hills, New York. In the first round, I drew former top 10 in the world player Pat Cash, who was coming off an injury and working his way back to the main draws of the ATP tour. Call it tennis' perfect storm, I played about as well as I could and his play had not returned to his top 10 form yet, helping me notch the biggest victory of my young career. Cash would go on to win Wimbledon the next year. The victory showed me that on the slow green clay courts upon which I developed me game, I could more than hang with many of the world's best players.

In my experiences playing professional tournaments, I could see there was more to being successful than just being able to play tennis at an elite level. The whole lifestyle was different. Traveling full time, getting used to losing every week, likely no coach or loved one in tow. The expenses for just an individual player were extraordinary, so adding in a support team was not good business. And a business tennis was. These guys were serious professionals with many of them international celebrities. These players were out here strictly to make a living and they conducted themselves so.

The vibe on the Forest Hills grounds was powerful for me. You never forget your first few times with a player's badge that gives you full access to the grounds. All these great players I had been watching on television all these years. Now here they all were, in the draw, walking the grounds, practicing next to me, watching me hit, and eventually standing across the net from me in competition. The whole experience was nothing more than thrilling for me. As much as I would try to pose and posture that I was one of the boys, there was always a little side of me that remained the wide-eyed fan.

I looked around the grounds with my "gaydar" tuned up high, guerrilla style. I had been around enough now to know the signs; what to look for in another. More than anything else, I was increasingly wary of those who seemed to be paying extra close attention to me. And so goes life living in the closet. Seekers and sought, predators and prey, a world of interactions and signals going on right before your eyes that only a gay person could decode. It's a murky world, being gay in a straight society. If we're good at being in the closet, you won't even know we exist. And if you don't know we exist, we fail to really exist to ourselves. We know our fellow travelers are out there. Oh, the hurdles we must go through to just meet a like-minded soul.

I had been on the sites of these tennis tournaments half my life by this point. This was as closeted an environment as you will ever see. But this was a whole different world, the professional ranks. I had learned enough by now to know that sexual orientation did not discriminate; world-class athletes had no immunity from nature's natural selection. I continued to look around me. A couple hundred players and coaches and staff and media, to say nothing of the thousands of fans walking the grounds. I knew I was not the only one. Was it worth finding out? This was no place to make my first mistake. Not unlike the gay bars of my Canadian summer, I needed to learn to get along here unde-tected in a different way, for it was in environments like these that I hoped to be making my living some day.

Subway ride from Forest Hills into Manhattan, after the biggest win of my life, over former top 10 player in the world and future Wimbledon Champion, Pat Cash.

After my match with Cash, I was ecstatic. I was also a filthy clay-court mess. I worked my way back toward the Players' Lounge simply beaming with pride at what I had just accomplished. I walked in to the bustling room to congratulatory hugs and handshakes from my new professional tennis peers. Players know what's going on; my big upset was being met with the notice-able curiosity from the tour veterans. Who was this unknown kid from Florida who just pulled the big upset?

In the corner was the media table, full of journalists and their typewriters. I see them. They see me. I just pulled about as big an upset as you could, former top 10 in the world player losing to random 500th in the world player that nobody knows. From across the room, a journalist starts walking toward me. Without a thought, I turn and walk away. His face looked familiar. Where do I know him from? From television? I was just at a gay bar the night before, could he recognize me from there? All I needed was to have my name and face in the sports section or the evening news and in my mind, my tennis career would be over before it barely began. I quickly surmise nothing good could come from talking to this approaching person as I head toward the locker rooms for safety.

Safety from what? This was the professional tennis world. This was everything I ever wanted. Fame, fortune, attention. Everything I worked my whole life to attain was right in front of me. And I ran away. There were so many ways to make a name for oneself out here on tour. So many players were either shy, introverted, not terribly attractive or not well spoken. But here I was, this great looking kid, a marketer's dream, making his first moves in tennis' big-time and when the cameras started to point my way with the people that present tennis to the greater viewing public, when one of those people approached me, I ran away. I was becoming so uncomfortable with any attention, so enmeshed with shame from my ever-expanding double life.

It seemed every new person I met, every new conversation I would have with people, began to carry a little extra weight. I was getting increasingly uncomfortable if conversations and questioning ever veered toward my personal life. I was on guard, trying to be sure that I knew exactly what to say to steer attention away from if I was dating, or who I was dating, or why I wasn't interested in this person or that girl. It was just getting harder to say, harder for me to lie. I felt I could not be honest with people, which meant I wasn't being honest with myself. I had studied some journalism in college, I knew reporters had a way of getting to the truth, of asking tough questions, of asking follow up questions, of keeping on a point until they got what they wanted. I did not want to be on the receiving end of an interview like that. Not now. Not when I was just on the cusp of possibly making it in my sport of tennis.

I escaped to a corner of the locker room to compose myself, looking for a secluded spot to shower and change. All the stars from my youth were there,

Ivan Lendl, Stefan Edberg, Boris Becker, me. The wide-eyed fan in me tried to listen in on their conversations, many of them getting ready to play, others winding down, some in groups just catching up with other players and their entourages. I started to undress when a pretty famous player I recognized instantly passed my way and paused. I looked up and caught his stare and before I could even muster a hello, he was giving me a good looking over from head to toe. I looked away embarrassed and somewhat surprised. A lot of people were checking me out for all kinds of different reasons, the new kid, the big upset, but I knew this look far too well from my youth to not be aware he was sizing me up.

I made it to the shower and began washing off the day's play from my weary and worn body when I looked up and there he was again, standing fully clothed for play while staring in at my showering naked self. He proceeded to look me up and down again. When our eyes met, I immediately looked away again in embarrassment. There was nowhere to hide in the open shower bays. By the time I turned back around to grab my towel and be done with this awkwardness he had moved on. Was I imagining all this? Had my years in the closet begun to wear on me? Was I getting paranoid?

Was I starting to assume that everyone was trying to figure me out, to see if I was gay or not?

Why would he do that to me? Was it that obvious that I was in play? Or had I been seen about town the night before? I remember thinking, what the hell was I doing? One minute I'm running away from a great opportunity to get my name in the papers, all from a fear of being discovered? The next minute I'm running away from a situation in the locker rooms for fear I have been discovered.

Here I was. I had been in New York City for all of 48 hours for the first time as an adult, but I had already checked out the NYC scene. The night before my match I had gone to a club called Rounds for dinner at the corner of 53rd and Second Avenue, known for great looking younger guys and wealthy older types. The place was beautiful. Before long I met a kind gentleman named Peter Copani, who invited me to join him for dinner.

He was a playwright on Broadway, an old friend of Judy Garland, with a successful ticket brokerage business in the Tri-State area. We spoke for hours that night, him giving me his sage advice about how to succeed living the gay life. He advised me to not worry about whether I was gay or not. As a   95 matter of fact, he never actually referred to me as gay. He thought I might be bisexual, the best of both worlds, someone who could make lots of people happy, boys and girls. Not that I didn't suspect this already, but hearing it from someone as established and wise as him; that maybe I was bisexual and not just gay somehow felt quite cathartic. I would grasp at anything if it seemed to ease my mounting shame.

I had a really fun time that night. I met all kinds of different folk. They shared openly and honestly about their lives. Several of the men I met were family men with wives and children at home. If ever there were any choices being made about whether one was straight or gay, the choices were being made by gay guys to live straight lives and not the other way around. As a matter of truth, in all my years I have yet to meet one single straight person who chose to be gay. But now I was starting to meet a lot of gay people who chose to live straight. Because it was easier to live straight. It's been an alluring trap for even the best of us. I ran around that night with Peter and a couple of New York's hottest young guys before I headed home early for the next day's morning match. Now, according to Peter, I was likely bisexual and not just into guys, so I tempered my desire to hook up that night with one of my new New York friends. I didn't want to seem too gay by just jumping at the first opportunity that arose.

But I met these guys at a gay bar. Sheesh, may the confusion someday abate. More importantly, a couple nights later after I lost in the main draw and had a few beers. I confided in Peter the truth about who I was. That I wasn't Mark from Florida, but that I was Bobby Blair from the U. of Arkansas in town to play the professional tournament over at Forest Hills. I knew it was risky, but I felt deep within me for the first time that I had more to gain from being honest with Peter and his friends than I did to lose.

At this point in my life, I was committed to living firmly in the closet to my family and tennis friends, but I was starting to get around a bit in the gay circles. I was aware of what happened to Billie Jean King and her being outed by a spurned lover. I did not want that fate to visit me. Again, I ran the numbers. There were thousands of people at this event and I had just spent many hours in plain view at one of the more elite gay clubs in all of New York. It's impossible that someone at that club those evenings was not at the tennis event that day. I know some of the people at Forest Hills had to be visiting these places too. They had to be. Why couldn't I have been more careful? In my head I was panicking. A stranger would look like a face from the club the night before and I would turn and walk quickly away.

An odd shift was occurring within me. I was beginning to trust the people I would meet in the gay clubs far more than the ones I would meet throughout the tennis world. How this was going to work out, I had not a clue. I was getting away with it for now, but every day my paranoia grew as the pressure of my being discovered kept mounting. Fortunately the tennis world was one big traveling side show, week to week, new city to new city. My escape from the mounting pressure I was feeling in New York was just mere days away.

I backed up the Cash victory with another big one over future top 30 player Christo Van Rensburg of South Africa, eventually losing first round of the main draw to South American clay court specialist Horacio De La Pena. I remember thinking while playing to a near-packed side court crowd what a thrill it would have been to have my player's box filled with all the important people in life. My family, my coaches, my close friends, gay ones and straight. Everyone sitting together in peace and harmony, full of love and acceptance for each other, brought together by their love and support for me and my tennis and my hopefully flourishing career.

Most of the top players traveled with their wives and girlfriends, their Player's Box full with the loves of their lives in full view. What if I had a partner at the time? What if I had a serious boyfriend who traveled everywhere with me? What if we were not in the closet, but out and proud about us and our love? What if my significant other chose to sit in my player's box and root for me just like all the wives and girlfriends? How awesome that would have been but what a circus that would have been. It was 1986 in America in one of the most homophobic arenas in all society: men's athletics. It seemed like such a small thing to ask for, to be able to have the person I loved sit in my box and root for me just like all the other loved ones. Yet society and no less myself were still miles away from being ready to accept that gay people deserve the same types of support as everyone else no matter what the endeavor. It's 2013 as I write these words and not much has changed in sports culture from my first matches on tennis' big stage, and I shake my head in wonder at just what it is going to take.

15

GOODWILL GAMES

I left New York exhilarated with how well I had done. But, had I really done that well? For all my success there, I received two total ATP points for my efforts, one for qualifying, one for losing first round. I had to turn down $1,800 dollars in prize money to retain my amateur status because I was still in college. The only reason I was even playing in New York was because the USTA was supporting my tennis financially with wild cards to events like Forest Hills. There was a limited supply of this support. Not having a big nest egg to fall back on I needed to take advantage of every opportunity granted to me. There was no bigger opportunity for players like me than the NCAA Championships to be held in Athens, Georgia.

The winner was granted a wild card straight in to the main draw of the U.S. Open to be played again in New York come summer's end. I was already having a great year; my victories over Cash and Van Rensburg catapulted me to the top of my Class of 86. My timing could not have been better. The U.S. Olympic Committee, in conjunction with the USTA, were in the process of selecting a five-man team to represent the USA in Moscow at the Goodwill Games in 1986. With the boycotts of the 1980 and 1984 Summer Olympic Games by both the U.S. and the USSR, respectively, the Goodwill Games were just that, an attempt at displaying goodwill between the two Cold War combatants. I got the nod over numerous soon to be famous American tennis players. A lot of attention was to be paid to our traveling team that summer. What an honor it would be to represent my country in such a prestigious international competition.

In Georgia, our team lost to the NCAA number one team SMU in the quarterfinals, after being moved indoors from the ideally slow hard courts to the screaming fast indoor ones. It was becoming apparent to me that my lack of physical strength and power game was going to make it tough for me on faster surfaces against what was becoming a steady stream of larger and stronger opponents. After the team championships came the individuals. I had a decent chance of winning the singles and the wild card into the U.S. Open, but I didn't have enough energy left in the tank after a grueling couple of weeks of playing and I lost in the second round.

All in all I had a great year, becoming an All-American for the second time, ending the year ranked NCAA number six in a talent-rich era of college tennis. I had a couple of weeks of well-deserved down time before heading over to Russia, with all kinds of options about how and where to spend them. Feeling the need to get away from the courts for a bit, I chose to visit my friend Jim back up in Louisville.

It had been four years since I first met Jim. I had pretty strong mixed feelings for the man. He was hard to define in a simple single sentence. As much as I knew he was a manipulative using predator toward a lot of young boys like myself, there was also a kindness and generosity and caring side to him I could not overlook. His actions toward my dying mother three years prior, regardless of what his ulterior motives may have been, provided my mom and me the greatest possible closure to her sadly shortened life. His benevolence at that most difficult moment in my family's life still carried quite a bit of weight with me.

I was still pretty young, 21 at the time, and did not know the full extent of his predatory ways when I was not around. As far as I was concerned, that was between him and the boys he would meet. As far as his actions pertained to me, he had not been cruel to me in any way and had only treated me with the utmost of kindness. So I chose to go to Jim's for a couple days. We partied pretty heavily at his house for the time I was there. I had a talk with myself as to what was OK for me to do and what was not before I arrived. As the partying intensified, eventually I would give in to his advances in ways I was not proud of. I never knowingly crossed any lines I had set those few days with Jim, but I will confess to adjusting my lines some.

Jim's generosity began to multiply. He offered to sponsor me for my tennis. I walked out of Jim's with a few thousand dollars in my pocket. He made it clear to me that there was much more of that if I needed it. But I drove away from Jim's that day never to return, for his assistance came with too high a price. That seemed to be the game. Pay to play. It all seemed so transactional. Wealthy older gentleman pursuing the hot young guys. Sex and money. The young guys doing as little as we could to get as much as we could. The wealthier older guys trying to get as much as they could for as little as possible. The unspoken rules of the game. I was starting to see I had a role in all this activity. I wasn't a victim anymore; if I ever really was. I chose to go to Jim's of my own accord. As convoluted as this sounds, around Jim I could be myself in ways I just couldn't around my tennis friends. I just didn't have any gay friends to talk to at that time in my life who understood what I was going through. It's not that Jim and I sat around all day and talked about the complexities of being in the closet. Often it was quite the contrary. Just to be around another gay person within the security of a private residence meant for a brief period of time we could let our guards down and get a well-needed break from the smothering fear and paranoia of our lived lies.

I knew my relationship with Jim was far from optimal. There were so many things wrong with it. For where I was on my journey, it was as good as it was to going to get for me until some things changed in my life and within me. Little did I know then how far in the future those changes were to be. I wondered about the day when I would meet someone who liked me just for me, who wanted to hang out with me just for me, and not have it always be about sex. I just knew I was beginning to crave a different type of attention; for everything I had learned up to this point in the gay life seemed to come with a price.

After leaving Jim's, I flew down to the NBTA to train on the clay before heading over to Russia. I was excited to see Nick after my great results in New York; I never stopped seeking his approval even well in to my adult life. His acknowledgement of my victories meant a lot to me, and to him too, that the time and resources he invested in my tennis had paid off. Once we concluded the feel-good congratulations, I expected him to put me with one of the academy's top players on the first court. Instead, he sent me off to a side court with some new 15-year old kid at the academy that he wanted me to play.

Slightly taken back, I did as Nick asked. I wasn't the biggest physical specimen back then, 5'10 155 pounds, but this kid was noticeably smaller than me, a couple of inches shorter, maybe 10 pounds lighter. We get to warming up and no more than a couple rallies in and I've never seen anything like it in my life. Who was this kid with all the long colored hair and makeup and finger nail polish hitting rocket after rocket by me? I walked back to the fence and asked Nick.

"Who is this kid, Nick?"

"Agassi" Nick growled. "Remember the name." I didn't have to remember it long. A month later Andre burst onto the tennis scene making it all the way to the quarterfinals of the Stratton Mountain pro event in Vermont. I had been among the best of my age group for some time now. I pretty much knew my competition, how well I needed to play to win, and what I needed to improve to have a successful career. But this was different. Some 15-year-old phenom absolutely crushing the ball like I had never seen before wiped me out in three straight sets. I always knew there was another level in tennis, but what Andre was doing was different. I came to the NBTA to train, riding as high as I ever had in my tennis life. I walked off that court with Andre three quick sets later wondering aloud that if this was the future of tennis, how was I ever going to have a chance at success?

I was not the only player who Andre Agassi made pause and think twice about the choices we were making in life. His tennis was amazing and was only going to get better. More significantly for me in my time spent with Andre was not so much how amazing a player he was but how he carried himself. He was such a free spirit and my absolute antithesis. He was an embodiment of inner freedom, with his kind and gracious personality and in his appearance. The long colored hair, the makeup, the fashion. It's not that he wasn't afraid of what people would think of him, he wasn't afraid of what he thought of himself, as outrageous as he may have appeared. And that inner freedom played out in his personality and how he viewed people, and I would even go so far as to say that it played out in how he played his tennis.

He wasn't afraid to play differently than everybody else, to go for it all the time with fearless and seemingly careless abandon. More importantly, he wasn't afraid of the big stage and of playing to win. Granted, if I had had his shot-making abilities I may have played more aggressively, too. But my super steady, never miss, play-not-to-lose style was pretty emblematic of my sense of self at that time in my life. I think about how restrained I was becoming in my public dealings and how I started to dislike crowds and how afraid I became when the interviewer wanted to ask me a few questions. He was everything I was not and that impression didn't pass once we went our separate ways. It stayed with me. My development and self-realization were getting worse, not better. Spending time around someone so seemingly liberated really brought that point home. As I left the NBTA after a couple weeks watching the younger, freer spirited and unbelievably talented players coming of age, another life lesson from those hallowed grounds was being brought home.

Andre Agassi (USA) at the 1988 French Open (Photo by Frank J. Sutton)

Leaving the academy in the summer of '86, I joined my USA teammates on a long flight to the former USSR. The Goodwill Games were a big deal back in 1986. Coming on the heels of the U.S. boycott of the 1980 Summer Olympic Games in Moscow and the USSR's boycott of the 1984 Summer Olympic Games in Los Angeles, the Goodwill Games were the brainchild of Ted Turner of CNN fame.

As Americans heading to Russia, we were under strict rules to keep our out-of-competition behavior in check, assimilating with the Russian people as little as possible. The importance of these Games was well beyond the athletic 103 competition; what mattered most here was that no Americans be involved in an embarrassing international incident. I got the message. There would be no cruising the gay parts of town on this trip.

The tennis was being played in Yelma, a village off the Black Sea. The weather was awful; cold, wet, dreary, making the whole country just seem so drab. The architecture, everything looked the same, like some military barracks housing project. There was minimal TV and radio, not that I could understand a word of it anyway. The famed state newspapers and magazines were also in Russian, making reading about the local news impossible.

Before we left for Russia, I had read up on the living conditions of the average Russian my age and was struck by the level of fear and control they lived under. The stark lack of human and civil rights available to the average Russian citizen sounded disturbing in the books I had read. But to see it firsthand like this was different. If it wasn't against the law to express yourself, everyone sure walked around like it was. My understanding was that the consequences of acting out against the Party Line were serious, with possible jail terms. That specter hanging over everyone's head resulted in an atmosphere of paralyzing fear emanating from the Russian citizens. A fear I oddly connected with, that it wasn't OK to express yourself or be yourself, and to do so had serious consequences; they all lived within a self-imposed prison out of fear of being discovered. And though I may have been living in a different type of self-imposed prison, I connected with them.

Political tensions between the two countries were quite high when we arrived. We were under strict instructions to be on our best behavior; there was to be no protesting of any kind permitted. To violate that creed would result in an immediate one-way ticket home. On the flight over, I read about past political protests at the Olympic Games. I was enthralled by the story of John Carlos and Tommie Smith at the 1968 Summer Games in Mexico City. Racial tensions in the United States were reaching a critical mass that summer. Smith and Carlos both medaled in the 400 relay for the USA and during the medal ceremony and the playing of our National Anthem, they raised their black gloved fists in the air in solidarity for the civil rights movement taking place in the U.S. then.

The two of them were on the next flights out of Mexico City, but they are a permanent part of Olympic history, prime examples of the power of political expression in the domain of sports. The long flight had me envisioning all kinds of different scenarios for my young self once afoot in the

USSR. I certainly was not ready to take a stand like Carlos and Smith did and make some type of statement regarding the state of human and civil rights discrimination that gays the world round faced. But taking inventory of where I was as a person compared to what I had just experienced being around the free-spirited Agassi and reading about the courageous Smith and Carlos and seeing the effects the overt oppression a nation had upon its citizenry, I knew something within me had to change. I was tired of living a lie, the worst kind of lie, for I could not to my own self be true. How much longer was I going to keep living in fear of people finding out that this was just the way God made me?

Goodwill Games U.S. Team, summer of 1986: (left to right) Beverly Bowes, Jay Berger, Ronnie Reis, Luke Jensen, Coach Sheila McInerny, Marianne Wendel, Caroline Kuhlman, Kelly Jones, Patty Fendick, Brad Pearce, Coach John Hubble and me crouching on the lower left.

What if I had come out then at the 1986 Goodwill Games? What would my life had been like? Oh, it would have been an international incident alright. The world was just so not ready for a gay male athlete representing the USA to take a stand against the discrimination and bigotry gays faced in all facets of life. And I was not ready to be that person to carry the torch for my similarly affected brethren.

It would have likely been the end of my tennis career; my need for outside financial support to keep playing would have dried up in an instant.

It would have been a media circus no doubt, with the mainstream media and sports world nowhere near as enlightened as they are today. And there is little doubt the general public would know my name. I would have been a civil rights pioneer, a trailblazer, hopefully not a martyr in the mold of Harvey Milk or Matthew Shepherd.

I think back now on all my years spent in the closet with remorse, as a waste, not just for my own self-realization but for the countless nameless and faceless gay athletes who came after me who chose to perform also in the closet because just like me they felt they had to, for fear of losing everything. It's a different time and place now for up-and-coming international competitors. The Winter Olympic Games returned to Russia early in 2014. Much was said and written about the host country's recent crackdown on free speech as it pertained to the visiting athletes and their views about gay rights. Even in 2014, still much of the world is just not ready to face and address their irrational fears regarding what it means to have gay people among them in our overwhelmingly straight world. But it's a different era today and with the Internet as it is, the world is connected like never before. Gay kids like I once was have all kinds of sites and resources available to them online for guidance and support. The days of feeling painfully alone with a shameful secret are gradually fading away.

In that context I felt hopeful about the Sochi Olympics, hopeful that someone would step forward, maybe even a group of both gay and straight athletes, and that they would protest Russia's restrictions on freedom of expression regarding gay rights. I looked forward to protests, done tastefully but with a forceful purpose behind them, declaring that the days of discriminating against a group of people based on their God-given sexual orientation must end.

I thought that if such a protest happened, it would be a circus again, but a different kind of circus, as athletes from around the world banded in unity to end the policies of bigotry that still plague our world. I imagined the headlines in the media, celebrating these brave men and women. What a powerful statement would be made to the world, a statement I wish I could have made myself in 1986, at the Goodwill Games. A statement I wished I could be making with them right there in that moment.

There was no such moment in Sochi. But I was proud of our Administration for selecting openly gay athletes as ambassadors and members of the Presidential Delegation to Sochi. I was prouder still that one of those athletes was a tennis player, Billie Jean King, and that the other, figure skater, Brian Boitano, already out to his family and friends, chose that selection as his opportunity to declare his sexuality and live his truth publicly.

CHAPTER

16

MY BOSTON ESCAPE

The Goodwill Games concluded without international incident. I was eager to get away from the cold, dreary and unfamiliar foreign customs of the USSR and back home to the States and its familiarities. Junior Davis Cup arranged a wild card for me to play the pro tournament VS Championships in Boston that summer. After a long flight home I remember deplaning at Logan Airport and being overwhelmed by a wall of heat and humidity. With only a day to adjust to the climate and my jet lag, I didn't have much energy on the courts, losing feebly in the first round of the singles. I had an extra day to acclimate before the doubles began. My junior peer Jay Berger and I had a winnable first round against UCLA's best, Dan Nahirny and Buff Farrow, with the world number one team of Andres Gomez and Hans Gildemeister waiting in the second round if we were to advance. Another great tennis opportunity was before me.

A couple days of down time on the road in a major U.S. city. After two weeks straight being embedded with my USA teammates, I needed a night on the town by myself to reset my sense of self. After losing my singles, just as I was leaving the tournament site, I overheard one of the volunteers from the tournament carrying on about how much fun she had the night before at a gay bar in town. Her gay uncle had taken her and a dozen of her friends to one of the nice gay clubs downtown and they had had a heck of a time checking out all the people. Great, just what I needed. Out of the closet, comfortable in their skin gay people do things like this, bring groups of their straight friends to the

107

clubs they like to haunt. Just my luck. Now I was going to be uncomfortable at the places I felt most comfortable for fear that half the tournament might walk in.

Fortunately Boston was a big city with a good assortment of places to go. I found a nondescript bar off the path a bit in one of the seedier parts of town. I decided to check it out that night. It was a Tuesday night, it was still light when I walked in from the long Northeast summer days. I entered through the saloon doors and came upon a completely empty bar. The bartender, in no hurry, slowly greeted me, filling my order without much enthusiasm before slipping off to the other end of the bar to resume his conversation.

It was still early; plenty of time for things to pick up. I sat at the bar alone, nursing my beer. I ordered another, and an hour later was still the only patron in the place. I had been asked by a couple of my teammates and their parents to join them in town for a nice dinner but something inside me felt the need to be by myself that night. I was used to going out alone on the road, but I wasn't used to the feelings of loneliness that enveloped me that Boston evening. I thought, "Was this it? Was this what my life was going to be like?" Same dingy bars in different cities with different faces. It was all starting to feel the same. The novelty and excitement of being the new kid in the new town had worn off. I was starting to not like how the clubs and bars were making me feel any longer.

I sat quietly listening to my picks on the jukebox. Each one played the same songs. Lionel Richie's "Penny Lover," Madonna's "Papa Don't Preach," Elton John's "Tiny Dancer." These songs became the soundtrack of my life that summer of 1986. I would travel a lot that year, different cities, different bars, but always the same songs. As my depression began to mount, those songs took on deeper lasting meanings for me. Was this as good as my life was going to get? Is this what God wants for me? To sit here alone in a bar in a strange city waiting...waiting...waiting, for something to happen, for some chance or circumstance; for someone or some opportunity to walk through the saloon doors of this bar and change my life's fortunes forever?

I knew I had a role in my increasing unhappiness; I just couldn't read the script to see what that role was. I was performing without direction, speaking without knowledge of my lines. I was acting with no sense of what my larger role was. I seemed to be going everywhere, tournaments, traveling, endless nightlife, but all of it without direction or plan, all the while leading me nowhere. The reality of where my life was and the growing fear about the unknown of where it was heading hit me that evening. I was descending farther and farther in to the closet and I couldn't see a way out for myself. The closet was wearing on me. In my suspicion, in my paranoia, in my anti-social behavior among my tennis peers, and ultimately in my growing depression that for the first time in my life I feared everything was not going to work out well for me. I seemed powerless to do anything to alter my fated course. It's hard for me to reflect back on those days, to hear those jukebox songs today and not have those feelings of loneliness and loss rekindle within me. In my increasingly distressed state of mind, I drank a fair amount that night before the place began to fill. After a few beers, or maybe a few too many beers, I met a gentleman. Within minutes, I was telling him everything about me; that I was Bobby Blair in town to play the pro tennis tournament and if he wasn't doing anything he should come on down to Longwood and watch my partner and me play the number one ranked team in the world in the Thursday afternoon session. He said he would. I sensed he wouldn't as we parted ways that evening.

On my way home, I chastised myself for being so forward with all my personal information. What if he did come to my match? Then what? I wasn't going to leave him a ticket to my box, so if he did come he would likely have to sit in the Grandstand away from my coaches, teammates and their parents. Thursday came. We were the last match of the day session,

Jay and I were warming up; I nearly had a heart attack as I looked over to our Player's Box and there was my new gay friend from a couple nights before sitting right next to my JDC Coach and teammates. This absolutely could not be happening. I couldn't hit two balls without looking over to the box; I just couldn't believe my eyes. I kept looking for the reaction from the coaches and parents in the box when they found out I met this guy at a gay bar and that I had invited him to come watch me play. What a way to end my career, I remember thinking, on center court against the number one team in the world.

The match began and Jay and I just could not have come out playing any better, winning the first set easily and racing off to a quick lead in the second. I was up to my usual fist-pumping high-fiving shenanigans, trying to keep Jay and me playing at our high level while getting under the skin of the veteran Gomez, who was not having a good time that late afternoon in Boston. Gomez was trying to intimidate me by trying to take my head off during some of our exchanges, but he kept barely missing. On the changeovers, he started 109 to dump the sawdust he used to keep his grip dry all over my head and body. That just got Jay and I more motivated to play harder as we closed in on the biggest victory of our careers.

They came on strong in the second set to force a third set. By this point it was getting late in the day, with the crowd filling up for the evening session featuring Ivan Lendl. I was doing the best I could on the court trying not to look over at our box too often when I was enveloped by a feeling I had never felt before regarding my sexuality. With my secret hanging precariously in the balance, I surprisingly felt suddenly at ease. For the first time in my life I gave in to my situation. The problems I was having being gay in a straight world were just too big for me to manage. Way too big. Too many variables, way too many aspects beyond my control. What was transpiring in my Player's Box as I played was going to happen again, and again, and again; my two worlds would collide away from me, away from my ability to intervene and do whatever I had to do to keep my secret a secret.

My dear friend Ricky Brown never knew of my internal struggles during this incredible tough time. I wish I had told him.

I started to think. Instead of spending all my time lying about who I was and hiding who I was, maybe that time would be better spent with me just explaining who I was. My primal fear in life, the fear that was the motivation behind all of my dishonest behavior all these years was that I was going to be suddenly outed, blindsided, totally caught off guard by someone in the most inappropriate way in the most awkward of places. I had run this scenario through my head so many times I couldn't even begin to count. I would panic over the results, envisioning the worst possible situation with the most extreme reactions and consequences. Friends and family gone, tennis opportunities squandered, unemployable and not to be trusted, a life of discrimination and bigotry, a lifetime of being labeled different, of being feared because I was different from my fellow man only in who I loved. As I played this great match against these great players, I just knew that was what was happening in my box. I sensed it was all over for me and somehow I gave in to it and just relaxed.

Every time I did look to my box to see what was going on, I saw that nobody was freaking out or acting differently. My new friend was still there in the middle of my team and coaches. I could only just imagine how all that was being greeted. What I feared most was the consequences of being found out to be gay. A close second was the visceral fight or flight reaction I feared about what I so didn't want to have, a difficult conversation; a conversation of being put on the spot and being asked direct questions from people who have known me my whole life.

I wish I had the life experience and wisdom to know then that everyone on this Earth has a difficult conversation they struggle to have with the people that are important to them. But the fact that I knew it was coming and that I had time to prepare for it made the angst of the moment dissipate for me. In a strange way it was perfect timing. I was tired, edgy, getting depressed and frustrated by the demands of living in the closet. If this was how I was going to be outed, let's get it over with. Maybe I invited this guy to my match because a growing part of me didn't care anymore what anybody thought. But here I was, mere moments from my being outed and knowing it was coming, and I felt calm.

Jay and I played our hearts out but ended up losing a tough three-setter to the world number ones. As we gathered up our stuff, I saw my coach and teammates walking toward us to congratulate us on our great effort. My heart sank as they approached, for all my deeply held fears were about to become reality. Everybody started talking all at once, a couple of the group addressing Jay while the other couple in the group addressed me. When my coach and teammates simultaneously turned to me and said what a pleasure it was to meet and watch the entire match with such a close friend of my father's, I nearly collapsed from relief. My new gay friend got it. He protected me. Likely protected himself too in the process, but he read the situation correctly, making up a story that protected us both. He saw that I was an in-the-closet athlete trying to make my way in the ultra-straight world of professional tennis. To have my cover blown now and be outed would come with consequences. For tennis wasn't ready for a gay male player. And I wasn't ready to come out as that gay male player. And he read that precisely without me saying a word to him about it, regardless of his position on whether gay people of prominence should be out or not. He knew that wasn't his call to make.

I left Boston as confused about my sexuality as ever before. Inches from being outed, I learned I could trust gay people with who I was. More importantly, I learned that the gay people I was meeting understood the complexities of living in the closet and that whether or when an individual chooses to come out was an intensely personal decision that must be reached by the individual himself, and not expedited along by other gay people on some sort of gay rights agenda crusade.

With tennis being structured in the transitory way it was, my desire to connect with like-minded souls was becoming a distraction. With each exploration deeper in to the gay life, I felt farther and farther apart from my fellow tennis players. I just wasn't feeling like one of the boys anymore; not in the innocent youthful ways that brought us together in the first place. We were all growing up. Tennis wasn't just fun anymore; it was our job. As with any vocation, having one's private life in order was tantamount to having any chance at long-term success, especially in a vocation so demanding as professional tennis. My margin for error in the tennis world was as slim as could be; with the choices I was making pushing my margins even slimmer. With a few weeks of summer tennis to go, I didn't like the direction my life was heading as I exited Boston.

CHAPTER

17

MY SLOW DECLINE

There were two more tournaments before the U.S. Open that summer of 1986. The USTA granted to me wild cards in to the qualifying, but I didn't have my best stuff and lost early. I had been on the road for four months straight by the time the U.S. Open came around at the end of August. I was under the assumption that being a part of JDC automatically included a wild card into the U.S. Open qualifying, hence my grave disappointment when my coach called informing me I was not offered one. My head automatically went conspiratorial; someone must have outed me or I had been seen with somebody. I was acting out more brazenly that summer of '86; exploring the gay scenes in every city, while not socializing much with my team. The staff's given reason for why I didn't qualify for the Open wild card was that my results from that summer just didn't measure up. I accepted their answer as graciously as I could, which wasn't very. Either way, I was tired. The training by day and running around at night while traveling every week was wearing me out. I looked forward to getting back home to Fayetteville and all the structure that school life provided.

I was entering my senior season at the University of Arkansas. I debated briefly on whether to turn professional that summer. Though I had not won the NCAA's, there was not that much left for me to achieve at the college level. Many of my peers were preparing themselves for the tour: Ricky Leach, Richey Reneberg, Jim Grabb, Patrick McEnroe, Brad Pearce, Derrick Rostag- 113 no, Jim Pugh, Luke Jensen, Patrick Galbraith, Michael Kures, Todd Witsken, Kelly Jones, John Ross, Jay Berger, Robbie Weiss, and others. The allure of the tour was tempting. After a few long talks with coach Hightower and my teammates, we collectively decided it would be best for us all to return and see what we could accomplish as a program. A national team title was our goal.

Martina Navratilova plays against Chris Evert Lloyd, 1984 in New York. Photo © Bettmann/CORBIS

At the Goodwill Games, I had caught the eye of renowned coach Mike Estep in my first round match against top Russian and French Open semi finalist Andrei Chesnokov. Full-time coach to world number one Martina

Navratilova, Mike liked what he saw in my game. He believed if I could develop an attacking net game to augment my strong backcourt play, I could earn a good living on tour. He offered to help me free of charge, inviting me to come down to Fort Worth to work out with Martina and him to see if we could add that new dimension to my game.

I was not back at school long before taking him up on his offer. After a few years of grown up college ball and enough professional level tennis, I knew Mike was right. I needed a little more offense to succeed at the next level. What he was suggesting was not an easy transformation for someone my size whose patient grinding style was well engrained from growing up on the slow green clay of Florida. I knew that. But what I was best at doing was only going to take me so far. I had a year of college tennis left to implement his suggestions knowing I could resume my old style of play if my new tactics proved futile.

More than the elite coaching Mike promised, I was excited to meet Martina. I knew I had so much to learn about her professionalism through her unrivaled work ethic; that was obvious. The hidden benefit for me was to be able to observe how she interacted with her partner at the time, Judy Nelson. Martina was the highest-profile athlete in the world to be out about her sexuality. In my brief and limited experience in the gay scene, I had not spent any sustained time in the company of an openly gay couple.

And what a sight it was. Judy, Martina, friends, family and their amazing array of dogs all scurrying around Martina's compound. Just like any other family would, normally, without drama, without self-consciousness, everyone just being themselves because what they had was so normal. They were two people in a loving committed relationship and they acted like it.

Laughing, joking, teasing, playing; they were great together, giving me hope that I could have a similar relationship someday.

I flew back to Fayetteville buoyed by the possibilities of having the full life yet a little maudlin about how far from attainable it all seemed. Arriving at school, there was immediate trouble. Too much tennis, not enough school; my grade-point average had fallen behind. I wasn't the only player either as several of my teammates were facing similar issues. Coach Hightower was also having some issues with the administration. The dominoes soon started to fall. Coach resigned, one of our top players, Joey Blake, turned professional. It became apparent that little good could come from staying in Fayetteville for my senior year, so like many of my peers from around the country, I chose to turn professional also.

Sort of. Didn't really have much of a choice. There was no announcement, no press conference, no contracts to sign. Everything I had worked so hard to achieve, to become a professional tennis player, happened more by default. This was not how I envisioned the moment. I had no master plan, no financial backing or strategy for getting the much needed support to survive on the road. I had no idea where the best tournaments to play were to improve my ranking. I had just started working with a new coach who was convinced I needed to fundamentally change my style of play to be successful at the next level. I was on board with this but knew such changes took time and an expected regression in results before the changes paid dividends. Time was not something I had the luxury of, and I just knew in my gut that this was no way for a player to turn pro.

That was just the tennis part of the equation. Emotionally I just wasn't ready either. Years of having to pretend to be straight was wearing on me. Not having a healthy gay mentor or friend in my daily school life left me feeling all alone and overwhelmed with my internal struggles. Compounding my loneliness was that I ceased being a good friend myself. All the lying and sneaking around created a profound cloud of shame that I lived under, pulling me farther and farther apart from my best childhood friends. I didn't feel as close to them anymore, nor did I want to be close to them for fear of being found out. All this mounting angst led me to seek out companionship and comfort more and more frequently when I would hit the road. Tired and lonely from my summer of acting out, the single-minded focus that my tennis required began to be compromised by the complex whirlwind of relationships I started finding myself entangled in. I left Fayetteville and found support and comfort from Mike and his wife, Barbara, some more coaching and on-court time with Martina. I was now a professional tennis player.

I secured some funding from my uncle Jim enabling me to get out on the road to play right away. Peers suggested I go play the Hawaii Satellite, five tournaments over five weeks on the various islands. What better place to start my career, I thought. First week I lost early. I tried playing my new style. It worked well at times, not so well at others. I lost a close match to a quality player, but the pro tour was no place for moral victories. Plus you don't get paid for losing. I hung around the site that first week and practiced hard on implementing coach Estep's new tactics. Week two. I lost early again. My frustrations on and off the court began to mount. I was back in that familiar place of being embedded full time with my tennis brethren. I loved many of these guys as friends, but I just didn't feel like one of them any longer. The years of my sneaking around and not being honest with them had affected our friendships adversely. Many of my traveling friends started to go out at night without asking me to join. Not because they didn't want me around. They just stopped asking me, for I had said no too many times before and they started assuming I didn't want to be around them. Part of what they felt was true, I didn't want to be around them, but it was not what they thought, that I was getting all stuck up, thinking I was hot stuff. The reality was, I just didn't want them to discover my secret.

My reality was crystallizing around me. Making it on the tour as a player was rough enough. How was I going to survive on the tour and be gay? I started getting the outer manifestations of anxiety. I wasn't sleeping well, spending countless nights and hours awake wondering how I was going to survive in this ultra-straight environment. Lots of my player friends had serious girlfriends and wives at home. Many of the tour guys had their wives and kids with them. What about me? I felt the meter running. How much longer could I legitimately stay single without having to explain it? I was getting tired of trying to figure outhow to answer to why I didn't have a steady girlfriend.

All the feelings of loneliness started to come back. I had another five days off between tournaments. I couldn't imagine another five-day stretch of hanging with my straight tennis friends and keeping up my false front, my fake image, my deceitful and dishonest other self. I needed an escape from that guy. Instead of working on all the new things coach Estep wanted me to, I started to spend my afternoons and evenings seeking comfort from my tennis reality, trekking cross island to scope out the local gay scene.

I met someone my first day in town, a great looking, life-of-the-party bartender named Curtis Ruud at a club called Hulas in Honolulu. Here I was, at age 22, and I didn't have a single gay friend my age to talk with, to share my feelings with, to ease my loneliness for being gay in such a straight world. Nobody. Anybody my age would do by this point. I hung out at all day and all night. This was the only gay bar in the only local village on this side of the island. I would sneak into town by day, enter the club through the back, be extra careful if I would walk outside for anything, and then sneak out of the club at night, trying to make it back to my housing undetected. The thrill of exploring my double life had passed long ago; all the carefulness and suspicion just left me bitter that this was what my life had become.

My mood continued to darken. The third week of the satellite I played my worst tennis of the trip. I was not happy. Instead of digging in and training harder, I looked to escape more. I resumed my trips to the other side of the island. My new bartender friend introduced me to a bunch of his fun-loving friends in town. I started to have a lot more fun running around with my new gay friends than I was at not playing well at my tournaments.

The nature of the gay society was the older/younger dynamic. I began to meet older, wealthier, more successful men. They all wanted me to be something for them; dinner date, arm candy, their evening's entertainment. I just wanted a friend to talk to. What I really needed was a mentor, for my tennis, for my life. I was starting to make bad decisions that were going to have lasting consequences. Upon returning home, I would look in the mirror at night's end, not sure who I was looking at any longer.

The fourth week was the worst of all, my new tactics and my old style haplessly in conflict. But where was my fight, my edge, my focus? This was not how I envisioned the launch of my pro career. I needed to reboot, and quickly.

The Hawaii satellite was the last remaining run of tourneys in the States that year. I checked the schedule for December satellites. Nothing was happening. My good friend Simon Robinson, my roommate at the University of Arkansas, suggested I fly to New Zealand to train with him for a month. I was already half way across the globe. I was not sure what was ahead for me there. What I did know was I needed to get off this island and away from my new friends promptly. Nothing good had come from my being here. Nothing good was to come from me staying here much longer.

New Zealand was an oasis of calm and happiness for me. And truly beautiful. The Robinson family welcomed we warmly. I basked in the reflected glow of what a happy family really looked like. Simon's parents had sent him far away to the U.S. to get an education and improve his tennis. That was their commitment and now he was home they surrounded him with love. Cushioned in a loving family, I found some equilibrium. There was no running around to bars, just some good tennis and some warm family time. But it also made me realize how much I had missed out in my own home life. I

missed my mom more and I resented my dad more for not being like Simon's, so supportive and caring.

A month in New Zealand and it was back to the States in January. I chose to fly to England to play the indoor circuit there. Total mistake. In the past two years I had been moved to faster indoor courts at the three most important times in my career, losing to bigger, more aggressive players than myself. What made me think I could compete successfully in those conditions now as a professional? A month of futility there and it was back to the States to regroup. My career wasn't going well and I was already running out of time.

The Florida clay court run began where the conflict between my two styles of play was never more evident. By the third week I was pretty frustrated, and I tried to revert back to my old grinding ways. The choices I had been making to deal with my inner turmoil on the road began to surface strongly in my sudden lack of physical conditioning. The partying, the lifestyle, the lack of sleep, the lack of training all began to have negative effects. I began to tire in my matches like never before, cramping horribly in my native Florida climate. The hot, humid conditions that used to be a reliable advantage for me were now becoming a serious liability.

I had started the Hawaii satellite circuit ranked around 500 in the world.

With my first full year of play under my belt, my ranking was not improving but falling. It was getting to be summer again, and now I had points to defend or my ranking would fall even lower. Guys I would always beat were having breakout tournaments. Guys much younger than me were already making names for themselves. The equipment was changing, the game was getting more global, larger, stronger, more powerful players began to dominate at every level. I was what I was, a 5'10" Florida clay court grinder who didn't have the firepower to flourish at tennis' highest level. All the world-class coaching wasn't going to change that. Coach Estep was right,

I did need to develop a more attacking game to compete with the pros, but I should have begun implementing such changes years ago. My dream was dying. All the hard work and lofty goals, all the hopes of tennis being my ticket out of my financial predicament were crashing down around me.

I needed money. I needed guidance. I needed some good luck. I needed some good results, something to give me hope that if I put in the work, this was all going to work out in my favor. I gave myself a hard reality check.

How could I have lost my way so badly in just a year? What was I doing with myself, with my game, with my life?

I needed to get into the Open and have a good run, but that didn't happen. Because my ranking had plummeted so low, I didn't even get in. I was staying in New York at an apartment arranged by my childhood friend from Orlando, Kevin Dinneen. I had a couple days in New York with nothing to do and nowhere to go. I had nowhere to live, I was really low on money. I was not entered in any tournaments and had lost close to 25 pounds from my playing weight. I looked terrible, I felt worse. I could barely eat, I could barely sleep. How did this happen? How did this happen? I hated what I saw in the mirror.

Kevin invited my friend Ricky Brown and me to dinner two nights later. We took the subway up from Wall Street to 43rd Street, we walked a couple blocks to this beautiful restaurant called Orso. It was a stylish crowd, Kevin and several others. Ricky and I took our seats at the end of the table.

Kevin wanted to talk to me; he knew I was struggling. He had no idea the extent; or maybe he did. I so wanted to tell him everything; everything I had been through since discovering I was gay. All the conflicts and struggles and the choices that I faced trying to make it in the tennis world. I just knew he would understand. And it kills me to this day that I couldn't, so in the closet immersed in shame I was.

As dinner began, I was greeted by a sharply dressed older gentleman seated to my left. I saw the look in his eye in an instant. I knew what that look meant. I was about to get hit on again. John Dupont was his name — a relative of his more notorious namesake and a real Dupont, heir to the Dupont family fortune. He was thunderstruck with me; couldn't take his focus off me, his attentive stare locked on me. I tried to look away and engage my friend Rick in conversation. Every time I would turn away, there John was, tapping me on the shoulder trying to re-engage my attention. He told me stories of Hollywood and fame, how he was closest of friends with Peter, Paul and Mary, how he sold James Dean the car he was killed in. How did he know I loved that LA/Hollywood stuff so?

He told me I reminded him a lot of James Dean, how I looked, how I spoke, how I carried myself and he asked would I like to go back to the Plaza Hotel with him after dinner? I was scared and said no. I came with Ricky, I was leaving with Ricky. To leave with John and not Ricky would certainly blow my cover.

John and I met up at the Open grounds the next day. He latched on to me again. Every time I turned around, there he was, taking a picture of me, telling me how beautiful I was, and all the things he could do for me. He told me I should come to Los Angeles with him after the tournament and see all the fun we could have together first hand. He was so brazen in his fawning over me I began to get paranoid others might be watching us. When I couldn't take it anymore, I asked if we could go and he agreed.

His limo picked us up. He took to me to Manhattan to shop, buying me thousands of dollars of clothes and jewelry. I started to get paranoid again. Ricky was to meet me in town later. How was I going to explain where I got everything from? Ricky knew I was broke. What the hell was I doing again? I had just told myself I wasn't going to do this anymore. Allowing these older wealthy men into my life, accepting their gifts was a dead end, leaving me so empty and alone, yet here I was doing it again.

John took a call. His plans for the evening changed causing him to leave abruptly. Or so he said. He left Ricky and me his limo for the evening. The game was on. I knew the game. I was being seduced. I had not let John touch me. I wasn't interested in him in that way at all, but he was as aggressive and relentless a suitor as I had yet to meet; I needed to calculate how best to go forward.

John was complicated. I found him smart, charming, worldly, obviously quite wealthy, but he was 30 years-plus my senior. I had told myself repeatedly I was done with this, the leading older men on for money and gifts. I didn't have to do this, I had seen enough by now to know that if I was patient there was a place for me in the gay world. A place for true love and partnership. I sensed my gay self-realization was not going to occur in the tennis world as a tennis player. That I knew. But it wasn't going to happen being the prize for older wealthy men like John Dupont either.

I wanted real love in my life. I had to be more than just a gay guy in the closet with a bunch of rich old men trying to secure me as their trophy. But John Dupont was a whole different level. He asked me to move to Los Angeles with him. I knew the game, I knew what that meant. This was Los Angeles, this was the good life, this was everything I thought I ever wanted -- travel, parties, all behind the security of a private gate. All I had to do was say yes and I was set.

The week progressed. It was time to leave New York. As I packed my bags to head to the airport, I still had no idea where I was going. John Dupont thought I was coming to Los Angeles with him to live out his fantasy.

I had told him I would go just to get him to stop talking about it. My friend Kevin knew something was wrong with me, he could sense it. He asked about my state of health. I told him the truth: I wasn't eating, wasn't sleeping, was drinking too much and had lost a lot of weight and I was thinking about going to Los Angeles with John Dupont to live for awhile.Kevin began to intervene. He wanted to help me. He didn't like the Los Angeles thing. Bad idea. We talked in circles. He avoiding asking me if I was gay, myself avoiding confessing I was gay. He knew what going to L.A. meant. It meant crossing a line that wouldn't be that easy to come back from. It also meant the onset of a life cycle borne of bad choices he knew intuitively never ended well for young guys like me, and in my gut I knew he was right. I knew that to go to Los Angeles with this wealthy older man, as intriguing as the Hollywood lifestyle had always been for me, and no matter how badly I needed the financial help, that the cost was way too high.

Kevin put his foot down, advising me against going. I tried to reason with him that John seemed OK. The more I spoke, the more he pushed back. I wanted to go, he wanted me to go home to Orlando. I now wanted to go home too, but I didn't know where my home was anymore. I started for the airport, still bound for Los Angeles when Kevin intervened at the last moment and said no. No more. You can't go there, it's the wrong thing to do. He said I should go back home to Florida, to Orlando, to see my dad.

Nothing good can come from going to L.A.. He wanted me to get well. He said, "Please go home to Orlando." I took Kevin's advice and flew home. I had little money. No place to stay. There was my dad's house but it was hardly a home. Upon landing, I went by there. I was deeply depressed; the Dupont assault had finished me off. I was already in a bad way before all that. Little good ever came from my dad; if there was ever a time I needed a strong male adult figure in my life, it was now.

Labor Day 1987. I walked in the house, weak and tired but dressed in all the sharp clothes John Dupont bought for me. Dad took one look at me and started. "Not playing very good are ya? Didn't see ya in the Open, what are you going to do now? How you supporting yourself? Where ya gonna live? Don't even think about asking to live here. What are ya gonna do, boy?"

He never had a good thing to say. My dad managed to make me feel even worse about myself. He continued to stare at the TV in his reclining chair, not even looking at me. I walked away and toward my old bedroom. I walked into
122 my mom's old room, saw the bed she had passed away on four years ago, and

I started to cry. How in the hell did I get here? What had I done with my life? I turned from her bed and saw myself in the mirror, a mere shell of myself with all this ridiculous clothing and jewelry, and something snapped in me. I hated what I saw. Hated, hated, hated. I wanted to hurt myself so badly; punish myself. I didn't know how or by what means but I just couldn't stand to be what I had become any longer.

I had enough sense to call my friend Kevin. He told me not to move as he flew over to my dad's house. He came in, took one look at me and said,

"Let's go." He piled me in to his car and took me straight to the hospital. I was in a bad way as they admitted me. Upset, agitated, talking fast. They gave me some valium to calm me down. Hours later after the doctors were sure I was alright, Kevin walked me out to his car. I literally had no money and nowhere to go. He asked me to come stay with him and his wife until I felt better. I accepted their gracious offer.

Late that night I lay awake. It was a hot, still Central Florida evening, the bugs buzzing outside my window. I had calmed down, partly from the medicine, partly from the grace and kindness of my friend Kevin. He gave me a wonderful pep talk that night; told me I didn't need to do a thing for a couple months but rest and heal up. He told me everything was going to be alright, and for some odd reason I believed him.

I laid there with nothing. Homeless, broke, jobless, the one thing I knew better than anything, my tennis, no longer able to sustain me in the world. I had no idea how I was going to be able to support myself in the future when I came to the realization that lying there with nothing was still better than going to Los Angeles or Europe or any of the other places I was offered. For me to accept their offers was a death sentence, a slow, degrading, by-the-install-ment-plan attack on my integrity, my dignity and everything I had worked so hard in my life to become.

I didn't need these people to make it in the world. Matter of fact, if I wanted to make it in the world, avoiding these types was the first step. They were takers, users, hyper self-centered people and deeply flawed. I saw first-hand what they did to others. I experienced firsthand what they almost did to me. And quietly, to myself that warm still evening, I made a vow to myself to never offer anything to anyone other than from a vantage point of wanting to help them. I would never ask or expect sexual favors in return, because I know what that almost did to me and the suffering I incurred by not knowing 123 better. The consequences of selling one's heart and soul for money for a young impressionable person like myself were severe. I couldn't bear the pain of bringing such discord upon another.

It was to be the beginning of a new day. Had I not learned my lessons?

CHAPTER

18

ROOKIE PRO TEAM

Back home in Orlando. Kevin and his wife, Tina, said I could stay as long as I needed. They also told me to try not to worry so much about everything. Not much chance of that happening. I was mere minutes from boarding a plane for Los Angeles with someone I had just met, to do God knows what to support myself before Kevin intervened. My reality was all my best thinking up to then had led me to look in a mirror in a seriously compromised state wanting to harm who I had become. Much needed to change in my life and quickly, none of which was to happen without some deep introspective thought.

I had hit an emotional bottom. When I considered putting my body and soul up for sale to the highest bidder, my sense of self-worth plunged to ever lower depths. It was one thing to feel the shame of being a gay guy in the closet; it was a whole new level of self-hatred and devaluation acknowledging to myself that I allowed people to believe they could buy me.

By doing so, I allowed myself to be treated as a commodity. I became objectified, someone who could be bought, someone who could be had for the right price. I ceased being a whole person to myself. I risked abandoning all the morals, ethics and values I was raised with; everything I had worked so hard to become and my innate sense of what was right in life. It should have come as little surprise then that others would treat me like I was treating myself; as disposable, easily acquired, easily replaced, and unworthy of real love. The whole cycle was immensely toxic. I felt spiritually damaged, unhealthy, 125 wounded. But I knew enough at that point in my life that to have any chance of ever being healthy again, I needed to heal first.

Randy "Moose" Koehnke: Randy helped me to get
my confidence and life back in order and was a huge part of the overall success of the Rookie Pro Team.

How to heal? I had enough sense left in me to know that a large part of the solution was for me to do stop doing what I had been doing. I was making terrible decisions with my life. Nobody was forcing me to go out at night, to look through the paper to see where the nightlife was. Nobody was making me party. Yeah, I dabbled in drugs a little bit and was drinking more than a professional athlete should, but I was far from being any kind of an addict or alcoholic where I had no control over my actions. Stopping the nightlife activities would be immediately beneficial to my overall physical health. As I reflected farther on how I had reached such a depressed state of mind, and on the actions I had engaged in to not feel so all alone, I encountered a loneliness hard to describe. Life on the road, especially the tennis road, was not the right fit for a young man like me. I needed to start looking at other options for how to spend my time. There was too much time to kill, too much temptation, all centered on destructive activities with often unhealthy people. What started out as fun and exciting had somehow morphed into behavior that was degrading and life-threatening. If I kept giving in to temptation, there was little doubt as to how bankrupt in every way I would be left.

I hated myself for what I had become. The time spent at my friend Kevin's house allowed me to see up close and practice another way to be. I began to see what it looked like to be a patriarch, a loving partner, a family man, and a giver. He and his wife did everything for me; they cooked, they cleaned, they listened when I spoke, they encouraged me when I seemed down. As I slowly began to get my strength back, the fog from my depression began to lift. I started to feel better, more optimistic, more hopeful, knowing that as I moved forward in my life I needed to conduct myself differently.

After a month of rest at Kevin's, I paid a visit to one of my old clubs, the Orlando Tennis Center. I hadn't hit a ball in four weeks, the longest break of my tennis life. I reconnected with the Director of Tennis at the time, a gentleman named Joe Scandli. I didn't feel I had much to offer the world at that time, but I still had my tennis. We got to talking and I eventually asked him if he needed any help around the club training some of his up-and-coming kids.

Joe asked me if I would help him with a strong junior he was working with named Randy Koehnke. All his friends called him Moose. I had little else going on and agreed immediately. A great looking kid who just loved tennis, was a sponge about tennis, couldn't get enough of it. I was by this point in my career a walking encyclopedia of tennis knowledge just waiting for somebody to share it with. I loved the feeling of being a mentor to someone in tennis. I loved the instant connection and friendship I developed with Randy. So it wasn't a big surprise that within a couple weeks, I started having feelings for him.

What started out as a pleasantly distracting minor crush however quickly grew into a full unadulterated, falling head-over-heels infatuation for my new charge. The problem with my love for Randy was that he was straight. One hundred percent straight. The girls loved him and he loved the girls. At first I thought I would be OK with it, I was so happy to have the feelings of love for another, even if they weren't being reciprocated.

Randy had a way with the girls I had never seen before. It wasn't a question of if he was going to hook up, but with whom and how many. He had the touch. I would play along as best I could, trying not to blow my cover when we would go out. I would do everything I could to run interference, trying to come up with reasons why we had to go home early or couldn't go over to their place. When Randy would ignore my attempts at messing things up and go away with whomever that night, it would rip my heart right out of me to the point that I would get physically sick to my stomach watching him walk away from me to go home with someone else.

I would end up going home alone quite distressed in those early days of getting to know Randy.

Why did I keep making choices with my heart that kept leaving me so devastated, often in great turmoil? I wasn't a clueless, hapless teenager any longer. I knew intuitively that to allow situations to affect me so much, they must have been doing a lot for me also. On the outside, loving someone who could not love me back in the way I desired was a certain prescription for pain. But on the inside, having someone to love, to feel so connected to; to give my best self to, it brought the best person out in me. I was a young man looking for love and connection in a world that wasn't setting up well for guys like me. My choices again seemed bleak.

Falling in love with straight guys had no chance for long-term success, I knew that. But neither did being someone's trophy, or being a party boy drinking and hooking up with whomever, or pretending to be straight by securing girlfriends, or taking private vows of celibacy and just staying to myself, inviting the suspicions of my tennis peers that I was somehow different from them in the mysterious and misunderstood field of sexual orientation.

I was stuck in the closet with no reasonable escape in site. Unrequited love was as good as it was going to get for me. As unfulfilled as I often felt, loving Randy did help heal me from the whole John Dupont experience. It also kept me away from all the triggers of the gay bars and all of the late-night hours of the nightlife behavior in which I no longer could engage. I was treading water; I knew that. Sad as it was to admit, anything was better than getting pulled down any deeper in the destructive direction I was heading.

And so it went in my complex closeted world. With a complete lack of out-in-the-open gay males to befriend in the tennis world, I had to manufacture objects of affection for myself. I had to create in my mind like-minded individuals like myself again and again. I would idealize my creations, projecting onto people like Randy all the best loving and virtuous qualities I admired in myself and others. In a way, I learned how to love myself by loving these human figments of my imagination.

It's complicated stuff; the psychology of being closeted. I was bursting
with feelings of deep love and affection, with no person to express them to. I

tried to be straight, I tried the bar scene to keep it fun, I tried the dating scene to see if there was a way to benefit from my desirability, I tried obsessing on my sport to see if I could put my feelings to the side a while longer. With Randy, I let myself go a bit, allowing my heart to feel what it wanted to feel in spite of knowing it had no chance for success.

I needed to believe there were people like me out there for my own self preservation; and where they were not evident, I created them. There was great reasoning and cunning behind such self preservation, much permitted deception in my truth; but to not have invented such like- minded souls would have crushed me at that vulnerable time. What I needed most for my cure and self-restoration was the belief that I was not so isolated and all alone.

Helping out my new friend Randy with his tennis lifted my depressed spirits quickly back to normal. It also helped get my own game back in order. I wanted to play again; competitive tennis was what I knew best. To what extent I would resume playing I was unsure. It was spring of 1988, I still had a few ATP points remaining as the pro tour came through Key Biscayne for the Lipton International.

I entered and was able to secure a spot in the qualifying. I got to the site a couple days early to get acclimated. Walking the grounds, I felt like I was a little kid going to my first tournament again with my mom. But not in the excited, I can't wait to get out there and play sort of way. This time I felt like I just didn't belong. All the players walking around with their team of coaches and hitting partners. All the hustle and bustle of the site, everyone talking about what they had been doing and where they were going next. Except me. I didn't want to have to explain my last six months of personal rehabilitation. As for what I was doing after Key Biscayne, I had no answer for them, let alone myself.

The match came. I had nothing. No fire, no focus, no fight. The last couple games were surreal. For all my struggles fitting into the tennis world, I could always count on feeling at home competing on the court. But not that day. I was done, burned out, finished. It wasn't supposed to end like this. Certainly not in my dream ending. This was a waking nightmare. I felt defeated in every way as the last couple games slipped away. My home town paper, the Orlando Sentinel, would run a piece the next week on my tennis decline. "Bobby Blair Washed Up at 23." How could this have happened? Less than two years earlier I was on top of the tennis world.

After spending the past six months recovering from extreme dehydration, weight loss and a pretty nasty depression, I had plenty of time to get myself locked back into making tennis my profession. But that didn't happen. It was clear that my game, my body, my head and my heart were just not capable of going to the next level. The symbolism of my final match at the Key Biscayne qualifying was not lost on me. It came against 6-foot-10 Greg Neuhart who bombed serves and returns down upon my frail body from all angles. All my years of being a grinder had taken their toll; there was a whole new generation of power players coming on the scene and it was not hard to conclude that my time had come and gone in my beloved sport.

Did I retire that day? You never would have known it. Just as unceremoniously as my turning pro was, so was my retirement. No plaque, no watch, no speech, no acknowledgment thanking me for dedicating my whole life to a sport. I returned that evening to the Hyatt bar in downtown Miami where the players were staying. It wasn't hard to tell who the winners and losers were at the players' hotel. The winners front and center accepting all sorts of applause and accolades, the losers like myself slumped away in a darkened corner of the bar with maybe a close friend there to help ease the pain. There was no avoiding the hard reality that my playing career was over.

My friend, tennis journalist Linda Pentz, accompanied me to the lobby bar that evening. She had always been so encouraging, supportive, optimistic and full of hope about me and the direction of my career. We had met in Palm Beach, when I was 18 and Aaron Krickstein and I had been selected by her then boss, Eugene Scott, to play in the International Club Senior and Junior World Championships.

Gene, as everyone called him, published *Tennis Week*, and Linda was its editor.

We hit it off right away as we sat at Gene's table during one of those rather formal, but still fun, tournament dinners. Linda was engaging and relaxed and she had what I viewed as a dream job. I was fascinated by journalism and Linda wrote and edited well. She was doing something that I privately aspired to. And she talked to me, and listened to me, like an equal, like there was no age difference.

And yes, I found her attractive. Very. In fact, over the years, as our paths crossed here and there, that attraction occasionally made me ask myself whether I was really gay after all?

Linda was at the 1983 Easter Bowl, where I finished third. She met my mother there and saw and understood what I was going through. We met again when she covered the Olympic Trials in New York where I reached the round of 16, and once I was in college and competing in the NCAAs.

Back in that bar in Key Biscayne, it was time for my tennis autopsy. It's hard not to feel a little sorry for yourself in these moments. Fifteen years of hard work essentially adding up to nothing and nobody there at the site or anywhere in the sport seeming to give a damn.

I knew that 99 percent of the tennis world would give a limb to have the success and opportunities that I did as a player. But among my peer group, I was right there at the cusp of great success and I just didn't make it. I looked around at the all the players coming in and out of the elevators with their family, friends, coaches, hitting partners, advisers, agents, and sponsors; all the people a player needs to help him win matches and plot out a successful career, and it struck me once again. Everybody just seemed to have more than I did.

And so the night went. Some reflections, a little remorse, lots of stories and laughter. It was becoming more of a wake than a funeral as Linda and I settled into our seats. Ordering one beer after another, reviewing my career from start to end. We relived some of the highs, commiserated over some of the lows. I kept coming back to what I would have done differently if I could do it all over again. What I wished I could have had to make this all work better.

The developing themes in our conversations were the haphazard planning and the inconsistent and uncertain levels of support in all the important areas of my tennis from the USTA on down. My list was long. Linda was as smart a tennis person as there was. For every idea I put forth she had an equally insightful idea to add to it. We ordered another drink and what had begun as the proverbial drown my sorrows at the bar conversation soon began shape into something far more constructive.

We were devising out of thin air a concept that had never been applied before for professional tennis: a rookie pro team. I had been retired from tennis for all of four hours now, but sitting across a small table with my friend Linda helped me decide right then and there. I was going to change the way amateur tennis players turned professional

I would raise money for top college players to play professional tennis in a structured team environment, train together, live together, travel together 131 and support each other every day in every way. The dream was to give top-ranked college players a real chance for an ATP tour career. I was not

exactly sure what the parameters were to ensure a player success, but after a thorough inventory of my own playing career, I clearly knew what didn't work. If we could provide an environment for players to avoid the pitfalls that befell me, we knew we could make our system work.

And work it did. Two months later in May, 1988, Linda and I were at the NCAAs signing players to the Rookie Pro Team. I thought the team might be a tough sell, trying to convince recent former competitors of mine to sign on to my new system. Much to our surprise, players flocked to the rookie pro team concept. We soon discovered that Linda and I were well liked and even more respected by my tennis peers. After explaining our system and selling them on it, we walked away from Athens that May of 1988 with a mixture of players, some playing as professionals and some still as amateurs but testing the professional waters before returning to college. Included on that 1988 team were Eric Amend, Shelby Cannon, Kenny Thorne, Bryan Shelton, Brandon Walters, Jeff Brown, Greg Failla, Patrick Emmet, Stephen Enochs, Donny Wood and Doni Leaycraft who was to go on and win the NCAA singles title for LSU the following spring. Others would join the squad over time.

All Star members of the U.S. Rookie Pro Team: (left to right) Bryan Shelton,
Kenny Thorne, me, Richard Ashby, Shelby Cannon.

We wasted little time organizing the team and implementing our plan. Famed coach Dennis Van Der Meer was 100 percent behind us, providing us with training facilities, agreeing that the USTA was not doing enough to support its young talent in their transition to the pro ranks. It seemed I had found my purpose. Coach, mentor, financial backer, friend, confidant; running the rookie pro team was the perfect setup. Early morning training during the week, van rides and tournaments on the weekends, team meals in the evenings. The responsibility and the time demands left little time for my past nightlife, and little desire really.

As the team heated up in the summer of 1988, I quickly realized it was more than I could manage by myself. I needed an assistant to help with the team's responsibilities. I knew it was risky, but I asked my new friend Randy if he would be interested in joining us full time. I was having a hard enough time managing my feelings for him seeing him on the courts as I did. Working with him full time sounded great because I liked him so much, but would it be too much to manage? I didn't have to do much convincing as he jumped at the opportunity.

Having Randy on the team as my assistant soon grew complicated. I had grown to love Randy with every fiber in my body. We traveled together and slept in the same hotel rooms together, we were together 24/7. I played along on some crazy nights out on the road, all night parties with girls in the room. We would often all end up naked together, myself, Randy and the girls of our affections. I could not have been happier, but I also knew it was not reality and not the life I wanted to live. The girls loved Randy, but so did I.

I knew I didn't want to live like we were, running around at night hooking up with someone different every evening. I wanted him to not date girls at all and to be my boyfriend.

My feelings for him were very strong. I never made a pass at him or did anything to show my love for him back then. Upon reflection, it's impossible for me to believe that those who observed us closely at that time, namely our team members, didn't suspect something was going on between us. My desire to be with Randy was only matched by my desire to not be caught wanting to be with Randy. I don't care how good somebody is at being in the closet, that's just too much going on at the same time to not attract some suspicions from those around them the most.

A couple strong years of climbing the world rankings and the team was starting to make a name for itself. Meanwhile, Linda Pentz, had returned to her full-time tennis career, having come with us on the road for the first Challenger circuit to help get the team established and, more importantly, get us publicity. At every stop we had been met by reporters and articles appeared in the local papers about this "new concept" rookie pro traveling team. We were more than a novelty, though. It was clear we had met a need and filled a niche that wasn't being provided by the USTA.

We arrived at the 1989 U.S. Open with five players in the main draw. My desired team unity was starting to begin to undergo some stress. Randy and I and the five team members had been together non-stop for 15 months. In spite of my talks about the importance of team unity, cliques were starting to develop. My paranoia about being discovered started to get the best of me. There were never any arguments or disagreements between me and the players. They just started to drift away from me and what I was trying to teach them. Maybe it was because I was with Randy nearly every minute of the day. Maybe the guys on the team were starting to pick up on my energy. Nobody ever said a word about what was bothering them. I never asked a question either for fear of their possible answers. Either way, as a cohesive unit, we began to drift apart as we descended upon New York for the 1989 U.S. Open.

We had a couple of strong Christian players on our squad who noticeably began to tune me out. In my paranoid state, I just knew they were on to me and my huge crush for Randy. A couple of the other guys started to direct some off comments my way about my life choice of traveling around the world all day and night with a bunch of hot young guys. On the court, we really could not have been doing much better. All the players on the team were having great years. Off the court, I began to feel the strain of keeping my sexuality and my true self a secret again.

It's hard to have an out-of-body experience, to see how others see and view you. But intuitively you can feel it when people begin to withdraw from you. I realize now I was so on guard with my secret by this point in my life that the new bonds I was making with people were never as close as I thought. I had a foot out the door at all times when I engaged new people more intimately on the tennis circuit. And people picked up on my energy.

They suspected that I was not giving all of myself to my personal relationships with them. That I was withholding something important about myself that nobody was going to be allowed to know. This was my first venture out in to the world of coaching, where I was learning that the quality of the personal off-court relationship was just as important as the quality of the work being done on the court. The guys were picking up that something was off in me, and that on some deeper level I was not being my true self with them; creating an atmosphere of distance and aloofness that never came to a head via discussion but hung in the unspoken spaces between us.

The Open commenced. In the second round, team member Bryan Shelton played a fantastic first set against the legendary Jimmy Connors on center court under the lights of the main stadium. He eventually lost a tough four setter. Word was beginning to spread that our Rookie Pro Team program was onto something. When Philip Johnson knocked off former top-five player Anders Jarryd in the second round to set up a feature stadium court match with Andre Agassi, the Rookie Pro Team and its coach Bobby Blair were all of a sudden the buzz of the tournament.

With our success came attention. Big attention. National television media attention. Before Philip's third-round match with Agassi, I was asked to come to the television studio to be interviewed by USA Network host, Diana Nyad. What an opportunity for the Rookie Pro Team. We needed the exposure, for securing consistent funding was proving to be a problem.

I should have been relishing the moment. All the vision, all the hard work, all the commitment to our system of how young American tennis players should turn professional. It was my time to shine in front of the world. Yet all I could think about just moments before my national television interview was how many people might recognize me from all the gay bars I had been to over the years. My head raced. I thought of canceling, feigning sickness or some other excuse. Such a struggle to accept attention for what I had accomplished while trying to deflect attention for who I really was.

In the studio it's freezing cold, air conditioning cranked up full tilt. I started to shake. Moments later, I started sweating profusely. I was really nervous, my stomach all in knots. The interview began. I could barely speak, giving shaky short answers to the easy questions Diana was lobbing me. I got the interview over as quickly as I could, hardly even mentioning the whole Rookie Pro Team concept and blowing a great opportunity to make a name for ourselves and myself in particular. Anybody familiar with me knew something was amiss.

I went down to courtside to watch Philip play Agassi. Tennis matches provide ample opportunities for coaches to be recognized by the 20,000 spectators. We sit in the Players Box, there are plenty of moments to stand up, turn around, wave to people. The TV cameras constantly pan to the box to see who is there. If you want to be recognized, it's an egomaniac's dream. I don't think I turned around once the whole evening. I kept my head down and my eyes on the court the whole match. Philip played hard but was outclassed by Agassi. In Agassi's Player's Box was my coach and mentor Nick Bollettieri. Yet today we were squared off against each other. A part of me beamed with pride for having reached his level.

I raced home from the site after the match, bypassing completely the post-match press conferences where I once again could have done the Rookie Pro Team a lot of benefit. I could barely sleep that night. My head raced out of control with fear that somehow, someway I would be outed the next day. Maybe by an anonymous phone call, maybe by somebody walking up to me at the site and planting a kiss on my cheek and saying "Hey Bobby, I never knew you were a tennis guy."

The tournament continued. There were other requests by all sorts of media establishments for my time. I turned them all down. I just couldn't face down the anxiety of it all, of having all we had worked for stained forever by someone outing me. Facing the public was getting harder and harder for me. Was this always going to be an impediment to my success?

One of our players, Shelby Cannon, went on to win the mixed doubles.

It was so exciting for us to have a Grand Slam tournament champion on our team. It came time to be interviewed after his victory. I was able to deflect attention from myself, letting Shelby and his partner have their moment.

I watched from the press gallery with Randy as Shelby proceeded to go through the whole lengthy interview and not mention myself or the Rookie Pro team once, not a thank you, not a reimbursement or an acknowledgment that we had financed and supported him completely during his past 15 months on the tour. Nothing. We were devastated. Would this have happened if I had been sitting next to him in the interview room like I was asked to? Of course not. My shame about being gay was not allowing me to be recognized for all I was accomplishing.

I was proud of what we had accomplished, five U.S. Open main draw players and a Grand Slam tournament champion in our second year. But I was more
ashamed of myself for how I handled that success. I balked badly on the big-

gest of stages at all the attention and leadership responsibilities that came with being successful in such a high-profile sport as tennis. And I knew why. And I knew I was no closer to dealing with my sexuality, and I knew that my shame about who I was had adversely affected my success in the sport I so loved.

We arrived home with little idea of what lay in store next for us. I wanted a break from all the travel; it had become tiring and monotonous. I needed a new challenge, I just didn't know what that would be. The phone soon rang. I stared at it a bit, I got up slowly, answered it just before voicemail picked up, said a lazy "hello" and just then the voice on the other end asked for Bobby Blair.

I asked who it was.

She said, "This is Billie Jean King."

One phone conversation later and I had my new challenge.

CHAPTER

19

I UPPED AND WALKED AWAY

My blunders with the press withstanding, I was making a name for myself as an up-and-coming coach in American tennis. My Rookie Pro Team concept was soon co-opted by the USTA, whose broad resources far surpassed anything we could offer.

The team needed a financial miracle to continue being a viable option for young pro players. Part of me was sad to see my project's imminent demise, having poured everything I had in to assisting young professionals so that they might have a better chance at success than I had. Another part of me was relieved. After three years of straight travel, I needed a break. From the travel, from the players, from the economic insecurity of the team concept, and from my friend and assistant Randy.

I had grown tired of the low-grade perpetual heartbreak I lived with working so closely with Randy. There was nobody to blame but myself; it was my choice to remain so attached to him. It would have to be my choice to move on from him. I was 25 now. It was time for me to grow up and start taking my personal life more seriously. Investing so much of my heart and soul in dead-end relationships that had no chance of ever being fulfilling was burning me out. Getting honest with myself then was not easy for me. I could no longer avoid my reality that the love I was putting out toward Randy was not coming back at me. It was time to channel my energies in to activities that would pay me a better return. Billie Jean King was calling, asking me to coach the new 139

World Team Tennis franchise in Wellington, Florida. It could not have come at a better time. I jumped at the opportunity. After retiring from competition, the natural transition for players like myself was to coach at the pro level before utilizing all our experience and credentials to launch a major junior tennis academy. The academy idea had been in the back of my mind for awhile. This seemed like the perfect segue.

Having the BJK WTT stamp of approval on my resume was as good a recommendation as I could get as I sought sites for my academy venture.

Randy had moved to Atlanta after the US OPEN 1990 to work with his brother Brandon who was in charge of the Atlanta Braves field as their head groundskeeper. (Brandon has excelled incredibly in that career since then. He has been head groundskeeper for the Cleveland Indians for almost two decades now and is recognized as one of the best in major league baseball.) I called Randy and asked him if he was interested in helping me start a tennis academy in Orlando. He said yes. A few days later I drove from Orlando to Atlanta to pick him up and we made the long haul back to Orlando mapping out our plan. I was hopeful I could keep my personal feeling in check and we could start a great academy together. We arrived back in Orlando and immediately set up brainstorming sessions at Randy's parents home. Together, every step of the way we created postcards, sent letters to every junior who was a USTA member and marketed our last several years coaching some of America's best players on our U.S. Rookie Pro Team.

Randy and I chose Orlando as the site for my first academy. I had a well-conceived idea in my mind, I just needed the right location to execute my plan. I had my eyes on a site in North Orlando called Sabal Point, a beautiful multi-court facility run by a childhood friend of mine named Tony Fernandez.

Again, our timing was great. Tony agreed that greater Orlando needed a big-name junior academy and that his club was looking to host one. We easily worked out the terms on a lease agreement. All that remained was for us to recruit and sign up the local Orlando junior talent and we were in business.

Opening day arrived. We waited nervously at 3:00 p.m in the parking lot for cars to arrive, praying that all our work would be rewarded. And rewarded it was. Car after car drove in through the entrance asking where the academy was being held. It was a hit from the start. I was now owner and chief operator of my own business and I couldn't have been more excited.

Securing a couple of the top juniors in the area did not hurt. Their presence made my academy the go-to place for Central Florida junior tennis. Like it or not, I was now a high-profile coach in one of tennis' hotbeds and getting noticed. My reputation in the local Orlando tennis community was excellent, with not even a murmur that something might be different about my private life. Families were coming from all over, entrusting me with their children's tennis and overall development, responsibilities I took quite seriously. This was no time to get careless with my sexuality. I quickly grew close to my new academy students, getting to know everything about them as well as their families. Subsequently, they all wanted to get to know me as well as they could also. That often involved questions about my love life and whether I was dating anybody seriously. I would give my stock answer, that my life on the road made it hard to settle down with anyone and with the business starting, I didn't have the time or desire. My answers would go right in one ear and out the other, as my clients tried to set me up with every single friend or family member they could.

It was all pretty flattering if I wasn't so confused about where my heart was to go next. The last thing I wanted to do was bring any of my love-life dysfunction into my new thriving work space. I did not go on one single setup date the whole time I ran my academy. With each request of my time to be social, I felt that gnawing old paranoid feeling come back that my matchmakers were somehow onto me, that they were testing me. A lot of the women they were trying to set me up with were nothing short of dynamite. How many times could I say 'no' before they began to suspect something?

I was able to remain hidden, this time behind my hard work. I had a business going full tilt with some great money rolling my way for the first time in my adult life. I couldn't have been happier in Orlando until the phone rang. It was the general manager from the club in Wellington where I coached the WTT Aces. He wanted me to move my academy from Orlando to their amazing facility in Wellington.

It was a tough decision, being asked to leave the Orlando kids and families I had quickly grown so attached to. Orlando was also my hometown. It was just a couple years prior that the local paper had deemed me washed up. I'd be lying if I said I didn't take particular pleasure at having high-profile success back in the town where they had deemed me finished. The Wellington offer was quite generous though, a real opportunity for me to lay down some strong roots in a very affluent part of South Florida. After a couple of tough 141 weeks of weighing out all my options, Randy and I decided to move the academy and started working in Wellington on January 1 of 1991. At the young age of just 26, I felt on top of the coaching world.

Kathy Rinaldi-Strunkle and I at Wimbledon in 1993. I coached my childhood friend and practice partner as Kathy began to wind down an amazing career, ranking top 10 in the world in singles and doubles.

"I have fond memories of Bobby and I together that go back to training together when we were just starting out as junior players. To hear his story and struggles is not only inspiring to me but sure to help others who are struggling with the same issues and feelings that Bobby has overcome. Everyone deserves to find happiness and I am glad to know that Bobby has found his."
— Kathy Rinaldi-Stunkle

The academy got off to a great start, drawing from the copious amount of talent in the South Florida area. Combine that with my good kids from Orlando who came down on weekends and my academy was quickly the talk of the tennis community. Summer came, my second WTT season in full swing at my Wellington club. *World Tennis Magazine* was putting a Collectors Edition together and wanted to interview me. At first I was a little hesitant, for I had no idea what they had in store for their article. I still was on guard around the tennis media; I just felt nothing good could come from talking too much about myself and my private life. Our team flew out to Los Angeles to play Jimmy

Connors and the Los Angeles Strings when the World Tennis piece came out. "Will Bobby Blair Be the Next Nick Bollettieri?" OK, game on.

I was now the center of attention in the South Florida tennis community. It was during my time at the club in Wellington when I met the person who became a great gay friend and mentor to me, a gentleman named Gene Conti. I assumed Gene was gay right away. It took me a little longer before I was able to confide to Gene that I was gay myself. Being cautious about my impending celebrity in the Wellington area, Gene and I started to sneak a half hour out of town to explore the South Florida gay scene, often ending up at a club called Roosters in West Palm Beach.

It was on these trips with Gene where I began to really learn what the whole gay life was about. When I say the gay life, I mean the real life local community issues of being gay. Everything I had experienced before was transitory, always out on the road, always at night, a different city each week with different people. If I didn't like the people in a certain place, I never had to come back. This was different. Roosters and a couple other clubs like it were the centers of gay social life near my new hometown of Wellington. These were the places to make friends and connections, for these people were the responsible civic leaders of the local gay community.

Gene took great care to keep my secret under wraps at the club and within the community. He taught me where to go and where not to as well as who was in the closet and who was not. He told me whom to avoid, who was strung out, who would rob you blind, and who very well might have the AIDS virus that was plaguing so many gays in our community. He also helped me greatly to get over my perpetual heartache regarding Randy and my inability to let him go. (As you'll see in the piece Gene wrote at the end of this book, he took a courageous decision to "out" me to Randy which ended all the tension and preserved my friendship with Randy which I had been jeopardizing with my infatuation for him.) I loved my life in Wellington but felt socially stuck with Randy still working for me at the academy. So when BJK called right at the end of my second WTT season in Wellington telling me she had a WTT franchise starting up in my native Orlando and would I be interested in becoming general manager and coach, I jumped at the chance. Maybe I jumped too soon. The Orlando franchise seemed a done deal, but something went wrong between BJK and the Orlando investors. I had already moved back home when the bad news hit. I was fortunate enough to be able to re- 143 launch my junior academy again with my longtime friend Hector Villarroel in Orlando after the WTT confusion settled. More importantly, this was the first time I had been away from Randy in four years. The feelings of freedom were exhilarating as I sunk all my energy in to rebuilding my academy, trying to make it Florida's best.

A few months later Billie Jean called again saying we were back on, but this time in Tampa and would I be interested? I couldn't move myself and my academy again, nor was I going to say no to Billie Jean. So began my endless days of commuting 90 minutes to Tampa every morning to do my general manager responsibilities, only to turn around after lunch and drive another 90 minutes back to Orlando to run my academy. Despite the endless days, I loved everything about the work of being an academy owner and a top- level coach to the pros. Off the touring road and away from Randy, I settled into my new life as successful coaching entrepreneur and was as happy and prosperous as I had ever been in my life. I thought I had finally found my place in the tennis world. With all the work I had, there was little time for the nightlife activities of my younger years. Of course I missed the excitement of the good times. I missed meeting like-minded men my age seeking connection, even if just for an evening. I was growing up now and moving on from that way of life. I had been around the gay scene for some time now and knew I had to avoid the traps and unhealthy aspects of the life. There was an inefficiency to the whole endeavor; so much time spent, waiting and seeking. When I reflected back on the whole experience, I still had not experienced what would be considered intimacy in all that time with anyone I would consider calling a boyfriend.

During the years of my WTT experiences, I spent a fair amount of time around BJK and her partner, Ilana Kloss. I saw what the full gay life could be, not that it didn't come with its share of complications. The reality was it was the late 20th century and the tennis societies I ran with were not ready for out-of-the-closet gay males like myself. If I wanted what BJK had, I was certain I would lose everything I worked my whole life to build in tennis. If I wanted the flourishing tennis career, I was going to have to give up on living a true authentic gay life. I just couldn't see how I could have it all.

I did an imaginary survey of the important people in my life. I thought about my family, friends, colleagues and employers and what their probable response would have been if I felt compelled to come out to them. My dad would have freaked; his vitriol against gays was a leading contributor to much of my shame. My brother would have freaked, but in time would likely have been cool, for we were very close. My tennis friends, I couldn't tell. I would have hoped they loved me more than they hated gays. The families of the kids I coached would likely have been a mixed bag also, with some accepting and others wanting nothing to do with me. As for my employers, it was hard to believe there was a club in South Florida in the early 1990s that would allow a major junior tennis academy to be run by an out-of-the-closet gay guy. Not then. I just couldn't see how I could do it.

I was 28 and starting to achieve the kind of success I always dreamed of.

Ten years in and out of the gay scene and I was no closer to finding my equal. It seemed everyone in the scene had some baggage that didn't jive well with how I wanted to conduct my life. So many were not living happy functional lives. Drug and alcohol problems were rampant in the scene and about to get worse. The older guys seemed terribly depressed and stuck, spending their time chasing hot younger guys around and living a lifestyle I never wanted to live and not likely them either. The younger guys were all a little traumatized by their circumstances, either having been thrown out by their families or the victims of the kind of abuse and molestation you don't just shake off that easily. So many of them were working dead-end jobs, living day to day, with no long-term goals and no way to emerge from their conditions. There were exceptions of course, which gave me hope that if I was unable to succeed in the world as a closeted gay, with a lot of work and a little luck, there might be a life for me in the gay scene. On one of my excursions in Orlando out on the town I met a young guy in his mid-20s named Wayne Favorite. He was a male dancer who caught my eye. I knew the game; he saw me as just another wallet at first. But over time, we got to khow each other very well. He was hoping to marry his girlfriend who was expecting their child. He was dancing at the club to make a few extra bucks in what he strictly called a gay-for-pay situation and I was cool with that. I was immensely attracted to him and was having a great time with him, so I was more than happy to help him out in whatever way I could.

As we spent more and more time together, we both grew to like each other a lot. I was beginning the shift into what was to become a new career in real estate and I was able to get him a job in that venture which helped him to get out of the dance clubs. Wayne and I spent a lot of quality time together for a few month's stretch. Though he was set to marry his girlfriend, the intimate 145 time we shared was like nothing I had ever experienced before. I was 29 and finally feeling what intimacy was all about. Just my luck he was about to become a father, but he was the first guy I ever felt those feelings for that I had heard so much about from my friends and through my readings. Again, it was a glimmer of hope that there were men in Orlando that were my age and together enough to have a relationship with.

I was getting older, the highly successful owner and chief operator of a thriving tennis academy as well as an up-and-coming entrepreneur in the real estate business. I began to feel pressure from my colleagues to settle down and look the part of an up-and-coming businessman. Which meant stop chasing guys around at the dance clubs and find myself a wife and a family like everyone else my age and make it work.

I felt I could do it; the hard part was making the decision. Of all my experiences meeting gay men who chose to live the married straight life, the hardest part for them was the decision. The decision to give up on having an authentic gay relationship and to never look back. It was a decision I had given much thought to, something I felt I had to do to keep enjoying the success I was having in the ultra-straight worlds of tennis and real estate. Then my childhood best friend and first crush, Dani Leal, called to announce he was getting married.

It was during the weekend of Dani's wedding that I met Candi Grey. Candi was the maid of honor. She was five years my senior and the mother of two young children, 5 and 7. And drop-dead beautiful. We hit it off immediately from the rehearsal dinner throughout the whole event. The timing could not have been better. My new friend Wayne was getting married, most of my straight friends were married and starting families. This was my big chance to try one more time to live the straight life. I knew I could love and provide for another. I just felt I needed to make the hard decision once and for all and to never look back again.

Candi and I started a relationship that wedding weekend that was to last a couple of years. I made a decision those first few weeks of dating that I could make this work, that I could live the straight life. I could love her and be a great husband and father to her children, maybe even have a couple of our own. The consequences of living any other life seemed just too much to take on.

After nine months of dating, Candi packed up and moved east to live with me in Orlando. She quickly picked up work at a local Merrill Lynch broker-age house and she and her kids moved in to my first home. We enrolled her children in the best schools in Metro West Orlando, her job was working out great, my academy was rocking and rolling, and I was becoming one of the nation's top single-family home investors. I really felt like I had found the life, my life, the life God would want for me. I loved being the partner, the father, the provider and took every moment of those responsibilities seriously.

Dani Leal's wedding picture and my first weekend with Candi Grey.

In the fall of 1996, I was hired on as a USTA National Coach for the Boys' 16-and-Under team. My childhood nemesis and former top 10 in the world player Jay Berger was in charge of the 18s. Super coach Nick Saviano was my boss in Player Development. Having coached against Nick Bollettieri, having been entrusted to run a WTT franchise by Billie Jean King, and now having the USTA ask me to help develop America's top talent, I had reached the peak of American tennis coaching at the young age of 32.

The appearance of the happy integrated household was set. With Wayne now married with a beautiful young child, he and I both agreed to scale back the intimate time we were having together. We both wanted to give our best efforts to living the authentic straight life, however inauthentic we may have been. With the distractions from my gay life put aside, in the two years I was with Candi I did everything I ever dreamed. I achieved great financial success 147 with my real estate as well as great personal gratification from the success of my tennis academy. But all was not perfect in my seeming domestic bliss.

I felt it from the beginning. Or better stated, I didn't feel it. What was missing for me were those deep feelings of being in love, of not being able to be without her, those deep gnawing feelings of passion truly-in-love people feel for each other. I waited patiently. We had a lot going on with moving, kids, business, all the stress of two people merging their lives into one. I worried we may be too busy, or that I was too consumed with being successful. I ran every possible scenario through my head. Was it her? No, she was awesome, amazing, I could not have been luckier. She was the best woman I had ever met.

I knew the answer; it was the same answer as before. I started getting depressed, distant, just like I had before with my Arkansas girlfriend Kim.

A loving, caring person gave her whole life to be with me. Yet I was not capable of being the person this commitment demanded. I felt terrible, partly for myself that I came so close to settling for a life that was not an honest life. But mostly for Candi and her kids who had come so far to be with me, believing I was the right man for her and to be a proper stepfather to her children. What a mess. Why did this have to be so complicated and why did I have to involve other people within my turmoil?

I had been around enough by now. I knew I didn't want to be that guy at 50 who finally comes out to his family that his whole life has been a fraud, living my remaining years with crippling guilt. I had done the best I could. I loved her as much as I could. There was nobody else I desired, I had been faithful to my commitment to her to make our relationship work. I was just missing that deep primal connection I felt to three people I had loved in my life: Dani from the academy as a teen, Randy as a young adult and my first intimate relationship with Wayne. A few months in the relationship I knew I needed out. The question now was how.

Did Candi deserve the truth? My truth. The truth that at age 31 I still wasn't clear with myself? I still seemed so far away from fully accepting myself for who and what I was. What I did know is I didn't want to end up like so many men I had met along my path. Men alone, older, divorced from their wives for either getting caught or no longer being able to live their lie. Men whose ex-wives will never talk to them again and whose kids hate them for destroying their mother's life. That I did not want to be. Which meant

148 breaking everything off.

I loved Candi and her two beautiful children, but knew I had made a mistake. I was not living with my truth.

I hadn't said anything to Candi yet. She knew something was up though.

We weren't talking like a couple in love. As is often the case with struggling couples, I began to spend more time away from the house. It was December, 1996, I just wanted to get through the holidays before I told Candi I needed to do something different. On my way home from work, I would pass by a club in the gay section of town called the Parliament House. It was one of a few local gay bars in town that I had made a point to avoid for all the aforementioned reasons.

I would drive by the bar, knowing what temptations lurked within. I knew from the dissolution of my feelings in my relationship where my true heart belonged. I wanted to go in to the club and just sit among my like-minded people. But I knew to go in could complicate my life in ways I didn't need. I developed a driving ritual, some nights passing the club, double back, pass it going the other way, knowing there were great young guys in there to take my mind off my struggles, also knowing I had a girlfriend and kids waiting for me at home. The struggles I would have with myself those days, so angst-ridden about what awaited me at home, equally angst-ridden by the possibilities of 149 meeting someone like myself and having to face my inauthentic life again.

One night I gave in to my curiosities, going inside for a beer. I had not been there long when a gentleman walked in, lighting up the room. His name was Keith, beautiful, articulate and quite flamboyant. He had just been fired as a bartender at one of the hottest gay clubs in all of Florida. He sat across from me at the bar as I sat quietly by myself, listening as he commiserated with his friends about what had just transpired with his firing. My first thoughts were he had to be a total wild man to be a bartender at such a happening place. My second thoughts were he was so obviously gay I could never be caught dead outside of a gay club with a friend like him. It would blow my closeted cover for sure.

We were soon introduced to each other and much to my surprise he could not have been nicer. Smart, articulate, in spite of everything he was going through that day, he was so welcoming and made me feel so comfortable. After a couple beers, he had to get up to meet people next door at a club called the Full Moon. He asked if I would join him. I didn't want to tell him the truth, that I had a fiancé and two children at home and needed to call it an early night, for I had a long day ahead in my ultra-straight job of tennis academy director and wholesale real estate developer.

Those first couple hours spent with Keith had a profound effect upon me. I was instantly smitten by him, but even more impressed by just how comfortable he was with himself. He was out and proud, very talkative, quite energetic, to an outsider very flamboyant and obviously gay. In many ways he was everything I was not. Yet he liked me a lot. When it came time for me to drive home, I had a decision to make. To follow up with Keith and build on what we just started, or head home and face the reality of what continuing to live my life in the closet would be like. I hesitated. Then I drove to the Full Moon, drove by it, turned back. I went in. And I knew what the decision was that I had to make.

It surprised me how much of my life flashed before me in that moment of decision. There were many moving parts to the attraction I felt for Keith. Going to the Full Moon and pursuing him felt like such a bold decision, that it represented the end of my trying to make it work with Candi, that it represented the possible end of my life in the closet, and with that the end of my life in my sport of tennis. But also it represented a possible beginning. Of having my first real relationship with another gay peer, and the beginning of my own personal journey of self-realization.

Over the next couple weeks I began to break it off with Candi. It had to be one of the worst experiences of my life. I hated the idea of hurting such a loving person. I hated even more the guilt I felt at knowing that I should have known better than to try to make it work as a straight guy. I wanted it to work so badly, but for all the wrong reasons. It just couldn't be all about me.

To live the straight life in mid-1990s America would have been so much simpler. But I just couldn't. And I couldn't tell Candi the real reason why I could not be her husband. I still had so much shame about my being gay. I felt great guilt at feeling I had to keep my world a secret, that my professional self-preservation depended upon it. To have Candi out me in a rage would have been devastating, for my livelihood was derived from straight, mostly evangelical people in the tennis and real estate worlds. I told her it just wasn't working, that I wasn't in love with her. It felt rotten. But I could think of no other way out.

With Candi resigned to our fate, she eventually left my home, moving back to her old life in Destin, Florida. I knew I had to be careful about how Keith entered my life. Fortunately he understood my situation, for many who are out in the gay community are not cool with partners like myself still in the closet.

I slowly moved Keith into my home in Orlando's Metro West area. We quickly realized it was 30 minutes away from all the Orlando nightlife. I soon rented that house out, moving Keith and I in to a beautiful home at the Orlando Country Club. In many ways, I came of age those first few months with Keith. My businesses both were at their peaks of success. I was for the first time in my life in a committed relationship with somebody oriented just like me. Keith quickly introduced me to the local Orlando gay scene. Being in Orlando made it easy for me to reflect on just how far I had come from my modest beginnings.

Yet at the academy, people wanted to know what had happened between Candi and me. We seemed so good, we never fought, we were everybody's favorite couple. My friends never suspected anything was wrong. Her friends even less. We seemed happy, in love, and that nothing could interfere with our engagement to be married.

Our breakup wasn't received well. Many of the academy kids had grown close to Candi and her boys. We would have them over on weekends for cook-   151 outs and days of play and games. She became like a second mother to many of them. Maybe I didn't explain our breakup well. How could I have? Obviously I had to lie to everybody and make up a full story none of which was based in fact. Some people pushed for more details. Was I telling the same story to everyone, or was I making mistakes and people were catching on?

A couple months after Candi left, many of my clients began inquiring about how I was doing. I would say fine, I'm OK. They would invite me out socially. I would decline, giving a multitude of reasons, none of which were true. They would ask me if I was seeing anybody. I would lie and say 'no'. They began again trying to set me up with their single sisters and friends. I showed no interest. Time moved on. A month, a couple months, soon it was six months. No sign of any social activity by me. People at my club soon began to talk behind my back.

It wasn't just my clients and club friends who were inquiring about me. I grew up in Orlando, my brother was there, my life-long friends lived there. They started asking questions too. A friend said I was seen leaving the Parliament House one evening. I quickly denied it. I told my friends I had moved to be closer to town and was living alone. Another friend drove by and saw Keith walking into my house. He asked who he was. I gave a vague answer that I knew didn't sit well. My closest confidants from the academy noticed my change of mood. They soon began to interrogate me.

They never saw me anymore, I never called to do stuff. I wasn't returning calls and when they did see me I was increasingly aloof, distant, like I was hiding something from them.

By this point I was six months into seeing Keith, for the first time in my life feeling like my true self. But only part of the time. My working relationships in the tennis world were beginning to suffer, with my behavior just as much a part of it as anything. I spoke to Keith about letting two of my closest straight tennis friends in on the changes in my private life — Randy and his long-time friend Travis. Keith was very supportive.

My request was we never discuss my private life with anyone but the two of them. As happy and fulfilled as I was now in my private life with Keith, being able to have love and intimacy in my life for the first time, I was nowhere near ready to share my private life in my professional life. It spelled certain financial ruin.

I thought back to my summers of exploring the gay scene across North

America. How at the end of the evening I would flip the switch, going from Mark from Florida, in town to visit, back to Bobby Blair tennis professional.

I wasn't consciously flipping that switch anymore when I would leave Keith in the morning and head over to the club to work. It's not like Keith had some secret gay thing that attached to me when in his presence. I was for the first time in my life in love with someone who loved me, and that's just not a switch I could turn off easily. Or should have to.

I was at the peak of my business ventures and for the first time in my private life happy, content, and in love. But so far apart were my two worlds from ever colliding. I had been in tennis my whole life. Everything I had in this world I owed to my sport. Everything that made me who I was, all the great coaches and mentors and friends and competitors, I owed to tennis. Yet I knew intuitively that the sport I loved with all my being would reject me completely if they knew the real me. And that wasn't going to happen. I was not going to allow that, either overtly by coming out and facing the consequences, or covertly, like what was happening then at my academy, the slow and gradual pulling away of friends and clients now that they knew or suspected that I was gay and in love with another man.

And with that I decided in 1997 that if the sport I so loved could not love me back for who God had made me, I could no longer be a part of it and face the judging eyes of a culture of ignorance. At the age of 33, after an illustrious junior and college career that took me everywhere representing the USA, after a coaching career that had the likes of Billie Jean King, knocking on my door and being compared to the great Nick Bollettieri in *World Tennis Magazine*, I upped and walked away from my sport, completely, vowing never to return.

CHAPTER

20

WOULD I SURVIVE WITHOUT TENNIS?

A major component to my living in the closet was having to hide my sexuality from those around me in my profession. Walking away from tennis changed that. My working relationships in tennis were quite intimate; daily on-court lessons followed by lengthy talks with parents about their kids' futures. We socialized together with cookouts, we traveled together for tournaments. We became part of each other's extended families, which meant being close enough that I needed to be careful about what I said and whom I chose to bring around.

My growing real estate business was a much easier work dynamic to negotiate. It had started when I met Jac Klemper. I was coaching his son, Kenny, and Jac was a leading foreclosure real estate specialist. In exchange for some extra coaching I gave his son, Jac took me with him and showed me how his business worked. It basically amounted to buying a foreclosed house, fixing it up at a small extra investment, then selling it for around a $20,000 profit. Another tennis parent at my academy, Tom Graham, whose son Matthew I was also coaching, made that first investment for me and we split the profit. I was up and running. The real estate business complemented the tennis academy. I could work the real estate in the morning, then open the academy at 3pm in the afternoon when the kids got out of school. It was fluid and simple and exciting and I was making some serious money as well.

Relationships with my real estate clients were brief, mostly over the phone 155 or via fax. I had an office surrounded by a hand-selected sales team of my closest friends and advisers. All of them knew my desire to keep my sexuality secret; several of them were also in the closet. For the first time in my life, the overwhelming majority of my time was being spent in the company of loving supportive like-minded gay men, with the overall effect being quite liberating.

(top row, left to right) Travis Smith, myself, Randy "Moose" Koehnke, Tim Sanders and wife. (front row) Jay Mays and Kevin Dinneen, who always kept an eye on me and successfully picked me up when I was down.

I still had to be careful. Perhaps because of the renown I had gotten balancing both the tennis academy and the real estate business, without a degree but on entrepreneurial skills and determination alone, *Success Magazine* had contacted me as a potential spokesperson. Shortly after they hired me, some people in upper management and on senior staff began to be inquisitive about me. Finally, the question came: "Are you gay." My reply was unhesitating. "Absolutely not!" I lied. Inside, fear gripped me. A lot of money was at stake now. Once again I was forced back into the closet, obliged to live a lie so that all my hard-earned projects and dreams could survive. I conducted real estate seminars for them, headlining their late night infomercials, making me the face and focal point for a major real estate company, eventually leading
to a featured story in *Success*. I was selling homes in the Bible Belt of the

USA, while representing a company with traditional American values among its board members. The situation was not optimal, but it was manageable. I felt no pressure or need to be honest about my private life to my colleagues and clients, — we were doing the Don't Ask Don't Tell well before our time — yet I knew there would be drastic financial consequences if I was outed, hence my continued caution.

Myself, Randy "Moose" Koehnke and Joe, always there with incredible love and support. I wish I had shared my struggles back then. I felt that, with Randy and my brother by my side, I could survive without tennis.

With my professional life safe and thriving, I spent my private time learning how to be a partner in my first-ever serious relationship. After Candi and Randy, it was time for me to start making better choices, no more trying to marry women, no more falling for straight guys. After 16 years in the dating world, I had finally found my equal to love and be loved by. I thought I finally had it made.

If only it were that simple.

Keith was problematic from the start. When we met, he had just been fired as a bartender at one of the hottest clubs in Florida, The Parliament House. I knew what that meant; he loved the nightlife, he had hot guys throwing themselves at him constantly, and he liked to party, which meant a lot of drinking 157 and drugs. In the beginning, I was ecstatic to have finally met someone that checked off so many of the right boxes I never seemed to be able to check before. I felt I could handle his nightlife activities; I was hardly a prude from my years in the scene. I enjoyed my beer as much as the next person and went through my experimental phase with drugs. I was never drawn to them as a source of entertainment, though. I never saw them as a vehicle for life enhancement. Maybe it was the discipline from my tennis, maybe it was my drive to be successful and be my best in business every day, or maybe it was the fact that I had never seen a single person's life get better when they started doing lots of drugs. Likely it was all three that kept me from ever going down that path. Now I was confronted daily with the scourge that drugs can be on one's life.

There was so much good and bad going on in my early days with Keith. I began to bargain with myself. I was learning so much from being involved with him. He was worldly in ways I would never be. He could cook. He was a voracious reader. He taught me how to dress and not always look like a retired jock. He introduced me throughout the Orlando gay scene as I met countless people just like us, young men trying to thrive in a world of shared adversity. Many of my best friends came from the circles Keith introduced me to during our time together.

All those positives aside, his partying began to dominate our relationship. The staying out late, the not coming home, the infidelity, the lying, the inability to put in a good day's work after a late night on the town. That's just not who I was. Nor did I sign up for that way of life. Having an alcoholic father, watching the effects that had on my mom as my father chose drinking over his family scarred me. I vowed growing up to never allow myself to be treated that way in any of my relationships. Yet here it was happening right before me. I tried to be patient, I tried to be helpful. I tried everything to help Keith see the error in his ways. But to no avail. I was getting my heart ripped out with some frequency during our tougher stretches. In the beginning I could balance it out for I was getting so much from the relationship too. But in the end, the endless nights of deceit and abandonment led me to fall out of love with my first real partner. All that remained seemed my exit strategy. Again, if it was only that simple.

By any relationship counseling perspective, I stayed too long with Keith. In our time together, though, we developed some strong bonds that were not simple to detach from. One of those bonds was his best friend Vicky from the Parliament House. Vicky had a daughter Marissa, who herself had three children. Marissa was losing the battle to addiction when she contracted the HIV virus. Keith, Vicky and I watched Marissa from the front row die a terrible death from the illness that was plaguing communities all across the world.

Keith and my former Orlando coach, Hector Villarroel.
Keith was very quickly accepted by all my friends and family.

Nobody from outside the gay community was rushing in to help us with the scourges of HIV and addiction. We were on our own. As I spent more time in the community, I saw what an extended family really looked like; people helping people. We were united together in fighting back this mysterious illness. A profound sense of family and connection began to develop within me as I witnessed so many acts of selfless kindness, a feeling that has stayed with me my whole adult life.

Beauty and grace in the comfort of others. Why was it so hard for many in the gay community to direct that loving kindness inwards toward themselves? 159

There was an epidemic of unhealthy behavior in our community: drugs, unprotected and irresponsible sex, toxic shame and self-hatred, often resulting in suicide or painful premature death. Everywhere I looked I saw that the same people who were the first to offer you help were the last to help themselves. It was these fractured conflicted people that populated the scene of our community. I wanted to help them, aid them in seeing a better way in life. Nobody was going to save us but ourselves.

When I began to see many of the same overt unhealthy behaviors in my partner Keith, I knew I had to try something. Staying out all night, sleeping in all day, was not working for my hyper-scheduled, hard-working self. The lying and cheating that went along with being out all night became too much for me to handle. I put my foot down, demanding he stop and get back to taking care of himself and our relationship. We had a great life with unlimited potential, the drugs and the nightlife had to end. It seemed so simple to me; stop for the sake of health and prosperity and family. Why would somebody choose to live that way?

A couple years of ultimatums and broken promises and wasted effort again had me looking for an exit. Unfortunately, my real estate empire began to plunge at the same time, catching me totally unprepared. Like most successful entrepreneurs, I thought that my business skills were recession-proof and that hard times only happened to other less fortunate people. Boy was I mistaken. My *Success Magazine* seminars were winding down, having run their productive course. With the market turning south rapidly, I needed my dream team of sales guys in tow to help me escape without too much damage. Unfortunately, in all my excitement over my financial success, I had let them slip away to start their own ventures, leaving Keith and me with 80 homes we owned in the greater Orlando area to liquidate ourselves, or lose everything.

The next two years were difficult. All the work ethic in the world couldn't compete with the dynamics of a plunging market. Try as we might, there was little Keith and I could do to arrest my impending financial ruin. Compounding my malaise was the knowledge that our relationship was over. He couldn't stay clean, I had spent all the time I was going to spend trying to help him. I started to do my own things too as I slowly fell out of love with Keith. These were tough times for my self worth. With all my seeming success in my private and professional life, I saw how quickly it could all disappear.

Losing most of my money was hard, but I understood my failings there.

I wasn't prepared for the downturn in the business cycle. I would take my lumps, learn my lessons, and be back in that winner's circle again someday. My already fractured sense of self took a serious beating around Keith's drug use. Was I not worth more than a line or a hit to him? I should have known better, growing up in an alcoholic household, how hard it was to stop. I just thought with all my personal success in tennis and now in business that I could find a way, that if we tried hard enough and long enough, we could conquer his addiction.

But I was learning in the most humbling of ways that I was up against something no human power could alter. That addiction was bigger and stronger than all the love and care in my heart. It was hard to reach that point of surrender, where I gave up on the person I loved ever getting better. But I wasn't loving myself staying in such a destructive downward spiral of a relationship. All the times telling my partner to decide, realizing far too late that the decision was not entirely his own to make, that Keith, just like my dad with alcohol, was in the throes of a progressive illness that no human power could affect. He was incapable of sustaining the changes I needed to feel safe in the relationship. If any changes were going to occur for us, they were going to have to come from me.

Enter Wesley Jamaine Cuyler, September 1999, having a beer at the Parliament House. Not much good was happening in my life. I was taking inventory of how far I had fallen when he walked in. Young, real young, nine days short of his 19th birthday young, Wesley walked into the room with an innocence and free spirit that I found magnetic. I wasn't looking to meet anybody that night, or any night for that matter. Sitting at the bar, I didn't feel like I had a lot to offer anyone as I calculated just how far off the tracks my life had veered. But Wesley and I hit it off great. He was a great kid with an infectious laugh; just the kind of life-affirming medicine I needed during those trying times.

We started to hang out some. Wes was only 19 and too young to even think about pursuing, but I was growing to like the kid. A lot. Call it timing, call it inner-child healing, whatever it was that was happening to me, I found myself feeling great when I spent time with Wes. I soon taught him how to play tennis and how to shoot pool. He was a McDonalds All-American high school basketball player, so he taught me a few things on the court. After a weekend of running around, I would try to teach him to drive. It should have been a lot easier than it was, but my car had the dents to prove otherwise.

There was an innocence to Wesley that was real and affecting. What I saw in him was what I wished my younger life could have been like. A young teenager, out of the closet, with gay friends everywhere, all offering their support and wisdom about how to make life work best in our often hostile surroundings. Though I was 34 at the time of our meeting and going through the worst of all professional and personal situations, my life regained its luster when I ran around with this kid. Days and nights thinking about how unhappy I was morphed quickly into fun-filled days feeling like I was a kid again. All the energy I was spending trying to save my financial life and my dying relationship seemed like such a waste when I was around Wesley. I loved being a mentor to him. I also felt a sense of responsibility towards him. I wanted him to be able to hold onto his youthful innocence as long as he could. I wanted to save him from many of the hardships I lived as a closeted young teen and show him there was a better path forward than the one so many other young gay men like him were choosing. He had all the hope and desire. All he needed was an opportunity, a chance, a chance to live a healthier authentic life than the one I had.

I began to feel a strong pull that I needed to be living a different life. Keith and I were on life support. I was liquidating my remaining properties to somehow avoid bankruptcy as the market tumbled further and further every day. I was spending less time with Keith and in the office, while spending more time with Wes and his insatiable zest for living as he helped me forget about my daily woes.

One afternoon after running around town with Wes all day, he confided in me something he had never told anyone before. An older camp counselor at the Boys and Girls Club in Winter Haven had molested him repeatedly as a child. My heart just sank. I knew what that felt like. I knew what that did to one's sense of self, how confusing an act like that can be to a young impressionable youth. To be victimized by an act you know is so wrong yet were defenseless to avert. As Wes shared his story, I absorbed his pain as my own childhood traumas were triggered. The acts themselves were bad enough, the most lasting pain of being assaulted was not having a single trusting person in my life to go to with my inner turmoil. I wanted to be that person to Wesley, to save him from drowning in his shame, yet also assist him in life and help him flourish. Despite telling myself not to, there was no turning back now, for

I was falling in love with my new young friend.

I soon told Keith what he already suspected; that I had fallen in love with somebody else and needed to move on. As Wesley and I began dating, I could feel he was becoming more to me than just a partner. Being around his youthfulness was like being reintroduced to my own youth. I felt like I was getting a chance to relive a portion of my childhood being so close to Wes. But it was different this time. With him, I experienced my youth the way kids are supposed to come of age; innocent, free from fear, with a wide-eyed hope toward a promising future. I was 35 when we began to date, many years removed from my awkward teenage self and the youthful angst that I thought I had safely compartmentalized away.

But that angst would remain hidden no longer. Wesley was everything I wanted to be when I was his age. My joy in him reminded me of the pain in me.

I was getting a chance to have another childhood with Wes. I could live vicariously through him, reliving parts of my childhood the way they should have been lived. Free. Free from fear, and judgment, and bigotry. The psychology was complicated. In loving the youthful Wesley, I began to make peace with my youthful self, a young self I fought a daily struggle to love despite the clear message from early on that I received from all the important influences in my life, the church, my father, and society at large, that in some way I was flawed.

I knew dating someone so much younger than me was inherently flawed. But in my quest for completeness, making peace with my younger self was becoming an imperative. So many years steeped in shame and self-hatred for just being how I was born. I couldn't go back in time and alter the events of those days. What I could do is stop beating myself up about how I conducted myself back then for all the dishonest and inauthentic behavior I engaged in. If I could love a young person like Wesley, how could I not love the young person I was at his age? What was the difference? I saw that same dynamic within the gay community, how they could heroically come together as one in a crisis, but struggled to show that same loving care inwardly to themselves. Was I that way, too? I was so full of love and empathy for my young friend yet I didn't feel an ounce of loving forgiveness for myself during my dark troubling years. Something had to give.

There was just so much I didn't know as a young person. Either I missed that day of class or I didn't get the memo, when all the possibilities were laid out before me of what life could be like growing up gay in late 20th century America. There was so much I just didn't know. But I was growing up now, middle-aged even, and now I did. Now I knew.

Getting honest with myself was becoming so much more about accepting who I really was. I had to learn to forgive myself for all the transgressions from my past. What greater good could come from holding onto deep rooted feelings of self hatred and shame for being born the way I was? I was having no problem loving others. If I wanted any chance of them loving me, it was becoming apparent I better learn to love me too.

Wes and I began to talk about our future. That future would only be possible with a fresh start. Wes and my extended family of sales people still on board decided it was time to move to a new place with new opportunities. August 26, 2001, we packed up my car and headed down to South Miami Beach to start anew. We took an apartment there and a small office and my close friend and confidant Patrick Cambell and my long-time bookkeeper Jerry Kessler began to brainstorm about what our next move should be in the real estate world. Low on cash and credit, we concluded during our inventory that of all our remaining assets, the most valuable of the bunch was our Success Magazine database of 23,000 names of people who had attended my seminars. Patrick, Jerry and I began brainstorming our next move. Evaluating all our skill sets and assets, we came to the conclusion that a turnkey real estate mentoring service for investors made the most sense. Atlanta popped out to us as the best market for this. We were off to the races. There were many early morning flights from Miami to Atlanta to we'd be able to juggle between both places. We were back in business and loving every minute of it.

This was a very special time for two of the most supportive people in my life, Patrick and Jerry, with Wesley rooting us on every step of the way.

Those early days with Wes were the best. He brought me back to life in adulthood while giving me back my childhood, as much as he could. I just so wanted to give him a great adulthood in return. As I and my sales staff readied for our move to Atlanta, Wesley had enrolled in college with the big hope of becoming our company lawyer someday. This soon began a challenging back-and-forth pattern between Atlanta and South Beach that proved hard on our relationship. We started making a killing almost instantly upon our Atlanta arrival. From the moment we concocted our business plan, it took us only 11 days to close our first property. There was so much to do starting anew like we were; come day's end I was wiped out and had little left for my partner Wes 500 miles away to the South. We weren't talking as much and began seeing each other even less, especially for a new couple. I began to sense the worst, that he was succumbing to the temptations of the South Beach lifestyle. So consumed in my own business,

I missed a few of the early red flags that all was not well with Wesley. It took a few months of being apart for me to finally realize he had fallen in to the same trap as Keith regarding the easy access to drugs at that time.

I was heartbroken. I was so angry with myself for leaving him in such a vulnerable state. I was also so disappointed in myself for not having picked up on the signals quicker, trying to address his usage early before it became a problem. By the time I caught onto what was going on, it was way too late. He was strung out on crystal meth and we were in for the fight of a lifetime. I was wrecked with guilt over bringing Wes along to a life he may not have been ready for. Seeing him in such pain triggered all of the repressed pain from my youth. How could another person's well-being have such a profound effect on me? I was becoming aware that in our short time together, I had developed an unhealthy bond with Wes. He had brought me back to life both professionally and personally, and I had unwittingly made him responsible for my own well-being.

He affected me in more ways than in just renewing my zest for life. I didn't realize how emotionally broken I had become over the years. In the early days with Wes by my side, I felt like I was flying. It was like seeing the world from a whole different perspective, from heights I never knew imaginable. I didn't know it was possible to feel the freedom and ecstasy I did during our best times together. So when he began to struggle mightily with his addictions, it was so hard for me not to struggle with him.

That's a lot to put on somebody, to make them responsible for your happiness. Wes never asked or applied for that position. Subconsciously I developed a fierce loyalty to Wes. I felt I owed him my life, or at least the happiness I was feeling in my life, which I found out the hard way was a pretty powerful dynamic when it all got pulled away. Wes was in for the battle of his life; my happiness was not a priority in his world as he lurched from bottom to bottom, his life beginning to circle the drain of addiction. I was too co-dependent on him to be able to provide for my own happiness on my own accord. I kept praying he would be saved; that he could conquer the scourge of drugs. If he could be

OK, I could be OK. It took me a long time to realize how unhealthy that was. All my hopes of him being able to change his behavior, that if he could just change his behavior, I could be happy. It was a hard-learned lesson, realizing it is a whole lot easier to change your attitude about someone's behavior than it is to get that person to change his behavior to appease your attitude.

As disappointed as I was, I had made the decision within the gay community that I did not shoot my wounded. Even my first boyfriend Keith, in spite of his using, was still a part of my extended family. Thus began a long torturous cycle of Wes getting clean, cleaning up, some recovery, some hope, relapse, rescue and start again. Everybody close to me told me that I was doing the wrong thing, that I was enabling him, that he never was going to get well until he hit some kind of bottom that I kept protecting him from. Yet I just could not let that happen. I could not kick him to the street, or shut off his phone. If something had happened to him during his struggles that I contributed to, I wouldn't have been able to live with myself.

Early 2003 I got a huge break in my business, becoming the spokesperson for a large real estate education company. Business was hopping. I had moved Wes up to my Atlanta home just to keep a better eye on him. Overdoses or suicide attempts seemed to come every couple months, cries for help that were inaudible and undecipherable. I had tried everything: rehab, counseling, letting him do what he wanted, kicking him out and coming down hard on him, only to feel so guilty and letting him back in to my life soon after. Living in that house with him became toxic. I eventually moved to downtown Atlanta into a condo at the Four Seasons Hotel with an office across the street, where I could do my work without all the domestic drama.

I tried to move on. I dated a little. One night on the town in the summer of 2003, I reconnected with Lz Granderson, a top up-and-coming journalist working for the Atlanta Constitution. We had met once before in a bar a few months earlier. In a matter of just a few weeks of getting to know each other I knew I wanted a relationship, a relationship I felt I could commit to completely. Lz was a wildly successful journalist but was also out. I fell pretty hard for him instantly and we started a whirlwind summer romance soon after. After a seven-day cruise, I remember coming back to the wonderful feelings of having met a healthy adult professional man who was out and seemingly all together. What was not to love? The problem is was I lovable? I was not out in

the gay community like Lz was and that I feel was an issue for him.

He had worked incredibly hard to get to where he was professionally and personally; dating an in-the-closet guy like me would be a step backwards in his evolution. I tried to explain to him how conservative my business partners were, that I risked losing everything again if I were to be discovered. Again, I felt trapped. From my perspective, I was as out as a gay guy could be. I didn't see the necessity to explain things to people who weren't asking any questions, and in my mind the answers were none of their business. But my being in the closet ever so slightly had less to do with letting outsiders in to my private world. It was about me getting right with my private world and not being concerned what outsiders thought about me any longer.

Compounding my problems for Lz I felt was Wesley's constant injection of himself in to my personal life, calling all hours of the night, showing up un-invited to the Four Seasons where I was living at the time, violating my bound-aries in every imaginable way. My inability to say no to Wesley became more of a statement about what I felt I deserved in life. Why would I allow such a destructive influence to interfere with the healthy progression of my adult life? On September 8, 2003, Lz told me was moving on. He didn't need to say why. I knew. I was still in the closet, still a long way from being complete.

I was devastated. The first time I had ever been dumped. I was 38 years old, seemingly on top of the world with my business and my increased stand-ing in the community. Yet I felt I was discarded because I wasn't being true to myself and ultimately the greater community. Once I got done crying about the whole thing, I began to see and better understand the possible reason Lz left me after our short whirlwind time together. You can't have something you are not yourself. If I wanted the perfect complete relationship, I had to be the complete partner. My reality was, for all the strides I had made over the years, my con-tinued belief that I needed to hide my sexuality from certain people or risk ruin. And this was going to remain problematic for me in my personal relationships.

On a boring autumn Atlanta evening, my friend Patrick and I were hav-ing an early dinner. I leaned over to him and asked, "Are you as bored here as I am?" He replied affirmatively. Within minutes I was on the phone mak-ing flight arrangements to Orlando for some old-fashioned good times in my youthful stomping grounds. We arrived at the Parliament House, checked into the hotel and settled in quickly; nothing had changed a bit as the night pro-gressed enjoyably when from across the room a friend from my past walked in.

What would happen next would change the course of my life forever. 167

CHAPTER

21

WHAT WOULD IT TAKE TO LIVE MY TRUTH?

In Orlando, back at the Parliament House. The site of so many important life events for myself. I met my first partner Keith here. I met one incredible young man named Wesley here. I also met my longtime friend Patrick Cambell here. I treated this place with reverence over the years, always knowing I would want to come back here in the future. So many great friends met here; so many great times had here. It was little surprise that upon settling into our seats, I would see once again a face to intrigue me.

We had met before, I was near sure. We spoke only for a moment, but just in passing. If I was right, his name was Brian. There he was again, sitting alone at my favorite place. I sent my friend Patrick over to ask if he was who I thought. He said 'yes.' We ended up inviting him to our table. I told him I had been looking for him ever since that night we met. He said he had been doing the same.

Brian Neal. He entered my life healthy, ambitious, caring and kind. He could see I had all kinds of messy personal and business stuff going on up my way in Atlanta, but he never flinched. Never had I met anyone so supportive of me and all my ventures. I thought, 'could he be the one'?

We did the long-distance thing for a while, but not long. I was not going to make that mistake again. Here was a young man with so much poise, so interested in and caring toward other people. And with goals. He was well-respected and popular in the hotel business where he worked. But he wanted more. 169

He wanted to be somebody. I admired that in him. At the same time, there was a calm about him. He centered me. Within a few months of dating, I moved him up to Atlanta to live with me and we began to work on what interested him as well; to build a personal training studio. From that moment forward, he has never left my side. My personal life was finally where I wanted it to be.

Professionally was a different story. My real estate company had been doing well. Really well. But this was the South, and my owners were quite conservative. The work atmosphere around real estate was not like tennis, where you're embedded 24/7 with your fellow players. Our interactions were more formal; dinners and social functions where we all would meet. Spending hours around a dinner table, celebrating with people you are making money with, invariably questions about my personal life would surface.

One night at dinner with the president of the company that was marketing my turnkey investor-friendly real estate company to the country, I excused myself from the table for a moment. The president leaned over to Tony, my right-hand man in real estate and asked him point blank if I was gay. Tony knew the response to give. He replied "I am just Bobby's business partner and I don't involve myself in anything about his personal life". Wrong answer. Maybe it was a loaded question, but anything less than an emphatic "No!" was going to be construed as confirmation that I was. Two weeks later, I was informed that my highly successful brand was being pulled off the market. They gave me a bunch of excuses as to why they were going in another direction. But I knew differently. Not all that different than the tennis world, a gay guy just didn't fit in with the crowd I was doing business with.

Disappointed, I continued to operate a successful Atlanta real estate investor business, focusing ever harder on hiding my sexuality from my remaining clientele. Would they have been accepting of my sexuality if they were to find out? I was still so far away from seeing the issue of my sexuality clearly. The hours sitting around worrying who would think what of my being gay, when all that really mattered was what I thought about myself being gay...it was such the wrong approach. I had lost two careers by now fearing exposure of my sexuality; I was scared about losing all I had left, so I went even deeper in to the closet, holding on ever tighter.

Brian and I soon settled in comfortably to a life together. I got him started with a fitness training dream of his. Within no time, he had a thriving successful personal training studio in the Atlanta area of Midtown. Life was good for us then. A couple of solid years together in Atlanta and my home state of Florida began to pull at me again. Born and bred there, it would always be my home.

In 2006, Brian and I pack up and headed south to Fort Lauderdale. I felt the real estate crash was coming. The irrational exuberance of the investment world was wearing off. I could not in good conscience keep pushing income properties with the doom and gloom soon upon us. I also was tiring of being in a business in which I had to hide my true self fearing it was just a matter of time before they found out and moved on. Pulling back from my investment business, I began to seek out new opportunities that would challenge me. We invested in Brian's training studio, making it one of the top in the area. A year later, with real estate going nowhere but lower and lower, a unique offer came my way.

I got a call from Ellen Friedman. She was the ad sales director for *BUZZ,* a gay men's entertainment magazine. I had been buying ads there to promote Brian's personal training studio. Her boss was tired of the industry and would consider selling for the right price. I knew nothing about publishing, especially LGBT publishing. But I took the business challenge of a lifetime, buying *BUZZ Magazine*. I loved the idea of promoting businesses every week, featuring stories on people doing great things in the LGBT community. Our distribution was from Atlanta to Key West, a business corridor I knew very well. Nervous yet excited, I dug in with both heels for a midlife career challenge.

There was a lot more happening within me than just buying a business. I was still in the closet, yet I knew I wanted to get more involved in the gay community. Somehow I thought buying an LGBT media company would automatically just make me "out." How much more of an emphatic statement can a person make? I wasn't hiding who I was from anyone, yet all the actions I was taking revolved around the outsides of my life.

I was living openly with my partner Brian. We had moved into an oceanfront condo on Fort Lauderdale beach. Just next door was Wilton Manors, a predominantly gay community in South Florida. This was the home of my advertisers. Over the years, it became the home of my friends. They soon became my close friends, expanding on my concept of having an extended family all throughout the gay community. Yet a part of me was still ashamed of who I was.

That same year of 2006, my tennis life came calling again. John Eagleton, 171 a former ATP tour player, was looking for a donor to play in Michael Milken's Prostate Cancer Foundation fundraiser at Donald Trump's Mar-A-Lago resort in Palm Beach. I was told many tennis friends from my youth would be there: Aaron Krickstein, Rick Leach, Luke and Murphy Jensen and many others. A part of me was mortified to go, for fear all the small talk and reminiscing would invariably come around to my private life. Another part of me was really excited to see my old friends, as well as support a cause near to my heart as my mother had died from cancer.

The event came. I was excited to put a sizable donation in my mother's name as a tribute for the amazing life she paved for me. But that was the easy part. What remained was who was to be my plus one. I had been with Brian for three years now. Our life in the gay community was out and thriving, with both of our business lives centered there. The tennis world was a different world, though. It was a world where I spent many hard years in hiding, it was a world I spent years succeeding in, but it was also a world where I felt I could not be myself, even in my thriving thirties. I left that world for fear of being discovered. I left that world to live a more honest authentic existence. Now here that world was calling again.

I did a quick inventory. My evolution in coming out to this point was strictly external. I had the partner, the business, the community, the foundation. I was living in a virtual bubble of safety and support in my South Florida social circles. Now I was being challenged. All these people from my past and present, people from whom I had hidden my true self for so long. Was I ready to man up and live my truth before them?

The answer was 'no'. After much painful debate with my partner Brian, I opted to take a female date with me that I knew would keep my secret. I rationalized my decision that this was my first time seeing these people in almost 15 years. Let me feel the scene out this time. Next time it will be different. And here I was in my early 40s saying the same things to myself that I was saying 25 years earlier. That someday I'll deal with it. That it's better if nobody knows my true self. That there's more to lose than to gain. That someday I'll get around to this…someday... someday…

Always someday…Yet that day never seemed to come. I just kept putting it off. To ease my mind, as long as I kept telling myself someday I'll do it, I could function in my day-to-day life without the crippling guilt that I was ashamed 172 to live my full truth. When Brian would ask me what I was so ashamed of, I could back him off by telling him someday…someday… someday…And I got really good at backing people off. And even better at convincing myself that I would do it someday…And here was one of those days I promised to act upon, yet I didn't do it. Not yet, because someday… someday…

The event itself went off without a hitch. It felt so good to see all my fellow fragile tennis competitors grow up so well into such strong upstanding adults. The shy kids all grew into their personalities. There was an unspoken respect we all had for each other; that we shared a common experience. We all met as wide-eyed young tennis players with all kinds of hopes and dreams. Some of us got a little farther than others, but that didn't seem to affect our dynamics at all. Just a bunch of grown up tennis players for whom the war was over; we could come out of the bushes, lay down our weapons, and all share a great evening of class and camaraderie with each other.

There were no questions about my private life that evening. Just a bunch of heartfelt, genuine… "it's great to see you's" and "hope life is treating you well." Nothing personal, nothing probing. I never had to lie, yet I didn't give myself a chance to tell my truth either. I walked away from the event con-fused. I could be among these people and be myself. They loved me for who I was, not how I was. I left convincing myself again one day I would be back. Honestly and authentically. With my partner Brian and without shame. Some-day…someday…

I was asked back to the event the following year. This time it was to be held in the beautiful Hamptons on Long Island, NY. I had promised myself and Brian next time it would be different. Yet the time came and it wasn't. All the positive talk about someday living my truth. Just more hollow words. Brian was really upset. How could he not infer I was ashamed on some level to bring him? I would try to explain to him I just wasn't ready, to which he would shoot back, "Ready for what? To accept who you are? To accept who we are? Is this what our future is? A conditional relationship, where being gay or not is a matter of convenience or comfort for you? How can I be proud of my partner when you're not proud of yourself?"

And for the first time in my life, I didn't have that quick response to back him off. I couldn't put the words together anymore to tell him next time it would be different. Because I knew they just weren't true. That once again the shortest distance between two points was unbearable. Three simple words. I am gay. At age 42, a full-grown autonomous man, incapable of being honest 173 with others about who I was. In Brian's pain, now I was seeing how not living my truth was no longer affecting only me.

As much as I was paying lip service to myself for years that I wanted to live differently, my truth was I was fundamentally incapable of taking the last step on my journey. I just didn't have it. I weathered that storm with Brian, or perhaps I should say Brian weathered it with me. He was such an outstanding young man. I would be proud to take him anywhere. Yet, out of fear and embarrassment I didn't take him anywhere that might risk betraying my secret. It sickened me, and I was afraid I was hurting Brian's self-esteem at the same time; that he might be confused about how I felt about him or wondering if I would ever make it right. At the age of 42 I was no closer internally to honoring my truth than I was as a teenager. Time was beginning to run out for me to get right with myself.

Later that year. May 2007. My father was in poor health. Diabetes, obesity, alcoholism; the unhealthy years had taken their toll even though he had managed to stay sober all those years. To address his steadily worsening health issues, he had chosen to try something radical; gastric bypass surgery. But there were complications. He didn't make it out of surgery alive.

It was never easy for us, dad and me. I knew he knew my orientation, but he never heard it from my mouth. He had been around many of my homes over the years, meeting my partners Keith and Wesley along the way. During a particularly icy stretch in our relationship, my half brother Billy from my father's first marriage told my dad that I was gay and that he needed to get over whatever angst he had about it. He somewhat did; it was always the topic that hung heavily in the unspoken air between us.

Why did I resist being honest with him? My knee-jerk answer was he was a bigot and a homophobe with his reaction certain to be offensive. I had been hearing his rants my whole life. I would also rationalize that since he knew, I never had to tell him directly. But I know now that wasn't right. It wasn't right for me not to fully own my life, nor was it right for me to assume his response. I should have been honest with him. I should have given him the chance to make that fundamental choice, to make him look his own son in the eye, and have him state he hates homosexuality more than he loves his own son. I never gave him the chance to make that choice. I made it for him, and that was not right to do, to him or me. For me to fear his answer was to fear him validating

what I, at the age of 42, felt about myself. That I was still ashamed to be gay.

My dad and I didn't have the greatest relationship. But I wanted him to know me, to be proud of me, to approve of me for who I truly was. But how could anybody ever truly love me if I refused to honor myself first? I walked away from my dad's funeral thinking about all the opportunities I missed with him to let him know who the real me was. It was too late with my dad. I would soon learn there is nothing worse than being too late.

Early 2008, my partner Brian and I went to the movies. The movie was *Milk*. My first real gay hero from my readings almost 30 years ago. Now there he was, played brilliantly by Sean Penn, up on the big screen, for all the world to see. I cried a lot during the film.

I cried even more later on at home. It was hard to look at myself in the mirror. How could I still be in the closet after all these years? People were putting their lives on the line in support of gay rights. I had been too afraid to do so, for fear of losing some income. Was this to be my legacy? A person who was gay when it was convenient, but not willing to stick his neck out for his community when the almighty dollar was involved? I harkened back to that day as a teen in the magazine store reading that article about him, how he was shot dead and how sad that made me. I remember vowing that day to fight for my community, to do everything I could to prevent another tragedy like Harvey Milk's from happening. Talk about a reality check. *Milk* made me further question the authenticity of the life I was living. All the hardships in our community, was I doing enough? The obvious answer was no, but that would soon change.

Brian and I had been in South Florida for a couple years now. His personal training studio was thriving in Wilton Manors while I learned my way around the publishing world. We were making great relationships throughout the gay community both personally and professionally. Like every gay community, there were good points and bad points. The lifestyle continued to take its toll, with HIV still a scourge. Yet it was different now. These were my clients, my friends, my neighbors that were getting sick.

We attended a funeral every few months. That doesn't make them any easier, especially in such a small tight-knit community like ours. Few people were dying of natural causes after a life well lived. Many were dying well before their time; from drugs, from suicide, from HIV-related illnesses. All of these deaths seemed like such a waste to me,. Something needed to be done in our community to stem the tide.

Brian and I got to thinking. So much tragedy, so little being done. Inspired by *Milk* to do more, we started a Health and Wellness Foundation, providing services six days a week for people living with HIV/AIDS or any other life-threatening illnesses. Life coaching workshops, nutrition classes, gym memberships, personal trainers and many other classes and workshops to ensure our recipients think right, eat right and stay active. We were becoming pillars in the gay community to so many with our charity work, yet I still was holding off on coming out.

2009 arrives I get a call from Dani Bollettieri, Nick's daughter. The NBTA was to have a 30-year reunion...Another gala event...Bobby Blair plus one...I was excited, but not in a great way. This was returning to my roots, to the man who made me, whose approval meant the most to me. More than that, here I would be, together again, with so many of the people from my childhood from whom I so desperately tried to hide my true self. I wanted to bring Brian so badly, I wanted to bring him to show the world what a great person he was, that for all my accomplishments in life, my relationship with him is what I am most proud of.

Again I could not. I went with a friend, Wayne Johnson, from my academy days and my longtime tennis friend in Fort Lauderdale. Again, so many of my friends had grown up in to great people. Everyone was so thoughtful and polite; what personal questions were asked of me were all so respectful. There was not a sliver of gossipy inquiry from anybody that great weekend.

During one of the events, I snuck out from the crowd to walk among the courts. Before I could see a player in action, I could hear the sounds of balls being struck. It transported me back to Holiday Park with my mom and the first time I had ever seen tennis played live before. How far I had come in so many ways, yet how far I had to go.

Walking around the grounds of my youth I saw the academy, just like all of us, had grown up. It was hardly recognizable, how modernized it had become. I still recognized the courts and where my old dorms were. Memories flashed.

Images from my youth passed before me. I came of age here at the NBTA. I thought back on all the formative experiences of my life. I remembered my first crush. I remember rehearsing in front of the mirror wanting to tell him I loved him. I remember telling myself to be patient, that all this gay stuff will work itself out in time.

Yet here I was, at age 45, afraid to bring the love of my life to this event for fear of what others may think of me. I guess I hadn't worked it all out yet. I looked out upon the dozens of courts, players and coaches and parents, all working hard and huddled around. I saw players who reminded me of my young self out there, working as hard as I could. As I continued to look out upon the courts, I ran the numbers. There had to be at least one gay kid in the closet out there. I noticed one that looked like he could be gay. He was so good. But he'll never have a chance if his life progresses anything like mine. A part of me hurt for him, that all his hard work and talent would go for naught because he won't be able be his true self in the tennis world. If I could just talk to him, tell him the importance of coming out and living a truly authentic life. He would need a mentor. But how could I tell anyone to live an authentic life if I wasn't doing so myself? I wasn't in any place to help anybody until I got my own house in order. If I wanted to make a difference, in a time where many needed someone like me to step up and live my truth, I needed to figure out how to come out and share my story and soon.

August 4, 2012. Brian and I were in Tampa for his brother's graduation when I got a call from Wesley. Wesley was living on the streets of San Francisco, homeless, strung out on crystal meth. I had stopped supporting him financially; the drugs were destroying him. I had kept a cell phone in his name all this time, all these years letting him know that home in Florida and sobriety with a fresh start on life with full support were only a phone call away.

It was hard for Brian, my not letting Wesley go entirely. But a part of him also understood, that we were all family sharing a common experience. And that I didn't shoot my wounded. Never. So when Wesley called that early evening saying he was ready to come home to give the clean life another try, my heart soared at the chance to help him. We spoke briefly about the logistics of getting him back to Florida; a flight was being arranged for him the next day. We spoke some more about what would be expected of him; that all my resources were available to him if he could get sober and turn his life around.

He concluded our conversation saying his years spent with me were the best years of his life, that he would make me proud upon his return, that he missed his friends and family in Florida and that the party life was no longer for him. He reminded me of our favorite song, Paul Davis' "Sweet Life," and how his time with me were the best years of his life. I had heard this before from Wesley, that he was ready to come back to a healthy way of life, only to be disappointed time and again when he obviously wasn't ready. But this time he sounded different, like he really was ready. We hung up, my heart buoyed that my Wesley was finally coming home to his family.

But that would be the last time I would hear Wesley's voice. He died that night from a drug overdose on the street at 2200 Market St. All alone. I was devastated when I received the early morning Facebook message from his sister Cheryl that the San Francisco coroner office called her to say he was deceased. My heart sank. I knew my life was never going to be the same. A few weeks later Brian and my great friend Patrick and I made the drive to Winter Haven for Wesley's memorial service. (Sadly, Patrick, too, would be gone just a few months later, struck down by a brain cancer related to HIV.) The church was filled with over 200 people. If he only knew how much he was loved. I brought pictures in frames for the alter. The morning of the memorial service I wrote a letter I was going to read at the service. A letter letting everyone know about the great times in his life, his wonderful personality, his warming smile and full of life laugh. When time came for me to speak I had to let the pastor speak my words. I was too broken up.

That day, that moment, I felt an overwhelming emotion that I needed to share my story. That by living my truth, I could be a true partner for Brian. This meant living my life, our life, in every area as a happy and loving couple with no barriers and no walls to overcome any further. Brian deserved better and I really do believe Wesley was looking down on me that day. A whole new meaning to our song "Sweet Life" as I believe he wanted me that day and every day going forward to live a life of true honesty and happiness. Wesley always said I was the greatest coach in the world. It was time for me to get myself true and authentic and make a difference. The same thing I always wanted for him. Something he may have been hours away from having. I was ready now. Finally. To come out. The only question that remained now was how.

22

MY DEFINING MOMENT

Returning home from Wesley's funeral, the remainder of the summer was challenging. A part of me felt responsible for his struggles. A part of me felt like losing him in the way we did was the biggest failure of my life. I know now that's not fair, but in tragedy comes soul searching. I took a hard look at my life. There was so much good in it, but still that one personal hurdle to clear. It was clear in my mind now that it was time to come out... To stop being part of the problem for young gay people, and become the solution.

It was hard to quantify precisely how my life in the closet affected the lives of those around me. I know it didn't help. All I had seen over my years.

As I contemplated how to move forward, the world rankings, the career achievements, the surges of wealth; I would give it all back to have Wesley back among us. My life in the closet did not just affect me. It affected everyone I touched, for I asked them all overtly or covertly to participate in my lie.

I gave Wesley a chance at a life he may never have had. But in all my best intentions, I failed to give him the most important aspect of a young gay man's life: the self respect and courage that comes with being proud of who you were born while owning your own life.

Short of calling every important person in my life to tell them my orientation, I was not sure how to come out to my tennis and real estate world. I continued my unintentional slow process of telling on myself. I got involved in the social media world, reconnecting on Facebook with hundreds of friends 179 from my tennis past. I began making public posts about my LGBT media company for all the world to see. Much to my surprise again, nobody seemed to be too concerned about my name being associated with all things LGBT.

Late 2012, I'm stuck again. I feel no need to hold up a flag to tell the world I'm gay. I keep looking for my chance. I'm trying to figure out how to take my life spent in the closet and give it some greater meaning for the next generation of young gay athletic hopefuls. Then my friend Barry Buss from my tennis youth started writing a book. Every day he would post a chapter online, telling his story in unflinching detail. I became enthralled by his tale, for it mirrored mine in so many ways.

Come Christmas of 2012, he had finished his book in a mere three months.

I got a copy, read it and shared my thoughts with Barry privately about the work he had done. Near the end of our exchange, he commented in passing how proud he was of me for fighting the good fight for LGBT equality issues.

Excited that he not only noticed my posts, but openly approved of them, I commented back that someday I wanted to tell my story and maybe he could write it for me. We left it there.

A few months pass and it hits me what I want to do. I want to tell my story but in book form. I want to come out, primarily to the tennis world, chronicling my rise and fall as a young in-the-closet aspiring player. I sent Barry a message late one night on his Facebook timeline. It was vague, a little cryptic, I stated I had a project if he was interested. I trusted he would know what I meant without exposing myself publicly. A couple quick messages back and forth between us had me on a plane to Los Angeles, California, for five days to tell him my whole life story. It was happening, I was finally coming out. The feelings were overwhelming. Within a matter of weeks, we began sharing snippets of my story with the public on the social media platform. We both held our collective breaths. At first, the response was tentative. People were unsure of what we were doing, of where we were going, of how much of my private life I was going to unfurl. But there it was. My young gay life unfolding in a public forum for the whole world to see. My first sexual encounter, my first crush, my first love, all being told in the tasteful informed way you just read in the pages here before. The support from my tennis world, past and present, soon grew to what I could only call unbelievable. Lifted by their overwhelming support, I saw only one hurdle remaining.

It's one thing to come out online in the social media. It's relatively safe behind the monitor of one's computer. It's an entirely different proposition engaging people you've known your whole life and come out face to face with them. The book was progressing well; all indications were my author and I were going to see this project through. What remained now was to make my public announcement. The 2013 U.S. Open was coming up at the end of the summer. What a perfect venue to officially come out. I thought very deeply who the perfect person would be to help me set the stage for this moment to tell the world my story.

One person kept coming to my mind. This woman has a heart of gold, tenacity like a tiger and a proven track record in the tennis industry of getting things done. Patricia Jensen, the mother of Grand Slam doubles champions Luke and Murphy. I decided to take a risk and reach out to Patricia. You cannot imagine the fear when you call someone you have known for over 30 years who has no idea that you are gay and then to ask them to go on the world's stage to support you and help you share your story, this kind of story. My fear disappeared in less than a minute on the first phone conversation with Patricia. She opened her heart and said this is exactly what tennis needs, it's exactly a moment in time to be on the right side of history and that she would be honored to help me in every way.

What a relief. I started to feel confident I could do this. Patricia began to help arrange a press conference for me and the book. We invited all the major influences in my life. Billie Jean King, Lz Granderson, Sven Groeneveld, Nick Bollettieri. Much to my excitement, everyone agreed to participate either in person or via words of support.

I also invited as many of my friends from my tennis life as possible. Again, so many came. A few people in particular were there who had been by my side since my teenage years as loyal friends and supporters. Like Linda Pentz-Gunter, who I love very much and in so many instances over the early years provided me with so much support and guidance. My longtime friends form the NBTA, MJ Landry and Lisa Pamintuan, were so supportive and helped me believe I could impact the world greatly with our mission. My incredible friend and mentor over the past several years Bob DeBenedictis was there so stoic and reverent as always. Bob has been my personal and business mentor for the past several years, a successful businessman, philanthropist and guiding light whom I have looked up to as a gay man in every way. He has guided me through so many life lessons by his actions. Everybody could not have been better. I arrived in New York with Brian and my brother Joe a few days before the event to ensure all progressed smoothly. But all the support by my side in the world cold not quell my nerves. I was a veritable wreck in those days leading up to the press conference. Fidgety, short, uneasy, anxious. I was having a hard time sitting still or focusing on anything for sustained periods. The Thursday morning press conference just could not get here quickly enough.

Wednesday night arrived. I had been good all week, trying to pace myself, wanting to be at my best for the big day. My author Barry, brother Joe, close friend Linda Pentz-Gunter and I were meeting one last time to go over final thoughts for the big day ahead. We sat apart and alone in the corner of a bar next door to where we were staying at the Roger Smith Hotel. All the work was done, we just needed to make it to the morning when I saw Carling Bassett-Seguso enter the lobby.

I had not seen Carling in person since the NBTA 30- year reunion in 2009 but was honored and excited to have her agree to speak on my behalf. I started to rise to greet her when at the last second I saw her husband, former childhood friend and tour great Robert Seguso. Instinctively, without a thought, I tried to hide from Robert. Neither of them had noticed me as I crunched down behind a poll until they passed.

A little shocked at my reaction, I told my friends at the table I just wasn't ready to deal with Rob, a real guy-guy type, whose possible reaction I feared the most from my playing and coaching days. He obviously knew, he was to attend the press conference the next day. I was pretty stressed by this point. Forty-eight years of living a certain way. The desire to remain hidden did not magically wash away with my online announcement of my coming out book.

Coming out in person was going to be a hard process I could tell. I could barely sleep that night. Thoughts flashed every which way. All the moments I wished I'd have come out. How would my life be different today if I had? I thought of all the people I would have invited to New York to share the moment with me. For those who couldn't make the event, it was being streamed live for all the world to see. For those key people in my life who were no longer with us, my mom, my nana, dad, Wesley, Angel, Father Bill, my Uncle Dave and Aunt Eileen and Aunt Mary. I said a little prayer to them all, hoping in my heart of faith they were somewhere safe looking down upon me. And proud of me for what I was about to do.

182 A lifetime of frustration, angst, turmoil, fear, all to be purged within the

hour. Enough was enough. I just wanted to be done with the guy who still felt the need to hide. I went down to the press room early to prepare the event. I walked in to a vacant room of empty chairs. There stood the podium where it all was to happen. I would be the last to speak.

People began to arrive in earnest a half hour before the event. Sven, Luke, Lz, Patricia, Carling and then Nick Bollettieri arrived. I had not seen Nick in some time. I was so nervous about asking him to participate in my coming out. Spending a lifetime seeking his approval, to fear his disapproval over such a sensitive issue. Nick was old school, macho, military, alpha male. Just the type of person I feared all my life. Then I heard through the grapevine he had just been the best man at a gay wedding. The pundits had been saying that there was no better time in history for young gay athletes to come out. I was now beginning to believe them.

The room quickly filled. Patricia Jensen opened the press conference with her customary warmth and energy and made everyone feel welcome. A couple of people had come up to me before the event. They all said the same thing. If we had just known, we would have done everything we could to help. Now there began a steady stream of tennis luminaries saying the same thing, all wishing they had known. And right there is the trap of living in the closet. If we're good at it, you don't know we exist. And if you don't know we exist, you have no reason to concern yourselves with our plight.

But worse than that, we gays in the closet so fear that what you say is not true. And that has nothing to do with you. It has everything to do with us, with our own self-image. For again, if we can't accept ourselves for who we are, how can we ever expect anyone else to? And therein lies the problem; two groups of people completely unaware of each other's views, for everything remains hidden in the shadows when living in the closet is in play.

The press conference continued in a blur. Lz Granderson, journalist extraordinaire from CNN and ESPN, took the podium and read a prepared statement from Billie Jean King, friend and colleague from my WTT days. What an honor. It's still hard to believe that it was me she was referencing in her words of praise and encouragement. Lz was his normal brilliant self, slicing to the heart of the equality issues confronting gay athletes even today in 2013.

Carling Bassett-Seguso spoke next, so movingly, from the heart and with a passion that was reminiscent of her on-court focus and determination. Next came Luke Jensen, all fire, funny, filled with an earnest integrity, once my 183 opponent across the net, now an advocate by my side. And my author, Barry Buss. Quiet, thoughtful, modest. When he talked about how much his eyes were opened by my story, a story he had to relive with me over many months, I felt so much gratitude for his commitment to telling that story so well.

Then came Nick. My idol growing up. My mentor on the court, my inspiration off the court. He started in on our history together. An anecdote here, a joke there. He was a brilliant speaker. When all of a sudden he stopped cold, overcome with emotion at the thought of me, Bobby Blair, one of his "sons" he liked to call us, suffering quietly while under his watch. It was a powerful moment, this larger-than-life figure, the man who gave me my tennis life, overwhelmed by my experience.

Nick's expressed emotions did little to calm my frayed nerves as I followed him to the podium. Buoyed by all the positivity that preceded me, I rose to the occasion to give the best talk I could under the circumstances. I sensed something profound was going on within me. That this was the end of something, yet the beginning of something entirely new too.

In my announcement I made a promise. I vowed to begin a mentoring program for young in-the-closet athletes of today as part of the Brian Neal Fitness & Health Foundation. We would help them on their journey, whether they wanted to stay in the closet or come out, and provide a support team to hopefully make that journey a little easier.

With the press conference behind me there was a palpable sense of relief. It was done. I was out. That evening a group of us celebrated at the bar in the hotel. And there was Robert Seguso, smiling, hanging, taking photos with all of us. Later on, I found myself side-by-side with him playing pool. He was supportive, cool. Why had I been so afraid of his reaction? Did he embody all of that male tennis world from which I had been hiding for so long? Had I pre-judged him and made assumptions about him as I had with so many others? Playing pool with Rob somehow brought home to me just how long I had waited and just how fearful of people I had been who were in fact just totally fine with me for who I am. My sexuality just wasn't even an issue.

There was relief for Brian, too. With the focus on the book, it had been all about Bobby for a long time. But now it could be about Brian and Bobby. No more hiding our love from the world. I felt a change in me, too. Less of a need to hustle the next deal. Success didn't mean embarking on the next great 184 business venture. It meant time with family, something I never really had growing up. Brian's family is my family. We spend holidays together. They are supportive of their son and supportive of us as a couple. In that we are very fortunate. I know it is far from that way for many.

After so many years of struggle, my greatest love enters and stays in my life.
Brian Neal, you inspire me every day.

Photo by "Big" Dewitte Loe

That night I realized more than ever that to be of any use to anyone else, I needed to take care of myself too. Forty eight years of living a lie does things to you. My greater understanding of the life I have lived up to now would emerge within the pages you have just read. I understand my wisdom on the fruits of coming out is limited to the time I've been out.

There is a veritable time stamp to the words I've just penned. The enlightened reader would likely be able to predict with great accuracy just how long I've been out when writing these words. To tell my story at the one-year mark or the five-year mark, though the circumstances of my past would not have changed, I may write for you an entirely different book. For the lessons of the life honestly lived are only now coming to me.

What I do know is the need for a dialogue, for the consequences of the hidden life are too severe for far too many. I hope in these pages I have begun to build a bridge between two parties that hardly know each exist. The scared closeted athlete and those among the straight, tolerant, loving, and accepting culture that surrounds their every step. We in the gay community need to help ourselves, but we could use a little help from the straight community. For as all the people of my past said, if they only knew, things would have been different for me. Well, now everybody knows.

I hope in my book to have given a heads-up to the next generation of athletes, coaches, and parents that other Bobby Blairs populate your clubs and the tournaments you play. Now you know this. Now we need to work together to ensure their path is different than mine, for in the closet is no way to live. These kids deserve better. It really wouldn't take very much.

As I stepped away from the podium, I was overcome by a sense of peace, a feeling I had spent a lifetime chasing. A deep personal battle had finally been won that morning, a battle no opponent, or business cycle, or homophobic employer could ever take away from me. What I took away that morning was my dignity.

More importantly, though, is what I aspire to give in telling my story: That is hope. That it gets better, that we young gay men and women can live the same rich full lives of our straight counterparts if to our own selves we be true. I know a person cannot live on hope alone, but without hope life just isn't worth living. My goal in sharing my story here today is that I will fill you with the courage you need to carry on, with just enough hope to someday live your truth too. No longer hiding from anyone...just like me..

I have great hopes in our life travels that you pull me aside when we cross paths and share your story with me. Use my story as inspiration to love yourself for exactly who you are. If you are a parent, family member, friend, teacher, coach, sponsor or fan of an LGBT athlete, my hope is you will express love and embrace your athlete for exactly who they are and encourage them to live their truth as they dream big and work tirelessly to achieve their athletic and personal goals. And I hope that this expression of love, support and acceptance of LGBT people in the sporting world will cross over to all LGBT people from all walks of life as they aspire to achieve success with their talents and passion while having the love and support they desire to be proud and happy to live their truth.

Let's make a difference together and do what my old friend Billie Jean King says we should do every day: " Go For It."

BOBBY BLAIR: ACKNOWLEDGMENTS

To my life partner Brian, without your incredible support and encouragement I would never have had the courage to tell my story. Together we embark on a life-long mission to make a difference to others as we try to pave a better future for this generation and future generations of young athletes aspiring to reach their personal and professional goals while living their truth.

A heartfelt thank you to my mother Margaret who was the greatest mom any young boy could ever dream of and hope for. You taught me to dream big and believe that with hard work and great people around you anything is possible. You always reminded me to say my "Hail Mary's" which I do every single night before I go to bed as I reflect on my day. Never a day goes by that you are not in my thoughts and prayers.

To the greatest nana anyone could have. When I was young and tried to better understand what love was, all I needed to do was look in your eyes when you spoke to me and I immediately knew what love was and how it felt.

To my father who had a difficult time his entire life. The older I get, the pain of our relationship softens as I realize this world we live in serves up some pretty tough obstacles to us all. Dad, you had more than your fair share and I am sorry for that.

To my amazing brother Joe and his wife Jamie, who have been by my side and supported me every step of the way. Joe, your support of me in every aspect of my life since the day you were born has helped me have the courage to do things that otherwise I would have been too afraid to challenge. To my nephew Bryson, who inspires me every day and reminds me of the importance of my story for his generation. To my nephew Bradley, who since you were a young boy, expressed your love and support of me. It has been amazing and so appreciated. I am so proud of what an outstanding young man you have become.

To my Uncle Jim and Aunt Margaret, Uncle Dave and Aunt Eileen, Father Bill and Aunt Mary, cousins Angel, Kathy, Pam, Mickey, Bill, Mike and Tim. All of you supported and encouraged me incredibly as I worked to make a better life for myself and my family as a tennis player and coach when I was a young man. I love you all very much. I hope you are not saddened you are learning about my personal secret and life-long struggles for the first time in these pages. I never wanted to disappoint any of you.

My heartfelt thank you to my first coach, Jim Kelaher, who gave me my start in life on the tennis court and provided me the opportunity to dream big dreams. Jim, you provided me an environment in which to plant many amazing seeds at the Orlando Tennis Center that I would have never had available to me if not for you and your generosity and love. Your from-the-heart letter to me at a time when I needed it most changed my life for the better forever. Thank you!

To my other amazing coaches over the years in Orlando, who include Murray Hough, Betty Pratt, Hector Villarroel and Nata Treise. Your amazing instruction and dedication to me at different times in my career were building blocks to many of my dreams coming true. Thank you!

To my dear Nick Bollettieri. Your support of me since Labor day 1980 up until today has provided me with an internal burning desire to do great things and never let you down as you stepped up and took me under your wing on and off the courts for more than three decades now. My love and respect for you is immense. Thank you so much for attending my press conference at the 2013 U.S. Open, where your incredible words gave me the fuel to announce my story with confidence and pride as I then knew I had your acceptance and loving blessing. Something I have worked to have since the first day I met you as you took me in and launched me to the world tennis stage. Thank you!

To all the coaches and staff at the Nick Bollettieri Tennis Academy. A heart-felt thank you as all of you looked after me 24 hours a day and committed endless hours in helping me develop as a young man, which prepared me for life in every way. Carolina Bolivar-Murphy, Julio Moros, Chip Brooks, Greg Breunich, Chip Hart and a special thank you to Steve Owens, who I spent thousands of hours with as he was my on-court coach for the better part of three years as Nick coached us from the baseline on our side of the court. Your encouragement, great insight into the game and overall dedication to me will always be remembered and so appreciated.

To Dr. Murray and Lois Gerber and their daughter Susan Hedgcock. My years at Bradenton Academy were the most significant years in my life off the courts. Your amazing unconditional love for me gave me the confidence to challenge myself in ways that were unknown to me. Making you proud is a daily effort for me and will be until the last day of my life. You believing in me helped me believe in myself. Thank you!

To all my amazing childhood friends I met along the way as I pursued greatness on the courts as a player. All of you played an amazing role in my development in so many different kinds of ways. Dani Leal, Ricky Brown, Tony Zanoni, Cary Cohenour, Alice Reen, Mary Dinneen, Robert Sojo, Rolph Bonnell, Stan Carpenter, Mike Gustafson, Ginny Dickinson, Wayne Johnson, Aaron Krickstein, Joey Perry, Robert Green, Jim Sutter, Jim Schaedel, Roger Blackburn, Sean Cartwright, Jim Kasser, Danny Granot, Carling Bassett, Darren Herman, Jimmy Arias, Pam Casale, and so many more. Thank you for making me better every time we hit the courts and for being a friend off the courts as we all bonded in our own way. Each of you made my struggles just a little easier.

Thank you to the University of Arkansas for an amazing three years of education and tennis development. A special thank you to my first college coach, Tom Pucci, and assistant coach, Jose Lambert, for believing in me and helping me through the toughest period of my life when my mother died my freshman year, first week of school. A big thank you to Ron Hightower for your amazing dedication to me and the endless hours you devoted in helping to take my game to the next level when coach Pucci left as head coach after my freshman year. A very special thank you to Pat Serrett, Tim Siegel and Pat Mehaffy, who took me under their wings when I arrived at college. Pat Mehaffy, your on-court presence with me guided me through some very big wins and memorable moments. You made me feel I could beat anybody. To my teammates Kelly, Pat S, Tim, Simon, Bobby, Joey, Pat M, Richard, Danny, Brad, Brett, Darren you all were incredible teammates and I love and thank you all for pushing me to be the best I could be. I am sorry for not living my truth with you. It was a mistake.

Thank you Mike Estep and Ron Jenkins for all your help when I turned professional.

To all the players who participated in the "U.S. Rookie Professional Tennis Team." It was an amazing journey helping all of you live out your childhood dreams of being a professional tennis player. Each of you made me a better coach and person. I am so proud of what all of you accomplished on and off the courts.

Linda Pentz-Gunter, you have been by my side with love and support for over three decades. Your passion to make a difference in everything you do has been incredibly inspirational to me. You guided and mentored me as we started the Rookie Professional Team together in the 80s. You helped me transition form player to coach on and off the courts. Today, you helped me tell my story with clarity and precision. Our relationship is one of the most special things of my life. I love you very much. My life is so much better for you being in it. Thank You!

A special thank you to my tennis academy students who made me a better coach every day. Rodrigo Gomes, Trey Adcock, Ali Dhanani, Jim Mulligan, Mark Urbainczyk, Ty Braswell, Tracy Kotseous, Julie Woods, Jason White, Ryan Higgins, Kenny Klamper, Kenneth Wasserman, Hurly Constaine, Molly Sigourney, Matthew Graham and all of the hundreds of students I had the amazing pleasure of coaching over the years as I tried to prepare every one of you for life in every way.

Thank you to Shane Hackett, Billy Cannon, Bill Grenier, Allen Kmiotek, Joe Roberts, Anthony Ricciardo, Bob De Benedictis, Peter Schonberger, Merrill Brick, Keith Collins, Jamie Forsythe, Patrick Cambell, Gerrard Kessler, Jeffrey Sterling, Kevin Hopper, Alan Beck, Eugene Conti, Randy Koehnke, Travis Smith, Portia Ramassar, Kevin Dinneen, Ernst Urbainczyk, Thomas Graham, Jac Klamper, Robert Gillispie, Hector Villarroel, Tim Sanders, Jay Mays, Peter Jackson, Matthew Mushlin, Larry Simon, Steve Decesare and so many others who helped me in business after my last ball was hit all while I was "Hiding Inside the Baseline" on and off the courts. All of you and many more not mentioned made my life better in many ways and helped me achieve success I would have only dreamed of as a young boy. Many of you knew my secret and allowed me the opportunity to find and live my truth on my own terms and for that I am forever grateful.

A special thank you to Joseph Koker, Eric Tan, Dr. Alan Shafer, Mario Careaga, Lionel White, Locke Roberts, Dr. Scott Pearl, Mary Ann Pearl, and Samuel Chenillo all shareholders in Multimedia Platforms, LLC. Because of you and your incredible support, together we have been able to build a LGBT media business that makes a difference for the community we serve.

Thank you to Peter Copani for your unwavering support and love since we met in New York in 1986. When I decided to become an LGBT publisher you once again provided moral and financial support. Thank you my great friend.

My dear friend Randy "Moose" Koehnke. I will be forever grateful and appreciative for the many years we spent together as we tried to make a difference for American tennis with our Rookie Professional Tennis Team. Your commitment to me and the players was nothing short of incredible. Your friendship to me personally, combined with your loyalty to me as a best friend along with your desire to help me in everything we pursued, which included our tennis academy and many years in real estate, will always be one of the most special memories of my life. Thank you for everything you did for me. I will always love you.

A special thank you to my mentor Bob DeBenedictis for your unwavering love and support and for being a role model to me in all areas of my life.

To my dear Wesley. Thank you for your amazing belief in me. When I was down you picked me up. You will never know how much you have impacted my life. Your smile, laugh and all around amazing kind heart has been missed every day since your passing. I think of you every day and pray you are in God's great hands. Hit a game winning three-pointer up there for me. I love you!

Keith, thank you for always being by my side. Thank you for loving me at a time when

I felt a loving relationship was for the rest of the world and not for me. Your loyalty and commitment to me and our friendship for almost two decades speaks volumes of our deep love for each other. I will be by your side every day for the rest of my life.

Lz, thank you for your love and support years ago and again this past summer as you stepped up and helped me announce to the world that an average guy who had an average career can make a difference and connect with the thousands of young gay athletes all around the world as they strive to achieve their goals at all levels being exactly who they are with pride and dignity.

Patricia Jensen, thank you for embracing me and doing such an incredible job in helping me share my story. Your passion to help me inspires me every day.

Billie Jean King, you have supported and inspired me since we met in the spring of 1990. The confidence you gave me when you hired me to coach your World Team Tennis franchise in Wellington, Florida, took my tennis career to another level. The lessons I learned in your presence have served me well for a lifetime. Your passion to make a difference every day of your life inspired me to attack everything I do with tenacity and a never-give-up attitude. You taught me "No" is not an acceptable answer. Your make it happen and "Go For it" mantra has stuck with me every day of my life since I met you. Billie Jean, once again as you always have, thank you for supporting my life story. Your statements of support will inspire the world and because of you more people will be inspired to live their truth. Thank you, Ilana Kloss, for your unwavering support throughout the years. The support you and Billie Jean have provided for "Hiding Inside the Baseline" is so appreciated. I love you both very much.

Thank you Patricia Jensen, Carling Bassett-Seguso, Luke Jensen, Lz Granderson, Nick Bollettieri and Barry Buss for speaking so passionately in support of my story at my press conference in New York at the 2013 U.S. Open. Thank you to my amazing friends from the NBTA, MJ Landry and Lisa Pamintuan, along with long-time friends Sven Groeneveld and Linda Pentz-Gunter, who all provided me with such love and support when I was in New York as the amazing events of that week unfolded.

A very special thank you to one of the finest tennis publishers and journalists in the tennis world, Jim Martz. You have been an amazing supporter of me for over 20 years. When I called you to edit my book you said yes before I could even ask. You also encouraged and assured me I was doing something special. Those words from you helped me stay focused and inspired.

Thank you to Dennis Dean for a terrific cover photograph for this book. All your years of loyalty and incredible photo shoots for our publications is greatly appreciated.

Thank you George Dauphin for the incredible dedication and endless hours you dedicated to brilliantly formatting and designing "Hiding Inside the Baseline."

Richard Hack, your invaluable advice and commitment to helping me this past year is so appreciated. Having your expertise and support gave me the confidence I could make this book possible. I also want to thank you for being the most incredible mentor for my publishing business. Your insight and guidance has made a big difference in how we serve our LGBT community with our media business.

Shawn Palacious and Anthony Ricciardo, you have done a great job preparing my story for distribution by creating an amazing website and social media platform to reach as many people as possible. Huge thank you.

I want to thank a very special friend and my personal business manager Jamie Forsythe who has been by my side since 2003 as I struggled to find my truth, develop business opportunities and create the personal life I always dreamed of. Because of you, Jamie, and your amazing help and support in every area of my life, I am now in a much better place. Thank you.

To my writer Barry Buss. I will never be able to thank you enough and no words can express my sincere appreciation for your relentless passion to tell my story. Your open heart to be on the right side of history and to share with the world my story for the sole purpose of making a difference to others so that they may be empowered by your touching words to live their truth is a sign of true character. The world this day and age needs more people like you, Barry Buss, who are willing to go out on a limb when it may not be the easiest thing to do or the the most accepted conversation of a generation or a lifetime. But you are special. Your insight to my struggles and fear will connect with readers, young and old alike. You will touch lives in ways you will never know because what you have done for me. The world is a better place because of you. Thank you, my friend.

In closing, I want to thank everyone who encouraged and supported Barry and me. We hope you have been inspired to help us make a difference. We hope in your circle of life you are encouraged to be a leader in your communities in showing support for a loving and supportive environment for all people from all walks of life.

Bobby Blair

BARRY BUSS: ACKNOWLEDGMENTS

It's not every day you finish a book, so if you'll oblige me I have a few things to say and a few people to acknowledge. When the idea of this book came up, my first thought was..."A straight guy writing a gay man's coming out story...

What could go wrong?" But like most things in life, if you look for the similarities instead of the differences, it's fascinating how much common ground you can find. What started as a story about a world of which I knew little became a coming-of-age story of a tennis player searching for love and meaning on a road less traveled. A situation quite a few of us can relate to if we take the time to look closely enough.

About that world of which I knew little. I considered myself a pretty educated guy going into this project. I have to admit I was a little embarrassed by how little I knew about the struggles for equality the LGBT community endures. I discovered an eclectic array of bright, courageous individuals out there on the front lines on this most human of rights battles. Dan Savage, Andrew Sullivan, Lz Granderson, the late Harvey Milk; this list could go on for pages. I learned a lot from these trailblazers. I hope through our book more people will find their work and learn from them too. They have a lot to teach those of us safely ensconced away in our hyper-straight worlds.

About the people I met a long the way. It was East Coast meets West Coast. Southern California meets the Nick Bollettieri Tennis Academy. And I thought we out west were crazy. What a crew. Total pleasure to learn about that special moment in time back in Bradenton... and then to be able to meet so many of the people themselves along the way. MJ, Lisa, Carling, Anne, Nick himself and many others. I felt like I was crashing someone else's 30-year reunion, yet everyone treated me as if I had been one of them all along. So a sincere tip of the hat to the grace of all who survived those Academy years.

About my client. Well, what could have been a total disaster I don't think could have come together much better. To have another person trust you with the most intimate details of his life is always an awesome responsibility. To be entrusted to put them into a creative form for all the world to see is a whole different level. So many things could have gone wrong. I'm proud of both of us for how we managed ourselves in what became an eight-month exercise in patience and compassion. We both picked up a new friend for life...and that's a good thing.

Finally, about our community here and abroad. A writer is nothing without readers. To all my supporters over the years: Ken, Rhonda, Gayle, Michael V, Scott, Dan, Brenda, Jon F. and all my extended family of friends from the social media world. None of our good fortunes here would be happening without your patience and support. So many great people answered the bell on this project.

What a gig. To be able to sit back here and spin out tales for your reading pleasure. It's a total honor to be able to do this, and to be sought out to do this.

What more can I say? I'm overcome with gratitude to be able to live this life with you. Just wanted to take a moment to let you all know that within a few words of acknowledgment...

Peace...

Barry Buss

About the author

Barry Buss is the author of a junior tennis memoir titled "First In A Field of Two"...His cutting edge tennis journalism can be read at Barrybuss.com. He can be reached at Barrybuss1964@ yahoo.com for all sorts of future writing projects.

"Coming out with pride and dignity would have happened for me years ago if I knew I would have been this loved and accepted. I encourage you to find the strength to dig deep inside to live your truth. My hope and expectation is you will be greatly loved and accepted by so many as I have been. I hope you find yourself empowered by these statements to go for it."

Bobby Blair

KENNETH WASSERMAN

(Former student at the Bobby Blair Tennis Academy)

"I met Bobby through tennis when I was a junior player out of Miami, Florida. At age fifteen, my parents shipped me off to Orlando where I would train at Bobby's tennis academy and finish out my junior tennis years. This was freedom for any young teenager, no parents to tell me what to do and tennis every day. My relationship with Bobby first started out as coach/ student but gradually turned into somewhat of a brother/mentor relationship. One day in particular changed everything in Orlando for me. I was kicked out of the house of the family that had taken me in while I trained at Bobby's academy, and I was either heading back to Miami or Bobby was finding me another place to live. So, Bobby took me in and let me crash in one of his rooms at his house. What was clearly a low point in my time in Orlando turned into the time of my life. In this house, there was Bobby in one room, his brother Joe in another room, one of our tennis coaches Randy in a different room, and me the skinny 15-year-old in the guest room. This was the ultimate bachelor pad. Girls were coming and going from each room on each weekend except from mine unfortunately. But I was still in heaven. If Bobby was gay, I sure as hell had no idea. I lived with Bobby until I graduated from high school at 17 and then headed off to college. Bobby had prepared me for life as though he was one of my parents. He knew that my folks had spent every dime they had on me and he wanted to make sure that he didn't let them down. After college, it only made sense that I moved back to Orlando to work for him. This time around, I stayed with Bobby for some time but there were no more girls running around. It still never occurred to me that Bobby was gay even then. After working with Bobby in the real estate business, it was only then that his secret was told to me by one of his workers. I couldn't believe it. I was probably the only person around Bobby at the time that had no idea. For whatever reason, Bobby thought it was best not to tell me. We never talked about it and I sure as hell never held it against him. Since I am not gay, I really didn't understand how a man could like another man. But that was irrelevant with me and my relationship with Bobby. I loved Bobby. I still love Bobby. He's family to me. This book explaining what Bobby went through while keeping everything tucked away inside him should help anyone else out there who is going through the same thing."

·

DAN NAHIRNY

(Member of the U.S. Junior Davis Cup Team 1984, National Indoor Champion
Boys 16s and 18s 1982-83, UCLA All America 1986-87)

"There was no tennis player as fierce or as competitive as Bobby Blair. It was a pleasure to play and compete against him. As a junior tennis player,I looked up to him, as did so many others.When I heard Bobby came out publicly in 2012 , I was so happy for him.I realized he became a champion at the game of life. Bobby is on a new mission now and I'm sure he will succeed , just like he always does. I believe his story will enable and empower other young men and women to come out, to live their lives openly and in peace!!"

DON PETRINE

(Leading South Florida junior and professional coach for over three decades)

"I have known Bobby since he was 13 years old. I watched him grow from a popular and talented tennis prodigy into an entrepreneurial adult. Bobby always had smarts, drive, good looks and charm. On the tennis court he was a highly skilled warrior. He is always enthusiastic and engaging.

The thought never crossed my mind that he was gay. Nor would it have made any difference in my perception of him anyway. But what a cross to bear growing up in our world. Bobby coming out has definitely made me more sensitive in coaching young people. I can only imagine the peer pressure he felt when he realized that he was different. It is paramount now in our culture to judge people by their character and not things that are not within their control. I am very proud of Bobby Blair and honored to know such a great human being."

RICKY BROWN

(Lifelong friend of Bobby Blair. Orange Bowl 18 and under winner and U.S. National Boy's 18
champion and world ranked player)
"Bobby was my best friend and my best man in my wedding. He has such a big heart and is the most giving person I have ever met."

ALICE REEN

(Lifelong friend of Bobby Blair and former All American tennis player at the
University of Georgia and Division 1 head coach)
"Bobby and I were the best of friends growing up in the late 70s. his friendship has remained strong and true.

Bobby was a blue collar I will out work you by practicing until the lights go off and the club shuts down and I will out grind you and annoy you until you leave in tears. Not nearly the talent of the other guys but a player that loved the game, studied the game and always had a plan!

I know his journey in life in addition to living a hidden and secretive life has been difficult. The next chapter in his life will be even more meaningful and will make an impact in the LGBT community. Just reaching one kid through all of this will make a difference. This second part of Bobby's journey will be special!"

SCOTT HILL

(NBTA student and friend of Bobby Blair)

"I met Bobby Blair in 1980 at the Nick Bollettieri Tennis Academy in Bradenton, Florida. We were both full-time boarding students when the academy was gaining its momentum to global prominence. In those days we lived in a 14-room motel that was so small one of our students literally had to sleep with his feet hanging off his bunk bed outside the window because of his height and the room being so small. Most all the students became familiar with each other, doing tasks together like making our next day's lunch out in the parking lot every evening by choosing either tuna fish, pimento cheese or egg salad.

For some reason that time period remains crystal clear in my memory.

One quality that I admired in Bobby, even before we met, was his ability to become friends with anyone and everyone. I, on the other hand, was reserved, quiet and shy. I was a young, naive, 14-year-old country boy from Kentucky and understandably somewhat intimidated by the older students and this new tennis academy that I had just seen on TV's prime time show "60 Minutes." When first meeting Bobby in the cafeteria at the academy he came across extremely polite and sincere. I could not tell he was a prodigy tennis star by the way he behaved. Unlike most kids who were ranked top 10 nationally, Bobby never boasted about himself and treated everyone with equal respect.

I got to know Bobby better one weekend when most of the students traveled to a tournament in Naples. I loved to watch Bobby compete. It was not just his level of play that was so impressive but the unique ability to turn on a switch from the moment the first point started. He played ALL OUT and fought for every single ball and every single point as if every point was match point. It was a blast to watch him play, flying around the court and ripping his two-handed backhand while overcoming opponents with his true grit and determination. My being on a full scholarship thanks to Nick's generosity, being ranked #1 in the South and tops nationally, I was by far the best 14-and-under at the academy while I was there, winning every tournament (7) Nick played me in; until another 14-year-old boy named Aaron Krickstein showed up on campus. So I quickly became a student of the game, a sponge, if you will. I studied everyone older than me and I soon noticed how Bobby would absolutely destroy an opponent on the court with his power, intensity and talent, but then once the match was over he could turn that switch off and be playing ping pong with the guy he just crushed 30 minutes ago and having fun. Then when his next match was called he would do it all over again. I learned a lot from watching Bobby play tennis. Not so much shot selection or strategy, but by the way he played with a calm intensity. His mind was composed and poised while his feet displayed a fist-fight intensity along with his explosive movement and killer instinct.

When Bobby called me recently to inform me of his decision to go public and told me about his new book coming out and inviting me to his press conference, I didn't even blink an eye. Unfazed. Although I knew nothing about any of this previously, it seemed absolutely normal to me. My aunt is a lesbian. Most people I know have someone gay in their family. It was just so easy to tell him,

"I love you, man. I'm behind you 100% and will do anything for you. How can I help?" We spoke for awhile, reminisced about being a teenager and that was it. He knows he has my total support; especially within the tennis community which, even globally, is small.

On Bobby being gay? To me, it's inconsequential. Brother or not. We are all God's children and He loves us equally and unconditionally. My generation and those to follow are so much more educated and understanding than that of, say my parents, who don't realize and perhaps can't even conceptualize that Bobby did NOT CHOOSE to be gay! That's simply how he was born. Do you think Bobby wanted to be different than his friends growing up? Are you serious? Not a chance. It's just the way he was brought in to this world. I'm just so glad that Bobby set himself free by going public. Now he can truly enjoy the rest of his life as he should: prideful, open, honest and just be himself. I am very proud of Bobby for many reasons I will soon explain. Being a Christian since age 10 and through college having preached sermons at my home church and abroad while in college, I would like to share some scripture for the people out there who choose to judge others. I'd like you to read James 4:11 where it says, "brothers, do not slander one another. Anyone who speaks against another or judges him speaks against the law and judges it. There is only one lawgiver and Judge, the one who is able to save and destroy. But YOU WHO ARE YOU TO JUDGE YOUR NEIGH-BOR?"Romans 14:10 "YOU, then, why do you judge your brother? Or why do you look down on your brother?" Romans 14:13 "therefore let us stop passing judgment on one another. In-stead, make up your mind NOT to put any stumbling block or obstacle in your brother's way." And my favorite verse of all, Matthew 7:1,2 "DO NOT JUDGE, or you too will be judged. For in the same way you judge others, you will be judged, and with the measure you use, it will be measured to you." The Golden Rule sums it up nicely. Matthew 7:12 "So in everything, do to others what you would have them do to you."

Our society looks at a person and is quick to express their opinion passing judgement like they are God. Be careful now! We tend to dwell on a person's outward appearance where God only looks at what's in our Heart.

Bobby Blair has a heart of gold that only God can see. He is paving the way for young and old. He is opening eyes as well as minds and making a difference in this world in many different ways. Not only by liberating our youth and people of all ages from having to travel down the same road Bobby did: feeling wrong, guilt-ridden, confused, embarrassed, self-es-teem issues and isolation. Wrestling with that decision of whether to go public or not must be so gut-wrenching with no certainty of who will understand and who will turn their back on you during your deepest time of need must strike panic through one's soul. But Bobby did it! The "fist-fighter" I watched destroy opponents on the tennis court came out as well as that poise Bobby possesses to think clearly through all the internal chaos and conclude that he needed to be honest with himself and all others.

It is also my hope that Bobby accomplishes more in this endeavor than he might possibly be aware. I can see Bobby planting seeds in our society concerning the enormous bigotry that continues to exist in America as the quintessential ELEPHANT IN THE ROOM idiom. Education and awareness are the answer. For example, if a person believes men should be paid more than women, they are by definition displaying bigotry. The official definition of bigotry is an intolerance to those who hold different opinions than themselves.

When Lincoln was president white men owned black slaves. I am proud of our Afri-can-American President for breaking down countless barriers that were once thought impossible. This transition to acceptance will eventually take place in a similar fashion in the gay community. What does a person's skin color, sexual orientation, ethnicity or gender have to do with one's character, work ethic, integrity and heart? Absolutely NOTHING! What business is it to anyone else what another person does on their own time as long as they are not hurting anyone? Bobby Blair is making a big impact by shining a spotlight on many important issues that are rarely brought to the surface; as well as what he is doing for himself personally along with his non-profit foundation and many other ventures. He is on a very important mission here to educate our society to accept gays as normal human beings; because that is exactly what they are, simply men and women.

I am here to remind the American people that bigotry is as prominent as ever, just in different fields and forms, including, but not limited to racial, ethnic and even gender bigotry. It will take time, education and people who are willing to stand up and fight for what is right, like prize money in men's and women's tennis; it was vastly unequal until approximately a decade ago. But there were women who stood up against this gender bigotry, fought and won. Bobby Blair is one of those people making a difference by standing up for what is right; today, and for future generations to come."

TONY ZANONI

(Bobby Blair lifelong friend and teammate of winning state high school tennis championships)

"I met Bobby in 1980 and immediately considered him to be like my brother. His huge heart and true passion for people has always inspired me and truly made me admire him as a person. I am so proud of his courage and tenacity in fulfilling his mission to help young people. He is absolutely creating a path for today's youth and future generations to follow. Bobby is a remarkable individual and is creating a legacy to last for generations to come."

PATRICIA M. JENSEN

(Marketing Architect and friend. Supporter of Bobby Blair for over 30 years.)

"I traveled on the National Junior Tennis Circuit at the same time that Bobby Blair competed in the same age group as my son. I followed his career from afar and was so impressed when at 23, he recognized the need to create the traveling professional team for his peers. When I received the phone call to assist him to announce to the tennis world that he was no longer hiding inside the baseline and wanted assistance in scheduling a press conference and reception during the 2013 U.S. Open, I accepted the role. I didn't realize at the time that I would learn so much from Bobby. His determination to share his experiences and challenges with the athletes of today via his foundation with effective mentoring is certainly a much needed vehicle for today's athletes. I am confident that his story will break down barriers and create a better understanding of the importance to love and embrace everyone equally with respect. Bobby inspires all who he comes in contact with his ideals, his vision, and boundless energy. Bobby's Foundation is destined to succeed and reach his objectives as evidenced by the support of the entire tennis world."

BRAD LOUDERBACK

(Wichita State University head men's tennis coach. Bobby Blair's Junior Davis Cup coach 1983)

"My first thoughts of Bobby Blair are his big smile and his big heart. Bobby made our prestigious 1982 Junior Davis Cup team (the top 12 Juniors in the USA) and he lived up to it. This tour of national junior tournaments was a grind in itself and Bobby had to endure one of the most difficult times in anyone's life, the passing of his mother. My heart was torn for Bobby and my respect grew tremendously as Bobby carried on what he learned from his mother and never stopped fighting on the court. He was a tenacious player with an incredible desire to do his best in every match. As I look back on those days, I wish Bobby would have felt he could come and talk to me about anything. We all have our special memories of those days in the 80s and when I think of Bobby, I always get a smile because he approached every day in a positive way and was fun to coach and have on the team. I love you Bobby and keep up the great work."

M.J. LANDRY

(NBTA friend of Bobby Blair)

"I first met you over 30 years ago when you came to live at NBTA. I remember that I was 12 years old and I thought that you were just the cutest boy, best tennis player and the coolest person that I had ever seen. I still have the diary entry to prove it.

For years we traveled to the same Florida tennis tournaments, we had the same friends and we shared the same dramas and first crushes and ups and downs as all teenagers do. Well at least I thought so at the time.

Years later, hearing your story and watching you share with the world the heavy burden of the secret you carried and battled with for all those years I feel really sad that you had to bear that burden all alone. It was a very different time back in the 1980s as is well known, but I wish there had been just one person who could've been there for you. I want to tell you now that your secret, though a burden to bear, did not define you. The core values and morals and convictions that your mother instilled in you throughout your life define you. Your work ethic defines you. Your good heart and the loyalty that your friends and loved ones feel towards you define you. The good that you and Brian are trying to achieve through your foundation defines you. And the courage it took for you to come out to the tennis community and the world at large defines you. We can't escape who we are.

I am so very proud of you and proud to be your friend. It takes tremendous courage to do what you have just done. I know that by writing this book and starting your mentoring program for other young gay athletes you will make a lasting impact on many people's lives, and that is an amazing achievement, my friend.

You have always been kind and respectful to me and besides all of your many achievements in tennis and in business what I love about you the most is your good heart and loyalty to your friends. You are one of the most positive people I know.

Good luck going forward Bobby, I know there are many great things in store for your future."

JIM MORRIS

(NBTA friend of Bobby Blair)

"I first knew of Bobby from my days at NBTA. Back in the late 80s he was a player I saw as phenomenon on the court and I was in awe. Seeing him at tournaments we played in we would talk about tennis and with his smile he would encourage me to take risks in my game. All these years later I'm proud of my friend that with that same bright smile is himself taking risks and wishing the rewards he so deserves."

MURRAY HOUGH

(Bobby Blair coach at the Orlando Racquet Club)

"I met Bobby in Orlando when he was about 12 years old. I was coaching him in tennis at Orlando Racquet Club and I can honestly say he was my favorite kid that I have worked with... and I have worked with many. I felt like his older brother because I had a lot of fun with him. He was full of life and always seemed to enjoy himself. I never knew he was gay when I was with him at Orlando Racquet Club and it doesn't bother me one way or another if he's gay or if he isn't. I heard through another close friend of mine in the tennis business several years ago.

Bobby was invited to play in the Orange Bowl Jr. Tournament because someone cancelled. And he got to the round of 16 or quarterfinals in the main draw. When he came home, he gave me a pro shop that was made of popsicle sticks with a sign that said tennis lessons $50/hour and that was back in the late ;70s. There was a nice note to go with it thanking me for all the coaching help. Another memory is he beat Pat Cash in a tournament and after he beat him he called me right away which made me feel really happy for him and all his hard work.

Everyone is the same in my eyes, regardless of what they are. Just go ahead and don't worry about what anyone else thinks."

TREY ADCOCK

(Student at the Bobby Blair Tennis Academy)

"Bobby coached me for about three or four years. In many ways I came to him a rough project. Under his tutelage, however, I went from being a pretty average junior tennis player to a top 10 national ranking and traveling the world. In doing so he taught me the importance of believing in myself and not allowing my own self doubts to become insurmountable. I will be forever grateful to Bobby for the time and energy he spent with me and the belief he showed in me. I am proud to have called him coach and equally proud to call him friend as he fights to tell his story. In doing so, Bobby continues to provide mentorship to me far beyond the baselines of the tennis court."

MIKE GUSTAFSON

(NBTA friend of Bobby Blair and teammate on winning state high school tennis championships)

I had the great fortune to have spent a few years at the NBTA in the early '80s. We were a special family from all parts of the world held together by a few essential pieces. Bobby Blair was one of these pieces. The smile that was ever present. The laugh that came from the heart. The endless enthusiasm and energy. And the knowledge that if Bobby is involved, it is with the deepest sincerity and caring that a person could have. The list could go on and on, but I know there is limited space. I truly believe based on Bobby's life history, and the obstacles he has overcome, that the LGBT community could not have a greater or more caring friend than that of Bobby Blair.

PAM CASALE-TELFORD

(NBTA friend of Bobby Blair and former top 20 world ranked tennis player)

"There are many unknowns when a teenager packs up their bags to move in with strangers just to follow a dream.....a dream to reach their potential in a very competitive, athletic sport. At age 15, many teenagers did just that. Moved from home to NBTA to find out if they could make it in the world of competitive tennis. We started out as strangers, maybe competitors, and ended up sharing life lessons and creating life-long friendships. Bobby and I had that relationship. We talked about our challenges, our successes, our fears and really enjoyed spending time together. I learned back then what a great guy Bobby is and I'm proud to call him my friend. He will always have a supporter in me."

DAN GRANOT

(NBTA friend and college roommate with Bobby Blair)

"We have been friends as long as I can remember. We met as kids playing tennis and immediately bonded. We were roommates at Nick's, roommates at the University of Arkansas and continued our friendship during your time in Atlanta. We dealt with many issues and emotions during our growth together, but none more important than when you had the courage to come out to me very early on.

Our friendship was, is and always will be an important part of our lives and never have I been more proud of you with how you have continued to move forward with your "truth" and use your popularity to make a difference in the world to others who are looking for their "truth"

Thanks for being a part of my life."

CHERYL YOUNG

(Wesley Jamaine Cuyler sister)

"I met Bobby when he and my brother Wesley invited me and my mother to Orlando for a Tina Turner concert. They made us feel very welcome, very comfortable. Bobby was the perfect gentleman. That was the first of many memories. Bobby and Wesley loved one another hard but yet unconditional. After spending time with them and their friends, I knew this was one of those types of love everyone prays and searches a lifetime for. I can remember Bobby sending Wesley to Winter Haven to pick me, my mother, and my daughter Tamyia for an impromptu visit down in Miami Beach. Bobby was so attached to my baby girl Tamyia while we there he took her to Publix and told her to get what she wanted and she ended up getting $400 worth of stuff. He played with her all night and made sure we had so much fun but also that we relaxed and got some much needed rest. We visited them in Georgia where they lived in a two-story beautiful home. Wesley and Bobby spoiled my children Ashley, D'Anthony and Tamyia rotten. Every Christmas they would buy all of the children's toys. Christmas was magical for them.

I cannot think of a time that Wesley and Bobby have not been there for me and my family. Always there to lend a hand with much love. I believe they brought the best out in each other and our lives and hearts will be forever grateful and our souls will forever be connected by love. Wesley was everything to me. He was my best friend and confidant. I will miss him everyday for the rest of my life. What a great life lived through such a extraordinary young man. He traveled and saw the world and loved basketball. This book should let others know that love has no race, creed or color. Never be ashamed to be you and live life to the fullest."

KEVIN GAINES DINNEEN

(Lifelong friend to Bobby Blair)

"From the moment nearly 40 years ago when I first meet Bobby, I knew that he was someone special. His tennis talent was obvious, but the innate twinkle in his eye hinted at his unique ability to befriend, motivate and convince others, often older and already successful, and all the while overcoming his distinctly dysfunctional and less than privileged background.

For one, I soon recognized his compelling desire to better his lot, not just in tennis but in life.

Quickly I became a mentor, big brother figure, and friend. Only much later did I come to understand the demons and insecurity that tormented his psyche. They both motivated and limited his future success.

This friendship, I trust, has helped him to be the better person he now is; I know it has helped me in my own journey. Hopefully Bobby's story will be an inspiration and life lesson to the youth of today confronting similar issues of their own."

JAMES FORSYTHE
(Close friend and business manager for Bobby Blair since 2003)

"When I first met Bobby I had been invited to his house by a mutual friend.

While I waited in his study, I noticed the wall covered with pictures dating back many years of people who were still with him at present. My first thought was that this was a man who valued loyalty and friendship. My first impression was correct! At that first meeting he explained to me his real estate business, and that his goal was to make a million dollars so that he could retire and start a tennis camp for disadvantaged youth. I went to work with him and that very next weekend saw the power of his ability to motivate people. He could get people excited about watching a group of ants move a bread crumb and give a pep talk on team work. Absolutely amazing.

I have been with Bobby for about 10 years, and it has always been a very interesting ride; not even a roller coaster has as many twists and turns and ups and downs. But through it all, Bobby remained focused, constantly adapting to each new situation and creating opportunities out of thin air. And all the while working with and guiding his staff and friends. He has ventured into new territories with enthusiasm and vision. He committed himself to not just making his world better, but to giving back to those around him and his community. He puts forth an incredible amount of energy to make his community a better place for all.

If I had to describe Bobby, three things come to mind. As I first guessed, he is an extremely loyal person, the best you could ever have for a friend. He is committed and dedicated to giving back and to making other people's lives better, both in action and by leadership. And he has never, ever, lost his love of tennis. He seems to view life as a tennis game, with both single matches and doubles. He uses his skill and talents to make sure that the team wins. He is a coach, a mentor, a player, and most of all, a friend!"

CARY COHENOUR
(Lifelong friend of Bobby Blair. Ranked number one in Florida in every age group. Ranked number three in the nation boys' 14s and 16s. Won four national gold balls, three silver. Easter Bowl champion 14s and 16s. Attained ATP tour ranking of 272 in the world. Owner/founder of the Celsius tennis academy in Sarasota, Florida. Co-founder of Dolphin Props real estate developers.)

"The first time I met Bobby Blair I was a hot-shot 11-year old tennis player playing up in the 14-and-under age group in a tournament in Orlando. Bobby and I met in the finals and I was assuming that I would have an easy win since I had never heard of this kid from Orlando. Low and behold Bobby took me out in strait sets! Instead of rubbing it in my face like most kids did in those days he encouraged me and instantly became my friend. Later that year he showed up in my home town of Bradenton, Florida, to attend the academy on a full scholarship. We later went on to win a high school state championship together and had a lifelong bond. By fate later in life when my tennis career ended and I had become extremely negative about my future, Bobby and I crossed paths again. Bobby told me one night that my life had not ended, that actually it was just beginning! Those encouraging words stuck with me several tough years, and through a little luck and hard work I have been more successful than I ever expected. As a firm believer in God and Jesus Christ, I believe we don't choose our sexual orientation. Bobby's book will have a positive influence on those who struggle with this, the same way he had a positive influence on my career!"

ANTHONY RICCIARDO

(Business partner and close friend to Bobby Blair)

"I first met Bobby at the end of 2001. I was fresh out of the Navy and looking for my first professional opportunity after college. He had a lot of tenacity and impressive public speaking skills that drew me to him. I remember thinking after meeting him, if I could learn to do in one month what he did in a couple days, then I would be really successful. I knew there was something I could learn from him. Since that day, we have worked side by side on many projects, and I am still learning from him. He is one of my greatest mentors, coaches, and friends.

Early on in working with Bobby, in the real estate business, we achieved a lot of attention nationally from different investment groups. We traveled doing seminars in front of several hundred people at a time. His incredible speaking skills allowed our business to gain a lot of respect and clients. However, he was not open about his sexuality. Bobby was certain it was bad for business. So, we spent a lot of time hiding his personal life from our clients and his friends from the past. We had long discussions and came up with strategies on how we would handle questions about whom he was dating and why he was single and had no kids. We even came up with a script for me to repeat should particular questions come up. It took up a lot of time away from our productivity and even caused a few conflicts between us. There is another book here with all our stories we could share, but that may be left for another time. We didn't become friends because we spent a lot of time working together; we genuinely liked hanging out and shared many common interests. Our drive to succeed was one of the reasons we worked so well together. Early on in our adventures, I saw Bobby going through a difficult time personally with his then partner Wesley, who passed away at the end of 2012. While they were together, there was a lot of turmoil and hardship for him. It was hard for me to see it happening, it was very surreal. The experience was more like a dramatic tear jerker I was watching on Lifetime television. I saw the transition from that relationship to Bobby's current relationship with Brian. That too was a striking chain of events. Despite all of the personal issues, we still went to work every day. We dealt with issues as they came up and we always looked into the future for a better and brighter day. I consider myself fairly resilient, so, when I see resilience in others, like I do in Bobby, I tend to have more respect for them.

I never judged Bobby for his personal life. We have had disagreements and differences, but we always seem to come back to common ground. I was there for him during some of his rough times and he was there for me during some of mine. One of the most painful experiences I went through is when I suddenly lost my mother. I knew he was one of the few who would understand, and after that moment I understood him a little more as well. That's how friends

205

grow together, though.

I was really proud and happy for Bobby when he finally decided to come out and tell his long-time friends about who he really was. It was a little bit of a relief too because I knew I did not have to spend the energy anymore protecting his secret. The fact that he was hiding for so long was really sad to me. So, I remember the day when I realized the impact his book could make. It was on one of the early days before he had a name for the book. At that time, a few names were being considered, but none of them rang too well for either of us. On top of that, I did not understand tennis very well nor did I know what the baseline was. After he explained it all to me, the name suddenly came to mind. As soon as we heard it out loud, we knew that was the name: "Hiding Inside the Baseline."

Today, I still consider Bobby one of my closest friends and mentors. He is like my brother and like an uncle to my daughter. We still work together and I am excited to think how we can help others with this book. In some ways now, I think we mentor each other a little now. I have grown, he has grown, we have grown together. I can't wait for what the future holds. I am very excited to see how this book impacts others and I will be there to support him in every way I can."

LINDA PENTZ -GUNTER

(Close friend and confidante to Bobby Blair since 1982 and former tennis journalist)

"Charm and determination: these were the qualities that most struck me about Bobby when I first met him. With courage in the mix as well, this book is the logical outcome. If no one wrote "most likely to succeed" in his school yearbook, this was obviously a gross oversight. Bobby has demonstrated that effort yields accomplishment. I suspect this book is just the precursor of more fine achievements to come."

ROBERT SOJO

(Childhood and lifelong friend of Bobby Blair from the Orlando Tennis Center)

"I remember when we met back in the Orlando Tennis Center in 1977! I remember all the great and competitive matches we had and the great friendship we built! I will never forget your mom and dad and the great times we had!!"

RIKARD BERGH

(Collegiate and professional tour friend of Bobby Blair)

"We met first in college and I thought he played a great game of tennis. We hit it off right away. Then we started touring at the same time having a blast living our dream of being tennis players. I admire his courage. Fantastic memories."

ROBBIE WEISS

(Long time friend and competitor to Bobby Blair. 13 time U.S. National junior champion and NCAA championships singles winner. Former top 100 player in the world)

"The first memory I have of Bobby is when we played in the quarterfinals of the 18-and-under Clay Court Championships in Louisville, Kentucky. I knew Bobby was a good player but was not aware of what an amazing competitor he was. I quickly found out. I remember it being a brutally hot day and we were running each other ragged. Late in the first set, I heard some weird noise coming from the other side of the net. I looked over and Bobby was hunched over in the corner of the court puking is brains out. Something he ate or drank was not sitting well in the stifling heat and it looked like the match was mine. No way he was going to keep up the pace of play he was demonstrating let alone finish the match. I guess I did not know the real Bobby. He finished puking and walked back up to the service line like nothing had happened and played with even more determination. It was a look of "nothing is going to stop me from kicking your butt today." After more than two hours of grinding in the heat, Bobby was just too tough mentally and physically for me and wore me down to win the match. I have always looked back on that match with the utmost respect for Bobby. He is a true warrior, an amazing competitor and showed he can and will persevere through anything on the court and in life.

A few years later, I was playing the Canadian Satellite Circuit which Bobby was playing as well. I had not spent much time with Bobby up to this point, but we quickly became good friends. We played doubles, traveled from city to city and also got housed together in each city. I had a great doubles partner, an awesome practice partner and also had a friend to hang out with during the five-week tour. After the Satellite in Canada, I knew I had a friend for life and to this day some 25 years later, I still consider Bobby a good friend.

I did not find out about Bobby's sexual orientation until a few years ago. I remember being surprised for about 30 seconds and then I just wanted to support him. It has not changed how I feel about Bobby even in the slightest and I am really proud of Bobby for having the courage to be true to himself. I feel bad that Bobby had to hide from his true self for so long and was probably in anguish for many years. My only thought is, I just want Bobby to be happy and live free, which he is doing today. My hope is that the book "Hiding Inside the Baseline" will help other athletes or young adults who may also be hiding from their true selves to be free to express to the world who they really are and not be scared. Bobby has been liberated and the outpouring of love and acceptance from his friends has been tremendous. Bobby can be a major inspiration to others that they too can be free and that they should not be scared and love and acceptance from others is around the corner."

KATHY RINALDI-STUNKLE

(Childhood friend to Bobby Blair. Former top 10 player in the world in singles and doubles)

"I have fond memories of Bobby and I together that go back to training together when we were just starting out as junior players. To hear his story and struggles is not only inspiring to me but sure to help others who are struggling with the same issues and feelings that Bobby has overcome. Everyone deserves to find happiness and I am glad to know that Bobby has found his."

HECTOR VILLARROEL
(Bobby Blair childhood Orlando coach and tennis academy partner)

"I have known Bobby since he was 14 years old when he walked on the tennis court and began training with Hector Villarroel's Tennis Academy. He immediately exemplified his hard work and dedication to becoming a great player. I've watched Bobby grow through the years into a man who is successful at whatever he attempts. I hope his book will be a stepping stone for young people to have the courage to be who they are and go after their dreams."

DANI BOLLETTIERI
(NBTA childhood and lifelong friend of Bobby Blair)

"I've known Bobby most of my life. He has always been one of those guys that shines in every way. Good looking, bright, out-going, kind and that was just off the court. On the court he was the superstar. Raw talent. Literally everyone loved him. As a teenager, he was one of my first crushes but above all he was like a trustworthy brother to me. Finding out that he was gay deeply saddened me. I felt like we all failed him. How could any of us have known? Our Bobby holding this secret for so many years was crushing to me as we would have all supported him and loved him just the same. Those years must have been quite lonely for him. I wish so much that I could have taken away what must have been some very lonely years. I hope others that read his story realize it's OK to be different. Your true friends will stick with you. You will be supported. You will be loved."

MARY CLAIRE O'BRIEN SIMPSON
(Former girlfriend of Bobby Blair)

"Hiding Inside the Baseline ... the perfect title. I am so proud of Bobby and to be a part of his story. What started as a fun young love developed into a close friendship. Sharing the experience with his mother as we watched him play the Clay Court finals was special. Special because it would be the last time she saw him play tennis and special because I could get to know her. She was so proud of him! I hope that by sharing his journey, Bobby can help others and that he can live everyday with his head up, shoulders back and be proud of himself!"

BOB DE BENEDICTIS
(Friend, mentor and business partner to Bobby Blair)

"Subsequent to most of the events related in his book, I met Bobby in conjunction with
his real estate ventures, of which I was involved in more than a few, some successful, some

not. These ventures led to a few business ventures, again some successful, some not. No matter what, there was Bobby, that same tireless, respectful, intelligent, quick-acting person to solve problems as they would arrive."

MARVIN NATHAN
(Longtime friend of Bobby Blair and Las Vegas entertainer)

"My friendship with Bobby should read as a Who's Who. Twenty years or so, we have been there through the best of times and some of the most difficult times. Never not being there for each other. I could not be more proud of him writing this book, not only for his true self to be front and center. More so all the young folks who are looking for there own enlightenment and self truth! Thank you Bobby...Proud."

ALYKHAN DHANANI
(Student at the Bobby Blair Tennis Academy and successful entrepreneur)

"I met Bobby for the first time when I was 14 years old to join his tennis academy in Orlando. I was just starting tennis and was not by any means a top-ranked junior as many of the other students, nor did I have any incredible talent. And there was no way my mother could afford the fees associated with playing in the academy. But gracious Bobby said OK, kid, work your ass off every single day -- and your in! And for four years, I was lucky enough to take part in Bobby's academy and become a part of a huge family. Bobby Blair, a man I barely knew, covered several of the tremendous costs associated with me taking part in the academy. But that's BOBBY!

He is one of the most generous, caring, and energetic people I have ever met and has always opened so many doors for young people, myself included, and it's wonderful to see that Bobby is still continuing to open more and more doors and make a huge difference. He made a huge difference for me.

I've since become friends with Bobby and even had the opportunity to work with him for a short while. I am so proud of his new endeavor and book that is going to be released.

I wish you all the best Bobby. You're an amazing, talented person and may you have all of the success you are seeking with your new cause!

Thank you so much for everything you have done for me."

JOE BLAIR
(Brother to Bobby Blair)

"From a very lucky and blessed brother: Bobby even at a very young age was a role model for me and still is the most influential person in my life today. His hard work and perseverance matched with natural ability helped him overcome obstacles at home as a youth that has made him the person I am so proud of today. Bobby and his unselfish personality made me his responsibility as a youth to get through some very challenging times. I will always be so grateful for he already had enough on his own plate. My brother has always found the good and the positive no matter what cards are dealt to him. I am so proud and happy for him for sharing his life story and totally support him in the passion he has to make a difference. Bobby through this platform will do what he does best, influence other people in a positive way. My wife Jamie, son Bryson, and stepson Bradley, share the same feelings as myself and are very fortunate to have him in their life. He has already been a major influence and role model to Bryson and Bradley, who are part of the next generation that Bobby is so determined to leave his mark upon."

ALAN H. BECK

(LGBT publishing mentor to Bobby Blair and Publisher of Fun Maps)

"Life is certainly a journey and Bobby Blair is experiencing the ride. Buoyant, always ready to put forth a new, exciting idea, exploring avenues that others fear to tread, Bobby continues to create a world where he is the chief showman, an extraordinarily talented leader and brilliant tactician.

When I met Bobby, he was taking over the publishing of a fledgling gay magazine to which he gave his devotion. He grew the publication to include a weekly newspaper and multi-media web platform serving South Florida's gay/lesbian audience.

This provided a challenge and conflict to Bobby as he was still "living below the net" to his straight colleagues and friends in the tennis world. I encouraged Bobby to "come out' fully and live his life with his partner and others so that he could completely be "himself." "No way," could this be at first, yet slowly he saw that it was possible. With a smile on his face, he came out to his peers in the tennis world and he was proud of who he was. His service sailed over the net with magnificence. When I came out to my mom, she said to me: "Alan,t's not what you are that matters, it's who you are; you are my son, you are smart, you are giving, you are a beautiful man and I love you." I wish these words to Bobby who is leading the life of a man who writes his own script and includes all in his life. I'm proud to be Bobby's mentor and friend as I've watched him grow in mind, spirit and heart.

Congratulations on your new book and for being who you are.

SHAWN FOLTZ-EMMONS

(NBTA friend and senior year prom date of Bobby Blair)

"I remember Bobby from NBTA as the first person to welcome me when I arrived there. He was funny, sarcastic, determined, and a leader for the younger players like me. His dedication to being the best player possible was clearly evident in his daily life at the academy. He was extremely kind to me, and very accepting to all around him, regardless of playing ability. Bobby is an extraordinary example of honesty, integrity, courage and faith. His vision for the future for all LGBT people is groundbreaking, and has the potential to radically change lives. I am very proud of Bobby, and he inspires me."

TIM SIEGEL

(College tennis team captain and close friend of Bobby Blair/Head Men's coach at Texas Tech University)

I met Bobby in junior tennis in 1979. I was impressed with his enthusiasm, competitiveness, and work ethic. Four years later I was excited to hear that Bobby was joining my teammates and me at the University of Arkansas. Bobby was one of the top recruits in the nation that year. Bobby's mom passed away just one week into his freshman year and I vividly remember sitting with him in his dorm trying to help him ease his pain.

Little did I know that he was dealing with a different kind of pain as well. The pain of keeping a secret from all of his teammates, friends and family. I wish I would have known then as I would have made sure that Bobby would have been accepted, embraced and respected as a teammate and friend.

As the captain of the team that's how I would have felt, just as I do today.

When I heard about Bobby's decision to let go of his pain and worry and announce that he was gay, my first reaction was I wish I were there for him back at Arkansas. How difficult that must have been.

As the head coach at Texas Tech University, I certainly hope that coaches like me from grade school to the professional level would create an environment without prejudice or judgement but rather acceptance and love and respect. Proud of you, Bobby.

GENE COLLINS

(Lifelong friend of Bobby Blair)

It was the summer of 1982 when Bobby and I met. I was 15 years old but not the typical 15-year old. I had been on the streets hustling to get what I thought would be a better life for myself, my mother and niece. I met a man who had a thing for young boys and was willing to pay whatever it took for him to get his fix. He was a very successful businessman and had the funds to support me and my family. He also supported several tennis players, you guessed it; to get his fix. That's where the journey began.

When Bobby and I met I remember thinking: I want what he has. I had been interested in tennis from an early age and in my eyes Bobby was the big tennis star. I remember watching him play in tournaments and thinking that could be me if things were different. What I did not know was Bobby was dealing with demons of his own. You see, I had demons of my own to deal with.

While I thought our lives were so different it turned out they were quite the same. We were in search of a better life with all the rewards we felt we were entitled to. Our search for a better life has not changed since the day we met over three decades ago, but the way we go about obtaining those rewards has come full circle. I can say this without any reserve whatsoever; Bobby is concerned about his comfort in life but more concerned about how his life's experiences can be of help to others. Now on a personal note, Bobby and I have been friends for over 30 years. He was my best man when Tammy and I got married, and I cannot think of any other person in my life whom I would rather have as a best friend, other than my wife, of course. Love you honey. I am so proud of the man Bobby has become, he has truly come full circle.

EUGENE CONTI

(Longtime friend of Bobby Blair)

I was fortunate to have met Bobby Blair back in 1990 on a golf course in Wellington, Florida. I remember that day like it was last week. My friend, Rick Davidson, was the teaching tennis pro at the Wellington Club and had recently met Bobby and his assistant Randy, so he made up a foursome for golf. Being the worst golfer of the four, I was like comic relief. Randy was an excellent golfer, Bobby and Rick were about equal...then there was me. The one thing I appreciated most about this first encounter was the laughing. We were just having fun. I remember missing a putt of less than a foot and we all fell to the grass in hysterics. By the end of the round, I knew that I had made two new friends.

Bobby was coaching the Wellington World Team Tennis franchise and would invite me to see the competitions, and I was there as often as possible.

Randy and Bobby would frequently come to my apartment for dinner, particularly on Sundays to watch NFL football games. Randy was a fanatic Green Bay Packer fan. We all started hanging out a lot. We became good friends.

As time passed, I noticed that Bobby had begun to lose some of his spunk, he seemed sad at times. We talked about it but he never really opened up about the reasons for his sadness. In the meantime, Randy would open up to me and ask me what's up with Bobby. "He is acting weird towards me."

Randy is a great all-around guy, loves women...to an extreme, and was a "player." Most times the conversations at the clubhouse were about this girl or that night out, etc. Randy and Rick were like two peas in a pod, both loved to talk about their female exploits. Bobby was mostly silent, as was I. We laughed respectfully at the stories but never added any real dirt ourselves. We were both closeted gay men, living, socializing and doing business in a straight world. I had come out to some friends, a very select few, and absolutely no family members (Italians of my parents' generation were not very accepting of the concept, much less the reality of a gay son). Actually, I had only recently come out to myself, accepting the fact that I was a gay man.

Bobby's relationship with Randy continued to deteriorate to the point of hostility at times, and I was the sounding board for both, a position I did not volunteer for, nor did I want. I knew Bobby was gay, not because he told me so, but I knew. Watching him react to situations was, for me, like looking in a mirror. I understood all his frustrations, desires and impossible dreams. I hated to see my two good friends becoming enemies in front of my eyes. Randy was really confused and angry. Bobby was getting more withdrawn and depressed. And I knew the reason why this was happening. What to do? Not an easy decision for me. Out a friend to save his friendship, lose a friend for outing him, cause a friendship to end, or remain silent while two great guys continued torturing each other because of this obstacle created by a heartless society. Well, one day Randy came to my apartment and immediately started about Bobby again, saying

that he was going to leave his job and couldn't take it anymore and didn't understand why. So, throwing caution to the wind, I outed Bobby. I will never forget Randy's reaction! He changed from an angry, confused young man instantly and his face became calm and a smile erupted! We talked some more and Randy left.Now I had to tell Bobby!!! I hadn't been that nervous since I went to an Anita Bryant concert. Bobby was not happy at the news, but after a long conversation, we started opening up to each other. Of course I outed myself to Bobby immediately. By the end of the day, we were all good and I drew a rather large sigh of relief. Bobby Blair was the first and only person I have ever outed, and we have remained great friends ever since.

I could continue with literally hundreds of other stories, experiences and shared "ups and downs" that Bobby and I have lived through during these 24 years of friendship, but I chose to share this, the first important one, with you, in the hope of perhaps shedding some light on the reality of being gay in a straight world.

I am extremely proud of my friend Bobby Blair for the way he has conducted himself throughout his life. He has fought through adversity on many levels and has emerged from this fight a better man. He now takes another, bolder step forward, I believe, by sharing his life's story in the hope of helping other LGBT people. Congratulations Bobby.

RON HIGHTOWER

(College coach to Bobby Blair at the University of Arkansas and lifelong friend and mentor)

I have had the privilege of knowing Bobby since he was 15. As a tough, scrappy Central Florida junior, I saw Bobby take advantage of his scholarship to the Nick Bollettieri Tennis Academy and use his drive and passion to compete daily with the best U.S. and world ranked professionals. It was five year later where I really watched Bobby grow and mature as an All-American at the University of Arkansas. As his Head Coach in college, I was so proud to watch Bobby become one of the best players in the country, and leading his team to an elite 8 finish in NCAA tournament. Bobby also represented our country at the Goodwill Games in Moscow in '86. Bobby played professionally beating the likes of Wimbledon champion Pat Cash and learned a lot more about the world stage. With his playing experience behind him, Bobby saw a need in the U.S. and pioneered his innovative pro traveling team in the 90's with our top U.S. players. (Gosh, does tennis need you now in this country.) Since then he has coached and managed teams for World Team Tennis, been a USTA National Coach and founded a successful real estate and media companies. Numerous successes and accolades later, Bobby is not close to the finish line. Bobby has a huge heart and has reached out once again in writing "Behind the Baseline" that will surely impact many people in a positive way. I'm grateful for our friendship, coach/player relationship, inspiration, and support you have given me over the years. Go Bobby Go! Love you!

DANI LEAL

(Lifelong friend of Bobby Blair and former top-ranked Junior and Collegiate and World-Ranked player.)

I'm happy to have had you in my life since we were around 12 years old. Battling through the junior competitions together was impressive despite our economic deficiencies compared to our rivals. We had nothing growing up, but you always made me feel like we could do anything and be anybody we wanted. You always made me feel like a million bucks without having anything. You will always be a blessing in my life and I am so grateful for your friendship. Thanks for being a best man in my wedding. I will always support you because you are my friend forever. Thank you. Coming out with your secret is just another blessing you can give and share with others who need your story to have courage and live life to their fullest with pride and dignity. Peace and love.

SUSAN HEDGCOCK

(Life-long friend and school teacher to Bobby Blair/head coach of 1983 state high school state tennis championships for Bradenton Academy, of which Bobby was co-captain)

On the court, in the classroom, in our hearts, we have always regarded Bobby as a special person with a sense of purpose. I never understood why he always seemed so self-critical and troubled. This book allows him to accept himself as he is, which we have always done. We love Bobby because of who we are when we are with him. We love Bobby because of his authentic struggle with life that he is able to share with others. Life has never been about him but all those he can impact.

SHANE HACKETT

(Business partner, mentor and dear friend of Bobby Blair)

I first met Bobby when he became the face of real estate investing for the Success Magazine Conferences. We worked side-by-side delivering training and workshops all across the country. We bonded quickly, as we were both athletes and shared an entrepreneurial passion. Bobby as a former tennis star and myself as a soccer player, we were now making our way in the business world.

Anyone who has met Bobby knows he is charismatic, upbeat, and a genuinely good person. He generously shares his energy and talents with others. Consistently at conference after conference, he channeled his charisma, motivating people to make positive life changes. It was really rewarding to be part of the process.

It was several years into our working relationship before someone first asked me if Bobby was gay. I replied, "I don't know. Honestly, I have never even thought about it."

I had grown up in a family that did not just tolerate diversity, rather we embraced it. My aunt had been openly gay from my earliest memory, and her long-term girlfriend was black. Looking back now, I realize that my family was boldly atypical for a 1960s/1970s white, Midwestern farm family, but it is just the way I was raised. My world was one of accepting people for who they are – regardless of race, color, creed, or sexual orientation.

The questions and rumors about Bobby's sexuality continued to occasionally surface in the office. I remember one of our co-workers, who also happened to be our friend, asked me if Bobby was gay. Like so many times before, again I replied, "I don't know. I never asked.

Why? What does it matter?" This co-worker had a general feeling that a gay man could not and should not be out speaking about the real estate business. After a short debate, we agreed to disagree, and I had the facts on my side: the years of successful seminars and real estate investing that Bobby had already accomplished.

Years later when Bobby and I were no longer working together, I wholeheartedly recommended him as a spokesperson for another training company. With his impressive resume, Bobby got the spokesperson role and entered into a business relationship with the company. Later that year, I got a call from one of the company's business associates. He was pretty animated as he questioned me, "Did you know Bobby is gay?" I responded, "I don't know that he is or that he isn't gay. Why, what's up?" I asked. "Well, we had dinner with him, and we asked one of his staff. He told us that Bobby is gay. We cannot have a gay person as a central spokesperson for our company. We are out promoting the 'American Dream' and 'family values.' Gay simply does not work." Months later, I learned they fired Bobby.

Interestingly enough, I cannot remember exactly when I officially knew Bobby was out of the proverbial closet. It may have been that phone call. Regardless, at some point in time, he had come out, and everyone seemed to know, including me.

It was natural. The biggest change I noticed was Bobby's self-confidence. He radiated confidence; he had grown so much. Being true to himself, living authentically, that was a game changer, a life changer. Through the years, Bobby and I have continued to be friends and business associates, and we have had time to reflect on our experiences – both good and bad. We are all on a path of self-discovery, acceptance, and celebration. For some, the journey is easier than it is for others, but for all, there is great meaning in finding yourself. Enjoy the book, and may Bobby's life stories bring you closer to your own truth.

RODRIGO GOMES NASCIMENTO

(Student of Bobby Blair Tennis Academy)

I can't see Bobby for being gay, straight or whatever. I see Bobby for the incredible human being and the huge heart he has, someone I love for taking care of me and others without expecting anything but hard work, someone that tennis misses because he is a hell of a coach with an incredible tennis knowledge who's definitely helped me to get where I am today. That's who Bobby is to me, and for the rest of my life I'm grateful for all he's done.

MARK KNOWLES

(NBTA friend of Bobby Blair and 3-time Grand Slam Doubles Champion and former Number One Doubles Player in the World)

I have known Bobby for over 20 years. Bobby has always had such an outgoing, positive personality that has allowed him to be successful in tennis at all levels as well as make a tremendous impact in other areas outside of tennis. I am so happy that Bobby is telling his story and allowing himself to be a role model for those that don't have the confidence to stand up for their beliefs. Bobby will continue to be a positive influence on our society. Bobby, I am proud to call you my friend!

T.J. JONES

(Longtime special friend to Bobby Blair)

I met Bobby over 25 years ago when he was a tennis instructor. We became friends beyond the tennis lessons and shortly learned that we had more in common beyond hitting tennis balls on the courts. Being a gay man was difficult and Bobby struggled with his sexuality. As most gay men fear at first, he anticipated that people would not accept him. This book shares his life experiences in hopes that someone will be inspired by this story of becoming comfortable with one's self. Enjoy this must read book.

CHUCK SWAYNE

(NBTA classmate/roommate and friend of Bobby Blair; former ATP Tour player, CEO/Founder of Imperial Properties Ltd.)

Bobby was the hardest working, most determined, fiercest competitor on and off the tennis court. A true winner! His story should be read by all compassionate people who compete. No matter where Bobby is "hiding" he is leading and making a difference!

JACK READER

(Lifelong friend and mentor to Bobby Blair, and ATP Tour Men's Professional Coach)

Late 70s, early 80s, I tried to help a wonderful and extremely talented young man with his tennis development. I knew he had problems but never recognized the true causes. I deeply apologize for not having the insight at the time Bobby.

If only I had had the opportunity to read some material such as your book. I know this will help a lot of people to recognize the true problem of some young person in the future. My compliments to you Bobby.

DR. LOIS GERBER

(Lifelong friend and mentor to Bobby Blair. Co-founder of Bradenton Academy.)

Good luck with your book. It is a statement meant to share. I'm sure it will be an inspiration to all. Your life is yours to hold. Keep tight in the palm of your hand! Love you, Mrs. Doc.

KEVIN HOPPER

(Special friend and associate publisher to Bobby Blair's media company Multi media Platforms, LLC)

Bobby has dedicated the last decade to the LGBT community in South Florida. It's wonderful to see him share his coming out story with the world. His story will pave the way for young athletes to live a more open life and create acceptance among their peers.